Annie's Favorite Baby Projects™

Editorial Director
Andy Ashley

Production Director
Ange Van Arman

Editorial
Senior Editor
Jennifer McClain

Editor
Liz Field

Editorial Staff
Shirley Brown, Donna Jones, Nina Marsh
Donna Scott, Ann White

Photography
Scott Campbell, Tammy Coquat-Payne

Book Design & Production
Coy A. Lothrop

Production Team
Joanne Gonzalez, Betty Radla

Production Coordinator
Glenda Chamberlain

Product Presentation
Design Coordinator
Sandy Kennebeck

Inhouse Designer
Mickie Akins

Design Copy
Linda Moll Smith

Sincerest thanks to all the designers and other professionals
whose dedication has made this book possible.
Special thanks to Quebecor Printing Book Group, Kingsport, Tennessee.

Library of Congress Cataloging-in-Publication Data
ISBN: 0-9655269-3-3
First Printing: 1998
Library of Congress Catalog Card Number: 98-72353
Published and Distributed by
Annie's Attic, LLC, Big Sandy, Texas 75755
Printed in the United States of America.

Cover: **First Portrait**, pattern instructions begin on page 98.

Contents

Toy Time

Bow Tie Teddy	8
Heirloom Dolly	10
Mimi The Mouse	14
Patchwork Pretty	17
Playtime Pals	18
Huggy Bunny	20
Snuggly Snail Pillow	24

Bonnets, Booties & Bibs

Ribbons & Lace Bib	28
Lovebuds Bonnet	30
Cottontail Cuddlers	32
Keepsake Slippers & Bib	34
Perky Puppy Bib & Pillow	38
Beary Warm Hat & Mittens	40
Buckaroo Booties	44
Quackers Please!	46

Afghans & More

Humpty Dumpty Afghan Set	50
Just Ducky Afghan	52
Carriage Cover & Pillow	56
Rainbow Puffs Baby Set	58
Mother's Love Blanket & Cap	62
Granny Bear Afghan	64
Bright Ribbons Mile-A-Minute Afghan	66
Sleepytime Bear	68
Tropical Treasures	70

Nursery Decor

Prancing Pony	76
Cottage Cushions	80
Carousel Filet	82
Bear Family Pillows	86
Cow & Moon Mobile	90
Tissue Train	92

Lovely Layettes

First Portrait	98
His & Her Finery	102
Antique Elegance	108
Winter Wonder Ensemble	114

Shower Stoppers

Baby Bow Trims	120
Baby Bunting & Bonnet	122
Bubble Bath Bear Bag	124
Bathtime Buddy	127
Sweet Tees Trimmings	128
Nannie's Paddle	132
Bootie & Basket Party Favors	134
Pretty Powder Puff	136

First Fashions

Play "Maties" Sailor Ensemble	138
Ribbons & Ruffles	142
Li'l Lamb Sleeper	146
Sugar & Spice	148
Rodeo Rider	152
Peach & Pineapple Dress Set	154
Stitch Guide	**160**

Gift Giving Diary

Gift Given to _____

Gift _____

Date & Occasion _____

Gift Given to _____

Gift _____

Date & Occasion _____

Gift Given to _____

Gift _____

Date & Occasion _____

Gift Giving Diary

Gift Given to _____

Gift _____

Date & Occasion _____

Gift Given to _____

Gift _____

Date & Occasion _____

Gift Given to _____

Gift _____

Date & Occasion _____

Dear Friends,

Scientists tell us that we are emotionally programmed to fall in love with babies: specifically with their peekaboo eyes, pug noses, rosebud mouths and starfish-like fingers that wave at us from their cradles and bassinets.

It doesn't take a scientist to tell us that from the humble swaddling clothes of the baby Jesus to the baby afghan made for us by Grandma, there is no more ancient and honorable nesting instinct than the wish to surround our own little lovebuds with the finest of handmade layettes.

With our hearts already eagerly captive, keeping baby cozy and coddled with beautifully stitched blankets, booties, bonnets and more, is pure delight for ardent crocheters like us! Especially when I've gathered all my favorite patterns, and yours, into this colorfully photographed, project-packed, collector's volume!

I turned to my own parenting experiences, and those of our extended Annie's Attic family, to bring you so many beautiful time-tested yarn and thread designs for the making and giving. In these seven chapters you'll turn to dolly and teddy toys, baby shower surprises and luscious layettes—not to mention lacy crochet to grace fashions, nursery decor, afghans and more. With this book you'll never say, "My baby just doesn't have a stitch to wear!"

And while crocheting, share the lullabies and nursery rhymes we've included in our chapter headings with your precious little ones!

Happy Crocheting,

Annie

CHAPTER 1

Toy Time

Dance to Your Daddy

Dance to your daddy,
My little baby,
Dance to your daddy,
My little lamb.

Baby shall have an apple,
Baby shall have a plum,
Baby shall have a rattle,
When Daddy comes home.

This ancient song for dandling (bouncing a baby affectionately on one's knee), is believed to have originated in Scotland and the North Country. It is often sung with an additional verse, "You shall have a fishy, In a little dishy, You shall have a fishy, When the boat comes in."

Bow Tie Teddy

Designed by Michele Wilcox

Finished Size: 15" tall.

Materials:
- ❑ Worsted yarn:
  - 6 oz. gold
  - ½ oz. off-white
  - Small amount black
- ❑ Sport yarn:
  - 1 oz. red
  - Small amount green
- ❑ White ½" button
- ❑ 2 gold 12mm animal eyes with washers
- ❑ Polyester fiberfill
- ❑ Tapestry needle
- ❑ E and G hooks or hooks needed to obtain gauges

Gauges: E hook and sport yarn, 5 sc = 1"; 5 sc rows = 1". **G hook and worsted yarn,** 4 sc = 1"; 4 sc rows = 1".

Basic Stitches: Ch, sl st, sc, hdc, dc, tr.

Notes: Work in continuous rnds; do not join or turn unless otherwise stated. Mark first st of each rnd.
Before fastening off, leave an 8" or longer end when needed for sewing.

HEAD
Rnd 1: With G hook and off-white, ch 2, 6 sc in second ch from hook. *(6 sc made)*
Rnd 2: 2 sc in each st around. *(12)*
Rnd 3: (Sc in next st, 2 sc in next st) around. *(18)*
Rnd 4: Sc in each st around.
Rnd 5: (Sc in each of next 2 sts, 2 sc in next st) around. *(24)*
Rnds 6–8: Sc in each st around. At end of last rnd, join with sl st in first sc. Fasten off.
Rnd 9: Join gold with sc in first st, sc in each of next 3 sts, 2 sc in each of next 16 sts, sc in last 4 sts. *(Last st made is at center bottom of muzzle—40)*
Rnd 10: Sc in each st around.
Rnd 11: Sc in first 4 sts, (2 sc in next st, sc in each of next 3 sts) 8 times, sc in last 4 sts. *(48)*
Rnds 12–17: Sc in each st around.
Rnd 18: Sc in first 12 sts, (2 sc in next st, sc in next 4 sts) 5 times, 2 sc in next st, sc in last 10 sts. *(54)*
Rnds 19–20: Sc in each st around.
Rnd 21: (Sc in next 7 sts, sc next 2 sts tog) around. *(48)*
Rnd 22: (Sc in next 6 sts, sc next 2 sts tog) around. *(42)*

Rnd 23: (Sc in next 5 sts, sc next 2 sts tog) around. Attach eyes to front of Head 2¼" apart between rnds 10 and 11 *(see photo)*. Stuff Head. *(36)*
Rnd 24: (Sc in next 4 sts, sc next 2 sts tog) around. *(30)*
Rnd 25: (Sc in each of next 3 sts, sc next 2 sts tog) around. *(24)*
Rnd 26: (Sc in each of next 2 sts, sc next 2 sts tog) around. *(18)*
Rnd 27: (Sc in next st, sc next 2 sts tog) around. Fasten off. Finish stuffing Head and sew opening closed.
With black, using satin stitch *(see Stitch Guide)*, embroider nose over top half of rnds 1 and 2; using straight stitch, embroider mouth over bottom half of rnds 1–4 *(see photo)*.

EAR (make 2)
Rnd 1: With G hook and gold, ch 2, 6 sc in second ch from hook. *(6 sc made)*
Rnd 2: 2 sc in each st around. *(12)*
Rnd 3: Sc in each st around.
Rnd 4: (Sc in next st, 2 sc in next st) around. *(18)*
Rnds 5–7: Sc in each st around.
Rnd 8: (Sc next 2 sts tog) around. *(9)*
Row 9: Flatten Ear; working through both thicknesses, sc in each st across. Fasten off.
Sew last row of Ears to rnd 18 at top of Head 2¼" apart.

BODY
Rnd 1: With G hook and gold, ch 24, sl st in first ch to form ring, ch 1, sc in each ch around. *(24 sc made)*
Rnd 2: (Sc in each of next 3 sts, 2 sc in next st) around. *(30)*
Rnd 3: Sc in each st around.
Rnd 4: (Sc in next 4 sts, 2 sc in next st) around. *(36)*
Rnd 5: (Sc in next 5 sts, 2 sc in next st) around. *(42)*
Rnd 6: Sc in each st around.
Rnd 7: Sc in each of first 3 sts, (2 sc in next st, sc in next 6 sts) 5 times, 2 sc in next st, sc in each of last 3 sts. *(48)*
Rnd 8: Sc in each st around.
Rnd 9: (Sc in next 7 sts, 2 sc in next st) around. *(54)*
Rnd 10: Sc in each st around.
Rnd 11: Sc in first 4 sts, (2 sc in next st, sc in next 8 sts) 5 times, 2 sc in next st, sc in last 4 sts. *(60)*
Rnds 12–20: Sc in each st around.
Rnd 21: (Sc in next 8 sts, sc next 2 sts tog) around. *(54)*

Continued on page 13

Heirloom Dolly

Designed by Michele Wilcox

Finished Size: Doll is 10½" tall.

Materials:
- ❑ 4 oz. tan worsted yarn
- ❑ 7 oz. white sport yarn
- ❑ 6-strand embroidery floss: Red, white, blue, black and brown
- ❑ 3¼ yds. white ¼" ribbon
- ❑ 3 white ribbon roses
- ❑ Polyester fiberfill
- ❑ Craft glue
- ❑ Tapestry and embroidery needles
- ❑ E and F hooks or hooks needed to obtain gauges

Gauges: E hook and sport yarn, 5 dc = 1"; 7 dc rows = 3". **F hook and worsted yarn,** 9 sc = 2"; 9 sc rows = 2".

Basic Stitches: Ch, sl st, sc, dc.

Notes: Work in continuous rnds; do not join or turn unless otherwise stated. Mark first st of each rnd.
Before fastening off, leave an 8" or longer end when needed for sewing.

HEAD & BODY
Rnd 1: Starting at top of Head, with F hook and tan, ch 2, 6 sc in second ch from hook. *(6 sc made)*
Rnd 2: 2 sc in each st around. *(12)*
Rnd 3: (Sc in next st, 2 sc in next st) around. *(18)*
Rnd 4: Sc in each st around.
Rnd 5: (Sc in each of next 2 sts, 2 sc in next st) around. *(24)*
Rnd 6: (Sc in each of next 3 sts, 2 sc in next st) around. *(30)*
Rnd 7: Sc in each st around.
Rnd 8: (Sc in next 4 sts, 2 sc in next st) around. *(36)*
Rnds 9–15: Sc in each st around.
Rnd 16: (Sc in next st, sc next 2 sts tog) around. *(24)*
Rnd 17: For **Neck**, (sc in each of next 2 sts, sc next 2 sts tog) around. Stuff. Continue stuffing as you work. *(18)*
Rnd 18: Sc in each st around.
Rnd 19: For **Body**, (sc in each of next 2 sts, 2 sc in next st) around. *(24)*
Rnd 20: (Sc in next st, 2 sc in next st) around. *(36)*
Rnds 21–33: Sc in each st around.
Rnd 34: (Sc in next 4 sts, sc next 2 sts tog) around. *(30)*
Rnd 35: (Sc in each of next 3 sts, sc next 2 sts tog) around. *(24)*

Rnd 36: (Sc in each of next 2 sts, sc next 2 sts tog) around. *(18)*
Rnd 37: (Sc in next st, sc next 2 sts tog) around. *(12)*
Rnd 38: (Sc next 2 sts tog) around, join with sl st in first sc. Fasten off. Sew opening closed.

ARM (make 2)
Rnd 1: Starting at Hand, with F hook and tan, ch 2, 6 sc in second ch from hook. *(6 sc made)*
Rnd 2: 2 sc in each st around. *(12)*
Rnds 3–5: Sc in each st around.
Rnd 6: For **Wrist**, (sc next 2 sts tog) around. *(6)*
Rnd 7: For **Arm**, 2 sc in each st around. *(12)*
Rnds 8–11: Sc in each st around.
Rnds 12–16: Repeat rnds 6–10. Stuff.
Rnd 17: (Sc next 2 sts tog) around, join with sl st in first sc. Fasten off. Sew opening closed.
Sew Arms over rnds 21–32 on each side of Body.

LEG (make 2)
Rnd 1: Starting at Foot, with F hook and tan, ch 2, 6 sc in second ch from hook. *(6 sc made)*
Rnd 2: 2 sc in each st around. *(12)*
Rnd 3: (Sc in next st, 2 sc in next st) around. *(18)*
Rnd 4: (Sc in each of next 2 sts, 2 sc in next st) around. *(24)*
Rnds 5–6: Sc in each st around.
Rnd 7: For **Toes**, (sc next 2 sts tog) 6 times, sc in next 4 sts, (sc next 2 sts tog) 2 times, sc in last 4 sts. *(16)*
Rnds 8–12: Sc in each st around.
Rnd 13: (Sc next 2 sts tog) around. *(8)*
Rnd 14: 2 sc in each st around. *(16)*
Rnds 15–19: Sc in each st around. Stuff.

• • • • • • • • • • • • • • • Continued on page 12

Heirloom Dolly

Continued from page 10

Rnd 20: (Sc next 2 sts tog) around, join with sl st in first sc. Fasten off. Sew opening closed.

With Toes pointing forward, sew Legs to bottom of Body.

FACIAL FEATURES

With red floss, using fly stitch *(see Stitch Guide)*, embroider mouth over rnd 14 of Head as shown in photo.

Using satin stitch, working over rnds 10 and 11 of Head as shown in photo, embroider white of eyes 1" apart with white floss and embroider iris of each eye with blue floss.

With black floss, using French knot, embroider pupil on each iris. With brown floss, using outline stitch, embroider around edge of each eye.

With brown floss, using straight stitch, embroider eyelashes and eyebrows as shown in photo and embroider nose on rnd 12 centered below eyes.

DRESS

Row 1: Starting at neckline, with E hook and white sport yarn, ch 31, sc in second ch from hook, sc in each ch across, turn. *(30 sc made)*

Row 2: Ch 1, sc in first 5 sts, (3 sc in next st, sc in each of next 3 sts, 3 sc in next st), sc in next 10 sts; repeat between ( ), sc in last 5 sts, turn. *(38) Front of row 2 is right side of work.*

Row 3: Ch 1, sc in first 6 sts, (2 sc in next st, sc in next 5 sts, 2 sc in next st), sc in next 12 sts; repeat between ( ), sc in last 6 sts, turn. *(42)*

Row 4: Ch 1, sc in first 7 sts, (2 sc in each of next 7 sts), sc in next 14 sts; repeat between ( ), sc in last 7 sts, turn. *(56)*

Row 5: Ch 1, sc in first 8 sts; (for **Sleeve**, 2 dc in each of next 12 sts), sc in next 16 sts; repeat between ( ), sc in last 8 sts, turn. *(80 sts)*

Row 6: Ch 1, sc in each st across, turn.

Row 7: Ch 1, sc in first 9 sts, (ch 3, skip next st, sc in next st) 11 times, sc in next 18 sts; repeat between ( ) 11 times, sc in last 9 sts, turn.

Row 8: Ch 1, sc in first 10 sts, (*4 sc in next ch sp, sc in next st; repeat from * 9 more times, 4 sc in next ch sp), sc in next 19 sts; repeat between ( ), sc in last 9 sts, turn. *(146)*

Row 9: Ch 1, sc in first 10 sts; for **Armhole**, ch 5, skip next 54 sts; sc in next 18 sts; for **Armhole**, ch 5, skip next 54 sts; sc in last 10 sts, turn. *(38 sc, 10 chs)*

Row 10: Ch 3, 2 dc in each st and in each ch across, turn. *(95 dc)*

Rows 11–17: Ch 3, dc in each st across, turn.

Row 18: Working this row in **back lps** *(see Stitch Guide)*, ch 1, sc in first st, (ch 3, skip next st, sc in next st) across, turn.

Row 19: Ch 1, sc in first st, (4 sc in next ch sp, sc in next st) across, turn.

Row 20: Working this row in **front lps** of last dc row, sl st in first st, ch 3, dc in each st across, turn.

Rows 21–23: Ch 3, dc in each st across, turn.

Rows 24–55: Repeat rows 18–23 consecutively, ending with row 19. At end of last row, fasten off.

Place Dress on Doll. Sew ends of rows on Dress together at center back.

Cut 45" piece from ribbon. Tie in bow around Dress below Arms *(see photo)*.

Cut two 18" pieces from ribbon. Tie each piece in a bow around Doll's Wrists.

Glue a ribbon rose to center of each bow *(see photo)*.

BONNET

Row 1: With E hook and white sport yarn, ch 15, sc in second ch from hook, sc in next 12 chs, 3 sc in last ch; working in remaining lps on opposite side of starting ch, sc in last 13 chs, turn. *(29 sc made)*

Row 2: Ch 1, sc in first 13 sts, 2 sc in next st, sc in next st, 2 sc in next st, sc in last 13 sts, turn. *(31)*

Rows 3–14: Ch 1, sc in each st across, turn.

Row 15: Ch 1, sc in first st, (ch 3, skip next st, sc in next st) across, turn.

Row 16: Ch 1, sc in first st, (4 sc in next ch sp, sc in next st) across, **do not turn.**

Row 17: Working in ends of rows, for **Bottom Edge**, ch 1, sc in each row across, turn. *(32)*

Row 18: Ch 3, dc in next st, (ch 1, skip next st, dc in each of next 2 sts) across. Fasten off.

Weave remaining ribbon through sts of last row on Bonnet. Place on Head and tie ends of ribbon in bow. ✪

Bow Tie Teddy

Continued from page 9

Rnd 22: (Sc in next 7 sts, sc next 2 sts tog) around. *(48)*

Rnd 23: (Sc in next 6 sts, sc next 2 sts tog) around. *(42)*

Rnd 24: For **First Leg,** sl st in first st, ch 3, skip next 20 sts, (sl st, ch 1, sc) in next st, sc in each st around to ch-3, sc in each of next 3 chs. *(24)*

Rnds 25–36: Sc in each st around.

Rnd 37: For **Foot Shaping,** mark center front of Leg; sc in each st around with 2 sc in each of 7 center front sts. *(31)*

Rnd 38: Sc in each st around with 2 sc in each of 4 center front sts. *(35)*

Rnds 39–42: Sc in each st around.

Rnd 43: (Sc in next 5 sts, sc next 2 sts tog) around. *(30)*

Rnd 44: (Sc in each of next 3 sts, sc next 2 sts tog) around. *(24)*

Rnd 45: (Sc in each of next 2 sts, sc next 2 sts tog) around. Stuff. *(18)*

Rnd 46: (Sc in next st, sc next 2 sts tog) around. Fasten off. Sew opening closed forming a seam lengthwise across bottom of foot.

Rnd 24: For **Second Leg,** join gold with sc in eighth st of rnd 23, sc in each st around to ch-3; working in remaining lps of ch-3, sc in each ch. *(24)*

Rnds 25–46: Repeat rnds 25–46 of First Leg.

Stuff Body and sew rnd 1 to bottom of Head.

ARM (make 2)

Rnd 1: With G hook and gold, ch 2, 6 sc in second ch from hook. *(6 sc made)*

Rnd 2: 2 sc in each st around. *(12)*

Rnd 3: (Sc in next st, 2 sc in next st) around. *(18)*

Rnds 4–21: Sc in each st around. Stuff.

Row 22: Working in rows, sc in first 9 sts, sl st in next st leaving last 8 sts unworked, turn. *(9 sc)*

Row 23: Skip sl st, sc in next 9 sts, sl st in next unworked st on rnd 21, turn. *(9 sc)*

Rnd 24: Working around outer edge, skip sl st, (sc next 2 sts tog) 4 times, sc next sc and next sl st tog; working in unworked sts of rnd 21, (sc next 2 sts tog) around, join with sl st in first sc. Fasten off. Finish stuffing.

Sew last rnd of Arms over rnds 5–9 on each side of Body.

VEST
Front (make 2)

Row 1: Starting at shoulder, with E hook and red, ch 5, sc in second ch from hook, sc in each ch across, turn. *(4 sc made)*

Rows 2–6: Ch 1, sc in each st across, turn.

Row 7: Ch 1, 2 sc in first st, sc in each st across, turn. *(5)*

Row 8: Ch 1, sc in first 4 sts, 2 sc in last st, turn. *(6)*

Row 9: Ch 1, 2 sc in first st, sc in each st across, turn. *(7)*

Row 10: Ch 1, sc in each st across, turn.

Rows 11–16: Ch 1, 2 sc in first st, sc in each st across to last st, 2 sc in last st, turn. At end of last row *(19)*.

Rows 17–20: Ch 1, sc in each st across, turn.

Row 21: Ch 1, sc in first 12 sts, hdc in next st, dc in next st, (tr, ch 1, tr) in next st, dc in next st, hdc in next st, sc in next st, sl st in last st. Fasten off.

Back

Row 1: With E hook and red, ch 36, sc in second ch from hook, sc in each ch across, turn. *(35 sc made)*

Rows 2–6: Ch 1, sc in each st across, turn.

Row 7: For **Armhole Shaping,** sl st in first 4 sts, (sl st, ch 1, sc) in next st, sc in each st across leaving last 4 sts unworked for armhole shaping, turn. *(27 sc)*

Rows 8–12: Sl st in first st, (sl st, ch 1, sc) in next st, sc in each st across leaving last st unworked, turn. At end of last row *(17 sc)*.

Rows 13–21: Ch 1, sc in each st across, turn. At end of last row, fasten off.

Matching sts and ends of rows, sew Vest Fronts to Vest Back at shoulders and sides.

For **Armhole Edging,** with E hook, join red with sc in any st at bottom of one armhole, sc in each st and in end of each row around, join with sl st in first sc. Fasten off. Repeat on other Armhole.

For **Outer Edging,** with E hook, join red with sc in st at center top of Back, sc in each st and in end of each row around with (sc, ch 2, sc) in each ch-1 sp and 3 sc in each front corner. Fasten off.

Place Vest on Bear *(see photo)*, overlap front edges and sew button over front corners through both thicknesses.

BOW TIE

Rnd 1: With E hook and green, ch 8, sc in second ch from hook, sc in next 5 chs, 3 sc in last ch; working in remaining lps on opposite side of starting ch, sc in next 5 chs, 2 sc in last ch. *(16 sc made)*

Rnds 2–5: Sc in each st around.

Rnd 6: (Sc next 2 sts tog) around. *(8)*

Rnd 7: Sc in each st around.

Rnd 8: 2 sc in each st around. *(16)*

Rnds 9–12: Sc in each st around.

Rnd 13: Sc in first st, sc next 3 sts tog, sc in next 5 sts, sc next 3 sts tog, sc in last 4 sts, join with sl st in first sc. Fasten off. Flatten last rnd, sew opening closed.

Gather rnd 7 tightly and sew to front of Body directly below muzzle *(see photo)*. ✪

Mimi The Mouse

Designed by Betty Blount

Finished Size: 10½" tall.

Materials:
- ❑ Worsted yarn:
    - 4 oz. gray
    - 1 oz. dk. pink
    - Small amount each of lt. pink, blue, white, black and red
- ❑ 2" square piece white plastic
- ❑ Lt. pink ½" pom-pom
- ❑ Polyester fiberfill
- ❑ Tapestry and large-eyed embroidery needles
- ❑ G hook or hook needed to obtain gauge

Gauge: 4 sc = 1"; 4 sc rows = 1".

Basic Stitches: Ch, sl st, sc, dc.

Notes: Work in continuous rnds; do not join or turn unless otherwise stated. Mark first st of each rnd.
Before fastening off, leave an 8" or longer end when needed for sewing.

HEAD & BODY
Rnd 1: With gray, ch 2, 6 sc in second ch from hook. *(6 sc made)*
Rnd 2: 2 sc in each st around. *(12)*
Rnd 3: (Sc in next st, 2 sc in next st) around. *(18)*
Rnd 4: Sc in each st around.
Rnd 5: (Sc in each of next 2 sts, 2 sc in next st) around. *(24)*
Rnd 6: (Sc in each of next 3 sts, 2 sc in next st) around. *(30)*
Rnds 7–10: Sc in each st around.
Rnd 11: Sc in first 7 sts, 2 sc in next st, sc in next 14 sts, 2 sc in next st, sc in last 7 sts. *(32)*
Rnd 12: Sc in first 8 sts, 2 sc in each of next 2 sts, sc in next 13 sts, 2 sc in each of next 2 sts, sc in next 7 sts. *(36)*
Rnd 13: Sc in first 6 sts, *(2 sc in next st, sc in each of next 2 sts) 2 times, 2 sc in next st*, sc in next 11 sts; repeat between first *, sc in last 5 sts. *(42)*
Rnds 14–15: Sc in each st around.
Rnd 16: Sc in first 6 sts, *(sc next 2 sts tog, sc in each of next 2 sts) 2 times, sc next 2 sts tog*, sc in next 11 sts; repeat between first *, sc in last 5 sts. *(36)*
Rnd 17: Sc in first 8 sts, (sc next 2 sts tog) 2 times, sc in next 13 sts, (sc next 2 sts tog) 2 times, sc in last 7 sts. Stuff. *(32)*
Rnd 18: Sc in first 8 sts, sc next 2 sts tog, sc in next 15 sts, sc next 2 sts tog, sc in last 5 sts. *(30)*
Rnd 19: (Sc in next st, sc next 2 sts tog) around. *(20)*

Rnd 20: (Sc next 2 sts tog) around. *(10)*
Rnd 21: 2 sc in each st around. *(20)*
Rnd 22: (Sc in next st 2 sc in next st) around. *(30)*
Rnds 23–29: Sc in each st around.
Rnd 30: (Sc in next 9 sts, 2 sc in next st) around. *(33)*
Rnd 31: (Sc in next 10 sts, 2 sc in next st) around. *(36)*
Rnd 32: (Sc in next 11 sts, 2 sc in next st) around. *(39)*
Rnd 33: (Sc in next 12 sts, 2 sc in next st) around. *(42)*
Rnds 34–43: Sc in each st around.
Rnd 44: (Sc in next 5 sts, sc next 2 sts tog) around. *(36)*
Rnd 45: (Sc in next 4 sts, sc next 2 sts tog) around. *(30)*
Rnd 46: (Sc in each of next 3 sts, sc next 2 sts tog) around. Stuff. *(24)*
Rnds 47–48: (Sc next 2 sts tog) around. At end of last rnd, fasten off. Sew opening closed.

ARM & HAND (make 2)
Rnd 1: With gray, ch 8, sl st in first ch to form ring, sc in each ch around. *(8 sc made)*
Rnds 2–9: Sc in each st around.
Rnd 10: (Sc next 2 sts tog) around. *(4)*
Rnd 11: 2 sc in each st around. *(8)*
Rnd 12: Sc in each st around.
Rnd 13: (Sc in next st, 2 sc in next st) around. *(12)*
Row 14: Working in rows, flatten last rnd; working through both thicknesses, ch 1, sc in each st across, turn. *(6)*
Row 15: For **Fingers,** (*ch 3, sc in second ch from hook, sc in next ch, sl st in next st on last row*, sl st in next st) 2 times; repeat between first *. Fasten off. Stuff.
Sew Arms to each side of Body over rnds 24–26.

LEG (make 2)
Row 1: With gray, ch 4, sc in second ch from hook, sc in each of next 2 chs, turn. *(3 sc made)*
Row 2: Ch 1, sc in first st, 2 sc in next st, sc in last st, turn. *(4)*
Row 3: Ch 1, 2 sc in first st, sc in each of next 2 sts, 2 sc in last st, turn. *(6)*
Row 4: Ch 1, sc in each st across, turn.
Row 5: Ch 1, sc in each st across, **do not turn.**
Rnd 6: Working in rnds, ch 14, sc in first st on row 5 to form ring, sc in next 5 sts, sc in last 14 chs. *(20 sc)*
Rnds 7–12: Sc in each st around.
Rnd 13: Sc in each of first 2 sts, (sc next 2 sts tog, sc in next st) around. *(14)*
Rnd 14: Sc in each st around.
Rnd 15: Sc in each of first 2 sts, (sc next 2 sts tog, sc in next st) around. *(10)*

Continued on page 16

Mimi The Mouse

Continued from page 15

Rnd 16: Sc in each st around, join with sl st in first sc. Fasten off.

FOOT SIDE (make 2 gray, 2 lt. pink)
Rnd 1: Ch 2, 8 sc in second ch from hook, join with sl st in first sc. *(8 sc made)*
Row 2: Working in rows, ch 1, sc in each of first 3 sts leaving last 5 sts unworked, turn. *(3)*
Row 3: Ch 1, sc in first st, 2 sc in next st, sc in last st, turn. *(4)*
Row 4: Ch 1, sc in first st, 2 sc in each of next 2 sts, sc in last st, turn. *(6)*
Row 5: Ch 1, sc in each st across, turn.
Row 6: Ch 1; for **Toes**, (3 sc in next st, sl st in next st) 3 times. Fasten off.
Matching ends of rows and sts, sew one lt. pink and one gray Foot Side together. Repeat with remaining Foot Side pieces.
Position rnd 1 on gray side of one Foot over rnd 16 of Leg and sew Foot in place. Repeat with remaining Foot and Leg. Stuff Legs.
Sew top of Legs over rnds 38–45 on each side of Body 1¼" apart at front in a sitting position *(see photo)*.

TAIL
With three strands gray held together as one, ch 25. Fasten off.
Sew one end of Tail to rnd 42 at center back of Body.

EAR SIDE (make 2 gray, 2 lt. pink)
Rnd 1: Ch 2, 6 sc in second ch from hook. *(6 sc made)*
Rnd 2: 2 sc in each st around. *(12)*
Rnd 3: (2 sc in next st, sc in next st) around. *(18)*
Rnd 4: (2 sc in next st, sc in each of next 2 sts) around. *(24)*
Rnd 5: (2 sc in next st, sc in each of next 3 sts) around. *(30)*
Rnd 6: (2 sc in next st, sc in next 4 sts) around, join with sl st in first sc. Fasten off.
For each Ear, hold one lt. pink and one gray Ear Side wrong sides together and lt. pink Side facing you; working through both thicknesses, join gray with sc in any st of last rnd, sc in each st around, join. Fasten off.
Sew to each side of Head over rnds 4–9 *(see photo)*.

TEETH
Cut Teeth from white plastic according to the full-size pattern piece. Using large-eyed embroidery needle and gray yarn, securely sew top edge of Teeth to center front of Head on rnd 13.

NOSE
Rnd 1: With gray, ch 2, 3 sc in second ch from hook. *(3 sc made)*
Rnd 2: 2 sc in each st around. *(6)*
Rnd 3: (2 sc in next st, sc in next st) around. *(9)*
Rnd 4: Sc in each st around.
Rnd 5: (2 sc in next st, sc in each of next 2 sts) around, join with sl st in first sc. Fasten off. Stuff.
Sew last rnd of Nose to Head over rnds 10–13, covering top of Teeth. Sew pom-pom to end of Nose.

MOUTH
With red, ch 8. Fasten off. Sew to Head in a U-shape around Teeth *(see photo)*.

EYE (make 2)
Rnd 1: With black, ch 2, 5 sc in second ch from hook, join with sl st in first sc. Fasten off.
Rnd 2: Join white with sc in any st, sc in same st, (sc in next st, 2 sc in next st) around, join. Fasten off.
Sew Eyes to front of Head over rnds 7–10 about 1" apart.

EYELID (make 2)
Row 1: With blue, ch 2, 4 sc in second ch from hook, turn. *(4 sc made)*
Row 2: Ch 1, 2 sc in first st, sc in each of next 2 sts, 2 sc in last st. Fasten off. Sew over Eye.

HAIR
For each fringe, cut one 4" strand of gray and one 4" strand of white. Fold both strands held together in half, insert hook in st, pull fold through, pull ends through fold. Tighten.
Fringe in each st of first two rnds on Head. Brush Strands to fluff.

SKIRT
Rnd 1: With dk. pink, ch 28, sl st in first ch to form ring, ch 1, sc in each ch around, join with sl st in first sc. *(28 sc made)*
Rnd 2: Ch 1, 2 sc in first st, sc in next st, (2 sc in next st, sc in next st) around, join. *(42)*
Rnd 3: (Ch 3, 2 dc) in first st, skip next st, (3 dc in next st, skip next st) around, join with sl st in top of ch-3. *(63 dc)*
Rnd 4: Sl st in each of next 2 sts, (sl st, ch 3, dc, ch 1, 2 dc) in next sp between 3-dc groups, skip next 3 sts, *(2 dc, ch 1, 2 dc) in next sp between 3-dc groups *(shell made)*, skip next 3 sts; repeat from * around, join. *(21 shells)*
Rnd 5: Sl st in next st, (sl st, ch 3, dc, ch 1, 2 dc) in next ch-1 sp, dc in next sp between shells, *(2 dc, ch 1, 2 dc) in next ch-1 sp, dc in next sp between shells; repeat from * around, join. Fasten off. Place Skirt on Body *(see photo)*. ✪

Patchwork Pretty

Designed by Debra Eckstein

Finished Size: 4¾" diameter.

Materials:
- ❏ Worsted yarn:
    30 yds. off-white
    5 yds. each of 20 desired colors
- ❏ Polyester fiberfill
- ❏ G hook or hook needed to obtain gauge

Gauge: Motif is 2" across.

Basic Stitches: Ch, sl st, dc.

MOTIF (make 1 of each color)
Rnd 1: Ch 3, sl st in first ch to form ring, ch 3, 2 dc in ring, ch 1, (3 dc, ch 1) 2 times in ring, join with sl st in top of ch-3. *(9 dc, 3 chs made)*
Rnd 2: Sl st in each of next 2 sts, (sl st, ch 3, 2 dc, ch 2, 3 dc) in next ch sp, (3 dc, ch 2, 3 dc) in each of last 2 ch sps, join. Fasten off.

ASSEMBLY
With right sides of Motifs facing you, working through both thicknesses, sc edges of Motifs together *(see illustrations)* to form Top Section, Bottom Section and Center Section.

Matching sts, sc Top and Bottom Sections to each edge of Center Section, stuffing firmly before closing last edge. ✪

TOP & BOTTOM SECTIONS

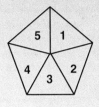

CENTER SECTION

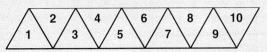

Playtime Pals

Designed by Lisa Michaud

Finished Size: Doll is 9" tall.

Materials:
- ❏ Worsted yarn:
  - 3 oz. lt. peach
  - ½ oz. brown
  - Small amount each of black and blue
- ❏ Pompadour baby yarn:
  - 1¼ oz. lt. green
  - Small amount white
- ❏ Pink embroidery floss
- ❏ 8" of white ¼" satin ribbon
- ❏ Polyester fiberfill
- ❏ Tapestry needle
- ❏ F and G hooks or hooks needed to obtain gauges

Gauges: **F hook and baby yarn,** 5 sc = 1"; 5 sc rows = 1". **G hook and worsted yarn,** 4 sc = 1"; 4 sc rows = 1".

Basic Stitches: Ch, sl st, sc, hdc, dc, tr.

Notes: Work in continuous rnds; do not join or turn unless otherwise stated. Mark first st of each rnd.
Before fastening off, leave an 8" or longer end when needed for sewing.

DOLL
Head & Body
Rnd 1: With G hook and lt. peach, ch 2, 6 sc in second ch from hook. *(6 sc made)*
Rnd 2: 2 sc in each st around. *(12)*
Rnd 3: (Sc in next st, 2 sc in next st) around. *(18)*
Rnd 4: (Sc in each of next 2 sts, 2 sc in next st) around. *(24)*
Rnd 5: (Sc in each of next 3 sts, 2 sc in next st) around. *(30)*
Rnd 6: Sc in each st around.
Rnd 7: (Sc in next 4 sts, 2 sc in next st) around. *(36)*
Rnds 8–12: Sc in each st around.
Rnd 13: (Sc in next 4 sts, sc next 2 sts tog) around. *(30)*
Rnd 14: Sc in each st around.
Rnd 15: (Sc next 2 sts tog) around. *(15)*
Rnds 16–17: Sc in each st around.
Rnd 18: 2 sc in each st around. *(30)*
Rnd 19: Sc in each st around.
Rnd 20: (Sc in next 4 sts, 2 sc in next st) around. *(36)*
Rnd 21: Sc in each st around.
Rnd 22: (Sc in next 5 sts, 2 sc in next st) around. *(42)*
Rnds 23–28: Sc in each st around.
Rnd 29: (Sc in next 5 sts, sc next 2 sts tog) around. *(36)*

Rnd 30: Sc in each st around.
Rnd 31: (Sc in next 4 sts, sc next 2 sts tog) around. *(30)*
Rnd 32: (Sc in each of next 3 sts, sc next 2 sts tog) around. *(24)*
Rnd 33: (Sc in each of next 2 sts, sc next 2 sts tog) around. Stuff. *(18)*
Rnd 34: (Sc in next st, sc next 2 sts tog) around. *(12)*
Rnd 35: (Sc next 2 sts tog) around, join with sl st in first sc. Fasten off. Sew opening closed.

Arm (make 2)
Rnd 1: With G hook and lt. peach, ch 2, 6 sc in second ch from hook. *(6 sc made)*
Rnd 2: 2 sc in each st around. *(12)*
Rnds 3–4: Sc in each st around.
Rnd 5: (Sc next 2 sts tog) around. *(6)*
Rnd 6: 2 sc in each st around. *(12)*
Rnds 7–9: Sc in each st around.
Rnd 10: Sc in first 4 sts, (sc next 2 sts tog) 2 times, sc in last 4 sts. *(10)*
Rnd 11: Sc in first 4 sts, 2 sc in each of next 2 sts, sc in last 4 sts. *(12)*
Rnds 12–14: Sc in each st around. At end of last rnd, join with sl st in first sc. Fasten off. Stuff.
Sew Arms over rnds 19–22 on each side of Body.

Leg (make 2)
Rnd 1: With G hook and lt. peach, ch 2, 6 sc in second ch from hook. *(6 sc made)*
Rnd 2: 2 sc in each st around. *(12)*
Rnd 3: (Sc in next st, 2 sc in next st) around. *(18)*
Rnds 4–5: Sc in each st around.
Rnd 6: Sc in first 6 sts, (sc next 2 sts tog) 3 times, sc in last 6 sts. *(15)*
Rnd 7: Sc in first 6 sts, 2 sc in each of next 3 sts, sc in last 6 sts. *(18)*
Rnds 8–10: Sc in each st around.
Rnd 11: (Sc next 2 sts tog) around. *(9)*
Rnd 12: 2 sc in each st around. *(18)*
Rnds 13–16: Sc in each st around. At end of last rnd, join with sl st in first sc. Fasten off. Stuff.
Sew Legs over rnds 30–35 on each side of Body.

Facial Features
With blue yarn, using satin stitch *(see Stitch Guide)*, embroider eyes on rnd 9 of Head about ¾" apart.
With pink floss, using straight stitch, embroider mouth over rnd 12 centered below eyes *(see photo)*.

Continued on page 22

see that no
...dle. To her
...ouse.
... On the
... the second
... as she felt
... porridge.
... hot. Then
... she said.

Huggy Bunny

Designed by Mickey Turner

Finished Size: 10" long.

Materials:
- ❑ 1½ oz. white fuzzy-type or regular worsted yarn
- ❑ 4" square piece pink felt
- ❑ Pink sewing thread
- ❑ White carpet and button thread
- ❑ 2 sew-on wiggly eyes
- ❑ 7" piece of ½"-wide elastic
- ❑ 2½" piece cardboard
- ❑ Polyester fiberfill
- ❑ Sewing and tapestry needles
- ❑ G hook or hook needed to obtain gauge

Gauge: 4 sc = 1"; 4 sc rows = 1".

Basic Stitches: Ch, sl st, sc, hdc.

Note: Sl sts are not used or counted as a st unless otherwise stated in instructions.

BODY BOTTOM
Row 1: Ch 7, sc in second ch from hook, sc in each ch across, turn. *(6 sc made)*

Row 2: Ch 1, 2 sc in first st, sc in each st across to last st, 2 sc in last st, turn. *(8)*

Row 3: Ch 1, sc in each st across, turn.

Rows 4–15: Repeat rows 2 and 3 alternately. At end of last row *(20)*.

Row 16: Sl st in first st, sc in each st across to last st, sl st in last st, turn. *(18 sc)*

Row 17: Skip sl st, sc in each st across leaving last sl st unworked, turn.

Rows 18–20: Ch 1, sc in each st across, turn.

Row 21: Ch 1, 2 sc in first st, sc in each st across to last st, 2 sc in last st, turn. *(20)*

Row 22: Ch 1, sc in each st across, turn.

Rows 23–24: Ch 7, sc in second ch from hook, sc in each ch and in each st across, turn. *(26, 32)*

Row 25: Ch 1, 2 sc in first st, sc in each st across to last st, 2 sc in last st, turn. *(34)*

Rows 26–28: Ch 1, sc in each st across, turn.

Rows 29–30: Repeat rows 16 and 17. *(32 sc)*

Row 31: Ch 2, hdc in each of next 2 sts, sc in each st across to last 3 sts, hdc in each of last 3 sts, turn.

Row 32: Sl st in each of first 3 sts, ch 1, sc in each st across leaving last 3 sts unworked, turn. *(26 sc)*

Row 33: Ch 1, sc in each st across leaving last 3 sl sts unworked, turn. *(26)*

Row 34: Sl st in first st, sc in each st across to last st, sl st in last st, turn. *(24 sc)*

Rows 35–42: Ch 1, skip sl st, sl st in next st, sc in each st across to last sc, sl st in last sc leaving last sl st unworked, turn. At end of last row *(8)*.

Row 43: Sl st in first st, (sc next 2 sts tog) 3 times, sl st in last st, turn. *(3 sc)*

Row 44: Skip sl st, sc next 2 sts tog, sl st in next st. Fasten off. *(1 sc)*

BODY SIDE (make 2)
Row 1: Ch 3, sc in second ch from hook, sc in next ch, turn. *(2 sc made)*

Row 2: Ch 1, 2 sc in each st across, turn. *(4)*

Row 3: Ch 1, sc in each st across, turn.

Row 4: Ch 1, 2 sc in first st. sc in each st across to last st, 2 sc in last st, turn. *(6)*

Rows 5–13: Repeat rows 3 and 4 alternately. At end of last row *(14)*.

Row 14: Ch 1, 2 sc in first st, sc in each st across to last st, sl st in last st, turn. *(14 sc)*

Row 15: Skip sl st, sl st in next st, sc in each st across, turn. *(13 sc)*

Row 16: Ch 1, 2 sc in first st, sc in each st across to last sl st, sl st in last sl st, turn. *(14 sc)*

Row 17: Skip sl st, sc in each st across, turn.

Row 18: Ch 1, sc in first 13 sts, sl st in next st, turn. *(13 sc)*

Row 19: Skip sl st, sl st in each of next 2 sts, sc in each st across, turn. *(11 sc)*

Row 20: Sl st in first st, sc in each st across to last st, sl st in last st, turn. *(9 sc)*

Row 21: Skip sl st, sl st in next st, sc in each st across to last st, sl st in last st leaving last sl st unworked, turn. *(7 sc)*

Row 22: Skip sl st, sl st in next st, sc in each st across to last sl st, sc in last sl st, turn. *(7 sc)*

Row 23: Ch 7, sc in second ch from hook, sc in each ch and in each sc across, turn. *(13 sc)*

Row 24: Sl st in first st, sc in each st across, turn. *(12 sc)*

Row 25: Ch 1, 2 sc in first st, sc in each st across leaving last sl st unworked, turn. *(13 sc)*

Row 26: Ch 1, sc in each st across to last st, sl st in last st, turn. *(12 sc)*

Row 27: Skip sl st, sc in each st across, turn.

Row 28: Ch 1, sc in each st across, turn.

Row 29: Ch 2, hdc in each of next 2 sts, sc in next 8 sts, 2 sc in last st, turn. *(13 sts)*

Row 30: Ch 1, sc in first 10 sts leaving last 3 sts unworked, turn. *(10 sc)*

Row 31: Sl st in first st, sc in each st across, turn. *(9 sc)*

Continued on page 22

Huggy Bunny

Continued from page 21

Row 32: Ch 1, sc in each st across leaving last sl st unworked, turn. *(9 sc)*

Rows 33–34: Ch 1, sc in each st across, turn.

Row 35: Sl st in each of first 2 sts, sc in each st across, turn. *(7 sc)*

Row 36: Ch 1, sc in each st across leaving last 2 sl sts unworked, turn.

Row 37: Sl st in first st, sc in each st across, turn. *(6 sc)*

Row 38: Sl st in each of first 2 sts, sc in each st across leaving last sl st unworked, turn. *(4 sc)*

Row 39: Sl st in first st, sc in each st across leaving last 2 sl sts unworked, turn. *(3 sc)*

Row 40: Ch 1, sc in each of first 2 sts, sl st in last st, turn. *(2 sc)*

Row 41: Ch 1, sc 2 sts tog. Fasten off.

Matching ends of rows and sts, sew straight edge of Sides together. Sew remaining edges of Sides to Bottom, leaving unworked sts at ends of rows 30 and 32 free for Leg openings. Stuff before closing.

FRONT LEGS

Rnd 1: Join with sc in any unworked st at one end of row 32 at bottom of one Leg opening, sc in same st, 2 sc in each st around opening, join with sl st in first sc. *(12 sc made)*

Rnd 2: Ch 1, sc in each st around, join.

Rnd 3: Ch 1, sc in first st, sc next 2 sts tog, (sc in next st, sc next 2 sts tog) around, join. Stuff. *(8)*

Rnds 4–5: Ch 1, sc first 2 sts tog, (sc next 2 sts tog) around, join. At end of last rnd, fasten off. Repeat on other Leg opening.

EAR (make 2)

Row 1: Ch 12, sc in second ch from hook, sc in each ch across, turn. *(11 sc made)*

Row 2: Ch 1, sc in each st across to last st, 2 sc in last st, turn. *(12)*

Row 3: Ch 1, sc in each st across, turn.

Row 4: Repeat row 2. *(13)*

Rows 5–6: Ch 1, sc in each st across, turn.

Row 7: Sl st in first st, sc in each st across, turn. *(12 sc)*

Row 8: Ch 1, sc in each st across to last st, sl st in last st leaving last sl st unworked, turn. *(11 sc)*

Row 9: Skip sl st, sl st in next st, sc in each st across. Fasten off. Using crocheted piece as a pattern, cut piece from felt ¼" smaller on all edges. Sew to front of Ear.

Lapping short straight edge at bottom of one Ear left over right and other Ear right over left *(see photo)*, sew folded edges to row 35 on each Body Side.

FINISHING

For **Nose**, cut a ½" × ¾" oval from felt. Sew centered over seam at narrow end of Body *(see photo)*.

For **Whiskers**, tie two 2" strands of carpet thread to a st on each side of Nose.

Sew wiggly eyes to Body above Nose ¾" apart.

For **Tail**, wrap yarn around cardboard 75 times. Slide loops off cardboard, tie separate piece yarn around middle of all loops. Cut ends of loops, trim to shape a ball. Sew to seam at row 10 of Body Side.

For **Bottle Strap**, overlap ends of elastic ½", sew ends together. Sew to seam at rows 25–29 on Body Side. ✪

Playtime Pals

Continued from page 18

SUNSUIT

Row 1: Beginning at top of Bib, with F hook and lt. green, ch 11, sc in second ch from hook, sc in each ch across, turn. *(10 sc made)*

Row 2: Ch 1, sc in each st across, turn.

Row 3: Ch 1, 2 sc in first st, sc in each st across to last st, 2 sc in last st, turn. *(12)*

Rows 4–5: Repeat rows 2 and 3. *(14)*

Rnd 6: Working in rnds, for **Pants**, ch 1, sc in each st across Bib, ch 50, join with sl st in first sc, **do not turn.** *(14 sc, 50 chs)*

Rnd 7: Sc in each st and in each ch around. *(64 sc)*

Rnds 8–10: Sc in each st around.

Rnd 11: For **First Leg**, sc in first 8 sts, ch 20, skip next 32 sts, sc in last 24 sts. *(32 sc, 20 chs)*

Rnd 12: Sc in each st and in each ch around. *(52 sc)*

Rnd 13: Sc in each st around.

Rnd 14: (Sc next 2 sts tog) around. *(26)*

Rnd 15: (Sc in next 11 sts, sc next 2 sts tog) around. *(24)*

Rnd 16: (Sc in next 4 sts, sc next 2 sts tog) around. *(20)*

Rnd 17: (Sc in each of next 2 sts, sc next 2 sts tog) around, join with sl st in first sc. *(15)*

Rnd 18: (Ch 3, 2 dc) in first st, 3 dc in each st around, join with sl st in top of ch-3. Fasten off. *(45)*

Rnd 11: For **Second Leg**, join lt. green with sc in next unworked st on rnd 10, sc in each st around. *(32)*

Rnd 12: Working in remaining lps on opposite side of ch-20, sc in each ch, sc in each st of last rnd. *(52)*

Rnds 13–18: Repeat rnds 13–18 of First Leg.

Ties
For **Bib Tie,** with F hook and white, ch 80. Fasten off. Weave through starting ch on row 1 of Bib.

For **Waist Tie,** with F hook and white, ch 125. Fasten off. Beginning and ending at edges of Bib, weave through ch-50 on rnd 6 of Pants.

Place Sunsuit on Doll. Tie ends of Bib Tie in a bow around neck and ends of Waist Tie in a bow at front of Pants.

BONNET
Row 1: With F hook and lt. green, ch 7, sc in second ch from hook, sc in next 4 chs, 3 sc in last ch; working in remaining lps on opposite side of starting ch, sc in last 5 chs, turn. *(13 sc made)*

Row 2: Ch 1, sc in first 5 sts, 2 sc in each of next 3 sts, sc in last 5 sts, turn. *(16)*

Row 3: Ch 1, sc in first 5 sts, (2 sc in next st, sc in next st) 3 times, sc in last 5 sts, turn. *(19)*

Row 4: Ch 1, sc in first 5 sts, (2 sc in next st, sc in each of next 3 sts) 2 times, 2 sc in next st, sc in last 5 sts, turn. *(22)*

Row 5: Ch 1, sc in first 5 sts, 2 sc in next st, sc in next 4 sts, (2 sc in next st, sc in next 5 sts) 2 times, turn. *(25)*

Row 6: Ch 1, sc in first 5 sts, (2 sc in next st, sc in next 4 sts) 3 times, sc in last 5 sts, turn. *(28)*

Row 7: Ch 1, sc in each st across, turn.

Row 8: Ch 1, sc in first 5 sts, (2 sc in next st, sc in next 5 sts) 3 times, sc in last 5 sts, turn. *(31)*

Row 9: Ch 1, sc in each st across, turn.

Row 10: Working this row in **back lps** *(see Stitch Guide),* ch 1, sc in each st across, turn.

Row 11: Ch 1, sc in first 15 sts, 2 sc in next st, sc in last 15 sts, turn. *(32)*

Row 12: Ch 1, sc in each st across, turn.

Row 13: Ch 1, sc in first 7 sts, 2 sc in next st, (sc in next 7 sts, 2 sc in next st) across, turn. *(36)*

Rows 14–15: Ch 1, sc in each st across, turn.

Rnd 16: Working around outer edge, ch 1, sc in each st and in end of each row around with 3 sc in each corner, join with sl st in first sc.

Row 17: For **Ruffle,** (ch 3, 2 dc) in first st, 3 dc in each of next 39 sts leaving remaining sts unworked. Fasten off.

For **Tie,** with F hook and white, ch 90. Fasten off. Beginning and ending at ends of Ruffle, weave through sts of row 15 on Bonnet.

Place Bonnet on Doll. Tie ends of Tie in bow at bottom of Head *(see photo).*

BOOTIE (make 2)
Rnds 1–4: With F hook and lt. green, repeat rnds 1–4 of Doll Head & Body.

Rnds 5–9: Sc in each st around.

Rnd 10: (Sc in each of next 2 sts, sc next 2 sts tog) around, join with sl st in first sc. *(18)*

Rnd 11: (Ch 3, 2 dc) in first st, 3 dc in each st around, join with sl st in top of ch-3. Fasten off.

For **Tie,** with F hook and white, ch 60. Fasten off. Weave through sts of rnd 10, tie ends in bow.

TEDDY BEAR
Head
Rnd 1: Starting at tip of muzzle, with F hook and brown, ch 2, 6 sc in second ch from hook. *(6 sc made)*

Rnd 2: Sc in each st around.

Rnd 3: Sc in each of first 2 sts, 2 sc in each of next 2 sts, sc in each of last 2 sts. *(8)*

Rnd 4: Sc in each of first 2 sts, (2 sc in next st, sc in next st) 2 times, sc in each of last 2 sts. *(10)*

Rnd 5: Sc in each of first 2 sts, (2 sc in next st, sc in each of next 2 sts) 2 times, sc in each of last 2 sts. *(12)*

Rnds 6–7: Sc in each st around. Stuff.

Rnd 8: (Sc next 2 sts tog) around, join with sl st in first sc. Fasten off. Sew opening closed.

With black, using French knot *(see Stitch Guide),* embroider eyes on rnd 4 of Head ½" apart; using satin stitch, embroider nose over rnd 1; using straight stitch, embroider inverted V-shape for mouth below nose *(see photo).*

Ear (make 2)
With F hook and brown, ch 2, 6 sc in second ch from hook, join with sl st in first sc. Fasten off.

Sew Ears to rnd 7 of Head 1" apart.

Body
Rnd 1: With F hook and brown, ch 6, sl st in first ch to form ring, ch 1, sc in each ch around. *(6 sc made)*

Rnd 2: (Sc in next st, 2 sc in next st) around. *(9)*

Rnd 3: (Sc in each of next 2 sts, 2 sc in next st) around. *(12)*

Rnds 4–5: Sc in each st around. Stuff.

Rnd 6: (Sc next 2 sts tog) around, join with sl st in first sc. Fasten off. Sew opening closed.

Sew rnd 1 of Body over rnds 6–7 on Bottom of Head.

Arm (make 2)
Rnd 1: With F hook and brown, ch 2, 4 sc in second ch from hook. *(4 sc made)*

Rnds 2–5: Sc in each st around. At end of last rnd, join with sl st in first sc. Fasten off. Stuff.

Sew Arms to rnd 2 on each side of Body.

Leg (make 2)
Rnds 1–5: Repeat rnds 1–5 of Arm; at end of last rnd **do not fasten off.**

Row 6: Flatten last rnd; working through both thicknesses, ch 1, sc in each st across. Fasten off.

Sew row 6 of each Leg over rnds 4–6 on each side of Body.

Tie ribbon around Bear's neck. ✪

Snuggly Snail Pillow

Designed by Jean Ford

Finished Size: 14" tall.

Materials:
- ❑ Worsted yarn:
  - 4 oz. rust
  - 2 oz. tan
  - 1 oz. blue
  - 1 oz. red
  - Small amount white
- ❑ Polyester fiberfill
- ❑ Small amounts of black, white and red felt
- ❑ Red and white sewing thread
- ❑ White embroidery floss
- ❑ 2 cups of dry rice or gravel sealed in a plastic bag
- ❑ Sewing and tapestry needles
- ❑ G hook or hook needed to obtain gauge

Gauge: 4 sc = 1"; 4 sc rows = 1".

Basic Stitches: Ch, sl st, sc.

Note: Work in continuous rnds; do not join or turn unless otherwise stated. Mark first st of each rnd.

SHELL SIDE (make 2)
Rnd 1: With rust, ch 2, 6 sc in second ch from hook. *(6 sc made)*
Rnd 2: 2 sc in each st around. *(12)*
Rnd 3: (Sc in next st, 2 sc in next st) around. *(18)*
Rnd 4: (Sc in each of next 2 sts, 2 sc in next st) around. *(24)*
Rnd 5: (Sc in each of next 3 sts, 2 sc in next st) around. *(30)*
Rnd 6: Sc in each st around.
Rnd 7: (Sc in next 4 sts, 2 sc in next st) around. *(36)*
Rnd 8: (Sc in next 5 sts, 2 sc in next st) around. *(42)*
Rnd 9: (Sc in next 6 sts, 2 sc in next st) around. *(48)*
Rnd 10: (Sc in next 7 sts, 2 sc in next st) around. *(54)*
Rnd 11: Sc in each st around.
Rnd 12: Sc in first 4 sts, (2 sc in next st, sc in next 8 sts) 5 times, 2 sc in next st, sc in last 4 sts. *(60)*
Rnd 13: (Sc in next 9 sts, 2 sc in next st) around. *(66)*
Rnd 14: Sc in first 5 sts, (2 sc in next st, sc in next 10 sts) 5 times, 2 sc in next st, sc in last 5 sts. *(72)*
Rnd 15: (Sc in next 11 sts, 2 sc in next st) around. *(78)*
Rnd 16: Sc in first 6 sts, (2 sc in next st, sc in next 12 sts) 5 times, 2 sc in next st, sc in last 6 sts. *(84)*
Rnd 17: (Sc in next 13 sts, 2 sc in next st) around. *(90)*
Rnd 18: Sc in first 7 sts, (2 sc in next st, sc in next 14 sts) 5 times, 2 sc in next st, sc in last 7 sts. *(96)*
Rnd 19: (Sc in next 15 sts, 2 sc in next st) around. *(102)*
Rnds 20–23: Sc in each st around. At end of last rnd on first Side, fasten off; at end of last rnd on second Side, **do not fasten off.**

Hold Shell Side wrong sides together; working through both thicknesses, join rust with sl st in any st, sl st in each st around half of edge; to balance Snail, place rice bag wrapped with fiberfill between Shell Sides, continue to sl st in each remaining st around, stuffing before closing. Fasten off.

Shell Rings (make 2 of each size)
With tan, ch 50. Fasten off. Sew to rnd 8 on each Shell Side.
With tan, ch 70. Fasten off. Sew to rnd 12 on each Shell Side.

HEAD
Rnds 1–5: Starting at center front of Head, with tan, repeat rnds 1–5 of Shell Side.
Rnds 6–7: Repeat rnds 7–8 of Shell Side.
Rnds 8–17: Sc in each st around.
Rnd 18: (Sc in next 5 sts, sc next 2 sts tog) around. *(36)*
Rnd 19: (Sc in next 4 sts, sc next 2 sts tog) around. *(30)*
Rnd 20: (Sc in each of next 3 sts, sc next 2 sts tog) around. *(24)*
Rnd 21: (Sc in each of next 2 sts, sc next 2 sts tog) around. *(18)*
Rnd 22: (Sc in next st, sc next 2 sts tog) around. Stuff. *(12)*
Rnd 23: (Sc next 2 sts tog) around. Fasten off. Sew opening closed.

NECK
Rnd 1: With tan, ch 35, sl st in first ch to form ring, ch 1, sc in each ch around. *(35 sc made)*
Rnds 2–6: Sc in each st around.
Rnd 7: (Sc in next 5 sts, sc next 2 sts tog) around. *(30)*
Rnds 8–13: Sc in each st around.
Row 14: Working in rows, sc in first 20 sts leaving last 10 sts unworked, turn. *(20)*
Rows 15–22: Ch 1, sc first 2 sts tog, sc in each st across to last 2 sts, sc last 2 sts tog, turn. At end of last row *(4)*.

Continued on page 26

Snuggly Snail Pillow

Continued from page 25

Row 23: Ch 1, (sc next 2 sts tog) across, turn. *(2)*
Row 24: Ch 1, sc in each st across. Fasten off.
With Head tilted up slightly, sew rnd 1 on Neck to rnds 13–20 on lower half of Head. Stuff Neck.
Positioning row 24 of Neck over seam about 1" above weighted bottom portion of Shell *(see photo)*, sew bottom edge of Neck over front of Shell.

NOSE

Rnd 1: With red, ch 2, 6 sc in second ch from hook. *(6 sc made)*
Rnd 2: 2 sc in each st around. *(12)*
Rnd 3: (2 sc in next st, sc in next st) around. *(18)*
Rnd 4: (Sc in next st, sc next 2 sts tog) around. Stuff. *(12)*
Rnd 5: (Sc next 2 sts tog) around, join with sl st in first sc. Fasten off.
Sew Nose to rnd 2 of Head.

TAIL

Row 1: With tan, ch 13, sc in second ch from hook, sc in each ch across, turn. *(12 sc made)*
Rows 2–5: Ch 1, sc first 2 sts tog, sc in each st across to last 2 sts, sc last 2 sts tog, turn. At end of last row *(4)*.
Row 6: Ch 1, (sc next 2 sts tog) across. Fasten off.
Fold in half lengthwise, sew ends of rows together.
Sew wide end of Tail on Shell opposite from Head and Neck.

ANTENNA (make 2)

Rnd 1: With tan, ch 2, 6 sc in second ch from hook. *(6 sc made)*
Rnd 2: 2 sc in each st around. *(12)*
Rnd 3: (Sc next 2 sts tog) around. Stuff lightly. *(6)*
Rnds 4–9: Sc in each st around. At end of last rnd, fasten off. Stuff.
Sew to each side of Head 3" from Nose and 2½" apart.

FACIAL FEATURES

For **Eyes,** cut two 1⅜" circles from white felt and two 1⅛" circles from black felt. With black sewing thread and needle, sew one black circle to center of one white circle. With white floss, embroider V-shaped highlight on black circle. Repeat with remaining circles.
With white sewing thread, sew Eyes to Head one rnd above Nose 1" apart.
For **Mouth,** cut ¼" × 1" strip from red felt. Trim strip to form smile. Sew Mouth to Head ½" below Nose.

NECK BAND

Row 1: With blue, ch 35, sc in second ch from hook, sc in each ch across, turn. *(34 sc made)*
Rows 2–3: Ch 1, sc in each st across, turn.
Row 4: Sl st in each st across. Fasten off.
Place Band around Neck and sew ends together at center front.

BOW

Row 1: With blue, ch 13, sc in second ch from hook, sc in each ch across, turn. *(12 sc made)*
Rows 2–5: Ch 1, sc first 2 sts tog, sc in each st across to last 2 sts, sc last 2 sts tog, turn. At end of last row *(4)*.
Row 6: Ch 1, sc first 2 sts tog, sc last 2 sts tog, turn. *(2)*
Row 7: 2 sc in each st across, turn. *(4)*
Rows 8–11: Ch 1, 2 sc in first st, sc in each st across to last st, 2 sc in last st, turn. At end of last row *(12)*.
Row 12: Ch 1, sc in each st across, turn.
Rnd 13: Working around outer edge, sl st in each st and in end of each row around, join with sl st in first sl st. Fasten off.
Rnd 14: Join white with sl st in any sl st, sl st in each sl st around, join. Fasten off.
Sew center of Bow to seam on front of Neck Band.

HAT

Rnds 1–6: Repeat rnds 1–6 of Shell Side.
Row 7: Working in rows, sc in first 15 sts leaving last 15 sts unworked, turn. *(15)*
Row 8: Ch 1, sc first 2 sts tog, (sc in each of next 2 sts, 2 sc in next st) 3 times, sc in each of next 2 sts, sc last 2 sts tog, turn. *(16)*
Row 9: Ch 1, sc first 2 sts tog, (sc next 2 sts tog, sc in each of next 3 sts) 2 times, (sc next 2 sts tog) 2 times, turn. *(11)*
Row 10: Ch 1, sc first 2 sts tog, sc next 2 sts tog, sc in each of next 3 sts, (sc next 2 sts tog) 2 times, turn. *(7)*
Row 11: Ch 1, sc first 2 sts tog, (sc next 2 sts tog) 2 times, sc in last st, turn. *(4)*
Rows 12–13: Ch 1, sc in each st across, turn.
Rnd 14: Working around outer edge, sl st in each st and in end of each row around, join with sl st in first sl st. Fasten off.
For **Trim,** with tan, ch 40. Fasten off. Sew around bottom of Hat.
Stuff Hat lightly. Sew bottom edge to Head between Antennae. ✪

CHAPTER 2

Bonnets, Booties & Bibs

Oh Dear, What Can the Matter Be?

Oh dear, what can the matter be?
Dear, dear, what can the matter be?
Oh dear, what can the matter be?
Johnny's so long at the fair.

He promised to buy me a pair of sleeve buttons,
A pair of new stockings that cost him two pence,
He promised me he'd bring me a bunch of blue ribbons,
To tie up my bonny brown hair.

This charming nursery song, first introduced at the end of the 18th century, probably helped nursemaids teach their young charges how to finish dressing themselves.

Ribbons & Lace Bib

Finished Size: 8" across front of Bib.

Materials:
- ❏ 90 yds. white size 5 pearl cotton thread
- ❏ 1½ yds. desired color ¼" ribbon
- ❏ Sewing thread to match ribbon
- ❏ Sewing needle
- ❏ No. 1 steel hook or hook needed to obtain gauge

Gauge: 7 sc = 1"; 8 **back lp** rows = 1".

Basic Stitches: Ch, sl st, sc, dc.

Note: Work in **back lps** *(see Stitch Guide)* throughout pattern unless otherwise stated.

BIB FRONT
Row 1: Ch 22, sc in second ch from hook, sc in each ch across, turn. *(21 sc made)*
Row 2: Ch 1, sc in first 10 sts, 3 sc in next st, sc in last 10 sts, turn. *(23)*
Row 3: Ch 1, sc in each st across, turn.
Row 4: Ch 1, sc in first 11 sts, 3 sc in next st, sc in last 11 sts, turn. *(25)*
Row 5: Ch 1, sc in each st across, turn.
Row 6: Ch 1, sc in first 12 sts, 3 sc in next st, sc in last 12 sts, turn. *(27)*
Row 7: Ch 1, sc in each st across, turn.
Row 8: Ch 1, sc in first 13 sts, 3 sc in next st, sc in last 13 sts, turn. *(29)*
Row 9: Ch 1, sc in each st across, turn.
Row 10: Ch 1, sc in first 14 sts, 3 sc in next st, sc in last 14 sts, turn. *(31)*
Row 11: Ch 1, sc in each st across, turn.
Row 12: Ch 1, sc in first 15 sts, 3 sc in next st, sc in last 15 sts, turn. *(33)*
Row 13: Ch 1, sc in each st across, turn.
Row 14: Ch 1, sc in first 16 sts, 3 sc in next st, sc in last 16 sts, turn. *(35)*
Row 15: Ch 1, sc in each st across. Fasten off.

NECK BAND
Row 1: Ch 13, sc in end of row 1, sc in end of next 14 rows, sc in first 17 sts of row 15, 3 sc in next st, sc in last 17 sts, sc in end of next 15 rows, turn. *(67 sc and 27 chs made)*
Row 2: Ch 14, sc in second ch from hook, sc in next 12 chs; working in **both lps,** sc in next 15 sts; working in **back lps,** sc in next 37 sts; working in **both lps,** sc in next 15 sts, sc in last 13 chs, turn. *(93 sc)*
Row 3: Working in **both lps,** ch 1, sc in first 28 sts; working in **back lps,** 3 sc in next st, (sc in next 17 sts, 3 sc in next st) 2 times; working in **both lps,** sc in last 28 sts, turn. *(99)*

Row 4: Working in **both lps,** ch 1, sc in first 30 sts; working in **back lps,** sc in next 39 sts; working in **both lps,** sc in last 30 sts, turn.
Row 5: Working in **both lps,** ch 1, sc in first 30 sts, 3 sc in next st; working in **back lps,** sc in next 18 sts, 3 sc in next st, sc in next 18 sts; working in **both lps,** 3 sc in next st, sc in last 30 sts, turn. *(105)*
Row 6: Working in **both lps,** ch 1, sc in first 32 sts; working in **back lps,** sc in next 41 sts; working in **both lps,** sc in last 32 sts, turn.
Row 7: Working in **both lps,** ch 1, sc in first 32 sts, 3 sc in next st; working in **back lps,** sc in next 19 sts, 3 sc in next st, sc in next 19 sts; working in **both lps,** 3 sc in next st, sc in last 32 sts, turn. *(111)*
Row 8: Working in **both lps,** ch 1, sc in first 34 sts; working in **back lps,** sc in next 43 sts; working in **both lps,** sc in last 34 sts, turn.
Row 9: Working in **both lps,** ch 1, sc in first 34 sts, 3 sc in next st; working in **back lps,** sc in next 20 sts, 3 sc in next st, sc in next 20 sts; working in **both lps,** 3 sc in next st, sc in last 34 sts, turn. Fasten off. *(117)*

EDGING
Row 1: Working in ends of rows and in **both lps** of sts on Neck Band, join with sl st in row 2, ch 5, skip next 2 rows, dc in next row, ch 2, skip next 2 rows, dc in next row, ch 2, skip next row, (dc, ch 2) 2 times in first st on row 9, (skip next 2 sts, dc in next st, ch 2) 11 times, skip next st, (dc, ch 2) 2 times in next st, skip next st, (dc in next st, ch 2, skip next 2 sts) 7 times, (dc, ch 2) 2 times in next st, (skip next 2 sts, dc in next st, ch 2) 7 times, skip next st, (dc, ch 2) 2 times in next st, skip next st, (dc in next st, ch 2, skip next 2 sts) 11 times, (dc, ch 2) 2 times in last st, skip next row, (dc in next row, ch 2, skip next 2 rows) 2 times, dc in last row, turn.
Row 2: (Sl st, ch 3, dc, ch 3, 2 dc) in first ch sp, *sc in next ch sp, (2 dc, ch 3, 2 dc) in next ch sp; repeat from * across, **do not turn.** Fasten off.
Row 3: Working in **both lps,** join with sc in first st, sc in each st and 5 sc in each ch sp across. Fasten off.

FINISHING
Cut 12" piece from ribbon and tie in a bow.
Weave remaining ribbon through sts of row 1 on Edging. Tack ribbon in place on wrong side at each end of row 1.
Sew ribbon bow to lower right corner of Bib above Edging *(see photo).* ✪

Lovebuds Bonnet

Designed by Patricia Mertes

Finished Size: Fits 0–6 mos.

Materials:
- ❑ 200 yds. size 5 crochet cotton thread
- ❑ No. 5 steel hook or hook needed to obtain gauge

Gauge: Rnd 1 = ¾".

Basic Stitches: Ch, sl st, sc, hdc, dc.

Special Stitches:
For **block,** dc in each of next 3 sts or chs.
For **mesh,** ch 2, skip each of next 2 sts or chs, dc in next st or ch.

BONNET

Rnd 1: Ch 8, sl st in first ch to form ring, ch 2, 23 hdc in ring, join with sl st in top of ch-2. *(24 hdc made)*

Rnd 2: Ch 8, skip each of next 2 sts, (dc in next st, ch 5, skip each of next 2 sts) around, join with sl st in third ch of ch-8. *(8 dc, 8 ch sps)*

Rnd 3: (Sl st, ch 3, 3 dc) in first ch-5 sp, dc in next st, 4 dc in next ch-5 sp, ch 3, skip next st, (4 dc in next ch-5 sp, dc in next st, 4 dc in next ch-5 sp, ch 3, skip next st) around, join with sl st in top of ch-3. *(36 dc)*

Rnd 4: Skipping ch sps, (ch 3, dc) in first st, *[2 dc in next st, (dc in each of next 2 sts, 2 dc in next st) 2 times, 2 dc in next st, ch 3], 2 dc in next st; repeat from * 2 more times; repeat between [ ], join. *(56 dc)*

Rnd 5: (Ch 3, dc) in first st, dc in next 12 sts, 2 dc in next st, ch 3, (2 dc in next st, dc in next 12 sts, 2 dc in next st, ch 3) 3 times, join. *(64 dc, 4 ch sps)*

Rnd 6: Ch 3, dc in next 7 sts, ch 5, dc in next 8 sts, ch 5, skip next ch sp, (dc in next 8 sts, ch 5, dc in next 8 sts, ch 5, skip next ch sp) 3 times, join.

Rnd 7: Ch 2, dc in next 5 sts, dc next 2 sts tog, ch 5, dc in next ch-5 sp, ch 5, (dc next 2 sts tog, dc in next 4 sts, dc next 2 sts tog, ch 5, dc in next ch-5 sp, ch 5) 7 times, skip ch-2, join with sl st in top of first dc. *(48 dc)*

Rnd 8: Ch 2, dc in each of next 3 sts, dc next 2 sts tog, *(ch 5, sc in next ch-5 sp) 2 times, ch 5, dc next 2 sts tog, dc in each of next 2 sts, dc next 2 sts tog; repeat from * 6 more times; repeat between ( ) 2 times, ch 5, skip ch-2, join with sl st in top of first dc. Fasten off. *(32 dc)*

Row 9: Working in rows, join with sl st in any center ch-5 sp between hearts, ch 3, 5 dc in same ch sp, 6 dc in next ch sp, (skip each of next 2 sts, dc in next st, skip next st, 6 dc in each of next 3 ch-5 sps) 5 times, skip each of next 2 sts, dc in next st, skip next st, 6 dc in each of next 2 ch-5 sps, turn. *(120)*

Row 10: (Ch 3, dc) in first st, dc in each of next 2 sts, (ch 2, skip each of next 2 sts, dc in next st) 38 times, dc in each of last 3 sts, turn. *(45 dc, 38 ch sps)*

Rows 11–21: Ch 3, work according to corresponding row on graph, turn. At end of last row, **do not turn.**

Rnd 22: Working in ends of rows, in ch sps and in sts around outer edge, ch 3, dc in first row, (ch 1, 2 dc in next row) 12 times, ch 1, 6 dc in next ch-5 sp, skip each of next 2 sts, dc in next st, skip next st, 6 dc in each of next 3 ch-5 sps, skip each of next 2 sts, dc in next st, skip next st, 6 dc in next ch-5 sp, (ch 1, 2 dc in next row) 12 times, ch 1, (5 dc, ch 1, 3 dc) in next row *(first front corner made),* ch 1, skip each of next 3 sts, *skip next ch-2 sp, (3 dc, ch 1, 3 dc) in next ch-2 sp; repeat from * 18 more times, ch 1, skip each of next 3 sts, (3 dc, ch 1, 3 dc) in last dc of row 21 *(second front corner made),* join with sl st in top of ch-3. Fasten off.

For first **Tie,** join with sl st in ch-1 sp at first front corner, ch 80. Fasten off. For second **Tie,** repeat in second front corner ch-1 sp. ✪

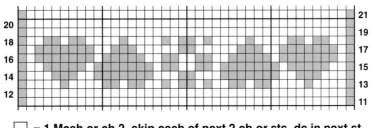

☐ = 1 Mesh or ch 2, skip each of next 2 ch or sts, dc in next st.
☐ = 1 Block or dc in each of next 3 ch or sts.

Cottontail Cuddlers

Designed by Michele Wilcox

Finished Sizes: Hat fits infant's 6–12 mos. Mitten is 4½" long.

Materials:
- ❏ Worsted yarn:
    - 5½ oz. white
    - 1 oz. pink
- ❏ Tapestry needle
- ❏ H hook or hook needed to obtain gauge

Gauge: 7 hdc = 2"; 3 hdc rows = 1".

Basic Stitches: Ch, sl st, sc, hdc.

HAT
Row 1: For **Ribbing,** with white, ch 7, sc in second ch from hook, sc in each ch across, turn. *(6 sc made)*

Rows 2–63: Working these rows in **back lps** *(see Stitch Guide),* ch 1, sc in each st across, turn. At end of last row, **do not turn.**

Row 64: Working in ends of rows across Ribbing, ch 1, sc in each row across, turn. *(63)*

Row 65: Ch 2, hdc in next 18 sts, skip next st, (hdc in next 20 sts, skip next st) 2 times, hdc in last st, turn. *(60 hdc) Ch-2 counts as first hdc.*

Rows 66–69: Ch 2, hdc in each st across, turn.

Row 70: Ch 2, hdc in next 7 sts, skip next st, (hdc in next 9 sts, skip next st) 5 times, hdc in last st, turn. *(54)*

Row 71: Ch 2, hdc in each st across, turn.

Row 72: Ch 2, hdc in next 6 sts, skip next st, (hdc in next 8 sts, skip next st) 5 times, hdc in last st, turn. *(48)*

Row 73: Ch 2, hdc in next 5 sts, skip next st, (hdc in next 7 sts, skip next st) 5 times, hdc in last st, turn. *(42)*

Row 74: Ch 2, hdc in next 4 sts, skip next st, (hdc in next 6 sts, skip next st) 5 times, hdc in last st, turn. *(36)*

Row 75: Ch 2, hdc in each of next 3 sts, skip next st, (hdc in next 5 sts, skip next st) 5 times, hdc in last st, turn. *(30)*

Row 76: Ch 2, hdc in each of next 2 sts, skip next st, (hdc in next 4 sts, skip next st) 5 times, hdc in last st, turn. *(24)*

Rows 77–78: Ch 1, sc first 2 sts tog, (sc next 2 sts tog) across, turn. At end of last row, leaving an 18" end for weaving and sewing, fasten off.

Weave end through sts of last row, pull tight to gather; sew ends of rows together forming center back seam.

First Flap
Row 1: With center back seam facing you, working in ends of rows on Ribbing, skip first 8 rows from seam, join white with sc in next row, sc in next 10 rows leaving remaining rows unworked, turn. *(11 sc made)*

Rows 2–3: Ch 1, sc in each st across, turn.

Rows 4–7: Ch 1, sc first 2 sts tog, sc in each st across to last 2 sts, sc last 2 sts tog, turn. At end of last row *(3).*

Row 8: Ch 1, sc 3 sts tog; for **Tie,** ch 35, sl st in second ch from hook, sl st in each ch across, sl st in decrease. Fasten off.

Second Flap
Row 1: Working in ends of rows on Ribbing, skip next 25 rows past First Flap, join white with sc in next row, sc in next 10 rows leaving remaining rows unworked, turn. *(11 sc made)*

Rows 2–8: Repeat rows 2–8 of First Flap.

Ear Side (make 2 white, 2 pink)
Row 1: Starting at bottom edge, ch 7, sc in second ch from hook, sc in each ch across, turn. *(6 sc made)*

Row 2: Ch 2, hdc in each st across, turn.

Row 3: Ch 2, 2 hdc in next st, hdc in each of next 2 sts, 2 hdc in next st, hdc in last st, turn. *(8 hdc)*

Row 4: Ch 2, hdc in each st across, turn.

Row 5: Ch 2, 2 hdc in next st, hdc in next 4 sts, 2 hdc in next st, hdc in last st, turn. *(10)*

Rows 6–13: Ch 2, hdc in each st across, turn.

Rows 14–16: Ch 2, skip next st, hdc in each st across to last 2 sts, skip next st, hdc in last st, turn. *(8, 6, 4)*

Row 17: Ch 2, skip next st, hdc in each of last 2 sts, turn. *(3)*

Row 18: Ch 1, sc 3 sts tog. Fasten off.

For each **Ear,** hold one pink and one white Ear Side together, matching rows and with pink Side facing you; working around outer edges through both thicknesses, join white with sc in end of row 1, sc in end of each row and in each st around with 3 sc in tip, join with sl st in first sc. Fasten off.

With pink inside, fold bottom edge on one Ear in half; sew folded edge together. Repeat with other Ear.

Sew Ears over rows 71–73 *(see photo)* on front of Hat about 4" apart.

MITTEN (make 2)
Rows 1–20: Work rows 1–20 of Hat. At end of last row, **do not turn.**

• • • • • • • • • • • • • • Continued on page 37

Keepsake
Slippers & Bib

Finished Sizes: Slipper Sole—small *(0–3 mos.)* is 3½" long, large *(3–6 mos.)* is 4" long. Bib—small is 7" × 8", large is 8" × 9".

Materials:
- ❑ Size and amount of white crochet cotton thread needed for desired size
- ❑ 2½ yds. white ¼" ribbon
- ❑ No. 9 steel hook or hook needed to obtain gauge for desired size

Sizes:
For **small** *(0–3 mos.)*, 220 yds. size 20 crochet cotton thread. **Gauges:** 11 sts = 1"; 12 sc **back lp** rows = 1"; 6 (sc, dc) pattern rows = 1"; 3 shell rows = 1".
For **large** *(3–6 mos.)*, 300 yds. size 10 crochet cotton thread. **Gauges:** 10 sts = 1"; 11 sc **back lp** rows = 1"; 6 (sc, dc) pattern rows = 1¼"; 3 shell rows = 1¼".

Basic Stitches: Ch, sl st, sc, dc, tr, dtr *(see Stitch Guide).*

SLIPPER *(make 2)*
Motif
Rnd 1: Ch 5, sl st in first ch to form ring, ch 4, 2 tr in ring, (ch 8, 3 tr in ring) 5 times, ch 8, join with sl st in top of ch-4. *(18 tr, 6 ch sps made)*
Rnd 2: Sl st in each of next 2 sts, (sl st, ch 1, 11 sc) in first ch sp, 11 sc in each ch sp around, join with sl st in first sc. Fasten off.

Sole & Top
Rnd 1: Starting at **Heel**, ch 23, 3 sc in second ch from hook, sc in next 20 chs, 5 sc in last ch; working in remaining lps on opposite side of starting ch, sc in next 20 chs, 2 sc in last ch, join with sl st in first sc. *(50 sc made)*
Rnd 2: (Ch 3, dc) in first st, 2 dc in each of next 2 sts, dc in next 20 sts, 2 dc in each of next 5 sts, dc in next 20 sts, 2 dc in each of last 2 sts, join with sl st in top of ch-3. *(60 dc)*
Rnd 3: Ch 1, sc in each st around, join.
Rnd 4: Ch 3, 2 dc in each of next 3 sts, dc in next 23 sts, 2 sc in each of next 8 sts, dc in next 22 sts, 2 dc in each of last 3 sts, dc in same st as ch-3, join. *(75)*
Rnd 5: Ch 1, sc in each st around, join.
Rnd 6: Ch 3, (2 dc in next st, dc in next st) 4 times, dc in next 21 sts, (2 dc in next st, dc in next st) 8 times, dc in next 21 sts, (dc in next st, 2 sc in next st) 4 times, join. *(91)*
Rnd 7: Working this rnd in **back lps** *(see Stitch Guide),* for **Top,** ch 1, sc in first 11 sts, (2 sc in next st, sc in next 9 sts) around, join with sl st in first sc. *(99 sc)*
Rnd 8: (Ch 4, 3 tr) in first st, skip next 4 sts, tr in next st, skip next 4 sts, (4 tr in next st, ch 3, 4 tr in next st, skip next 4 sts, tr in next st, skip next 4 sts) 8 times, 4 tr in last st, ch 3, join with sl st in top of ch-4. *(81 tr, 9 ch sps)*
Rnd 9: Sl st in next 4 sts, ch 4, skip next 4 sts; for **shell,** (4 tr, ch 3, 4 tr) in next ch sp *(shell made),* skip next 4 sts, tr in next st, skip next 4 sts, shell in next ch sp, skip next 4 sts, tr in next st, skip next 4 sts, 4 tr in next ch sp, ch 1; holding this piece and Motif wrong sides tog, sc in sixth sc of any 11-sc group on Motif, *[ch 1, 4 tr in same ch sp on Top as last tr made], skip next 4 sts, tr in next st, skip next 4 sts, 4 tr in next ch sp, ch 1, sc in sixth sc of next 11-sc group on Motif; repeat from * 2 more times; repeat between [ ], (skip next 4 sts, tr in next st, skip next 4 sts, shell in next ch sp) 3 times, join. *(9 shells, 9 tr)*
Rnd 10: Ch 4, (shell in next ch sp, tr in next st) 2 times, tr in same sc on Motif as first joining sc, shell in sixth sc of next 11-sc group on Motif, tr in sp between last 11-sc group worked and next 11-sc group, shell in sixth sc of next 11-sc group, tr in same sc as last joining sc on Motif, tr in next st on rnd 3; repeat between ( ) 2 times, shell in last shell, join. *(7 shells, 9 tr)*
Rnd 11: For **beading rnd,** ch 9, tr in next shell, ch 4, **dtr** *(see Stitch Guide)* in next tr, ch 4, (tr in next shell, ch 4) 2 times, tr in next st, ch 4, (tr in next shell, ch 4) 2 times, ch 4, (dtr in next st, ch 4, tr in next shell) 2 times, ch 4, join with sl st in fifth ch of ch-9. *(12 ch sps)*
Rnd 12: Ch 1, (sc, hdc, 3 dc, hdc, sc) in each ch sp around, join. Fasten off.
Cut 18" piece from ribbon, weave through sts on beading rnd. Tie ends of ribbon in bow.

BIB
Row 1: Starting at top edge, ch 56, sc in second ch from hook, sc in next 26 chs, 3 sc in next ch *(center made),* sc in last 27 chs, turn. *(57 sc made)*
Front of row 1 is right side of work.

• • • • • • • • • • • • • • • • • • • Continued on page 36

Keepsake Slippers & Bib

Continued from page 34

*NOTE: Work rows 2–23 in **back lps**.*

Rows 2–14: Ch 1, skip first st, sc in each st across to second st of center, 3 sc in next st, sc in each st across leaving last st unworked, turn.

Rows 15–22: Ch 1, 2 sc in first st, sc in each st across to second st of center, 3 sc in next st, sc in each st across to last st, 2 sc in last st, turn. At end of last row *(89)*.

Row 23: Ch 1, 2 sc in first st, sc in each st across to second st of center, 5 sc in next st, sc in each st across to last st, 2 sc in last st, turn. *(95)*

*NOTE: Work rows 24–31 in **both lps**.*

Row 24: Ch 4 *(counts as first dc and ch-1)*, skip next st, dc in next st, (ch 1, skip next st, dc in next st) 22 times, (ch 1, dc) 2 times in next st, ch 1, dc in next st, (ch 1, skip next st, dc in next st) across, turn. *(50 dc)*

Row 25: This row will have 12 Diamonds worked in rows as follows:

Row 1: For **First Diamond**, ch 7, skip next dc, sc in next dc, turn. *(1 ch sp)*

Row 2: Ch 3, 4 dc in ch-7 sp, turn. *(5 dc)*

Row 3: Ch 3, dc in each st across; skip next dc on row 24, dc in next dc, **do not turn.**

Row 1: For **Second Diamond**, ch 4, skip next dc on row 24, sc in next dc, turn. *(1 ch sp)*

Row 2: Ch 3, 4 dc in ch-4 sp, turn. *(5 dc)*

Row 3: Ch 3, dc in each st across; skip next dc on row 24, dc in next dc, **do not turn.**

For next 4 **Diamonds**, repeat rows 1–3 of Second Diamond 4 times; for **Tip**, (ch 1, dc, ch 1) in next ch sp on row 24, dc in next dc.

For last 6 **Diamonds**, repeat rows 1–3 of Second Diamond 6 times. At end of last row, **turn.**

Row 26: Ch 7, sc in top of ch-3 on First Diamond, ch 4, dc in next dc between Diamonds, *(ch 4, sc in top of ch-3 on next Diamond, ch 4, dc in next dc between Diamonds)* 5 times, (ch 4, dc in next dc) 2 times, repeat between first * 6 times, turn. *(26 ch sps, 15 dc, 12 sc)*

Row 27: Ch 4, dc in first ch sp, ch 1, dc in next st, (ch 1, dc in next ch sp, ch 1, dc in next st) 9 times, ch 1, dc in next ch sp, *ch 1, (dc, ch 1, dc) in next st; ch 1, dc in next ch sp*; repeat between first *, ch 1, (dc, ch 1, dc, ch 1, dc) in next st, ch 1, dc in next ch sp; repeat between first * 2 times, ch 1, dc in next st, (ch 1, dc in next ch sp, ch 1, dc in next st) across, turn. *(59 dc)*

Row 28: Ch 1, sc in first st, ch 5, skip next st, sc in next st, (ch 5, skip next st, sc in next st) across, turn. *(29 ch sps)*

Row 29: Ch 1, 7 sc in each ch sp across, turn. *(203 sc)*

Row 30: Ch 6, skip next 2 sts, sc in next st, (ch 5, skip next 6 sts, sc in next st) 28 times, ch 6, skip next 2 sts, sc in last st, turn. *(30 ch sps)*

Row 31: Ch 1, 2 sc in first ch sp; for **picot**, ch 3, sl st in second ch from hook *(picot made)*, 2 sc in same ch sp, (2 sc, picot, 2 sc) in each ch sp across. Fasten off.

Right Sleeve

Rnd 1: Ch 45; with right side of work facing you, join with sc in end of row 1, sc in same row, (sc in end of next row, 2 sc in end of next row) 11 times, join with sl st in first ch of ch-45, **turn.** *(45 chs, 35 sc made)*

*NOTE: Work rnds 2–7 in **back lps**.*

Rnd 2: Ch 1, sc in each st and in each ch around, join with sl st in first sc, **turn.** *(80 sc)*

Rnds 3–7: Ch 1, sc in each st around, join, **turn.**

*NOTE: Work rnds 8–15 in **both lps**.*

Rnd 8: Ch 4, skip next st, (dc in next st, ch 1, skip next st) around, join with sl st in third ch of ch-4, **turn.** *(40 dc)*

Rnd 9: This rnd will have 10 Diamonds worked in rows as follows:

Row 1: For **First Diamond**, ch 7, skip next dc, sc in next dc, turn. *(1 ch sp)*

Row 2: Ch 3, 4 dc in ch-7 sp, turn. *(5 dc)*

Row 3: Ch 3, dc in each st across; skip next dc on rnd 8, dc in next dc, **do not turn.**

Row 1: For **Second Diamond**, ch 4, skip next dc on rnd 8, sc in next dc, turn. *(1 ch sp)*

Row 2: Ch 3, 4 dc in ch-4 sp, turn. *(5 dc)*

Row 3: Ch 3, dc in each st across; skip next dc on rnd 8, dc in next dc, **do not turn.**

For next 7 **Diamonds**, repeat rows 1–3 of Second Diamond 7 times.

Rows 1–2: For **Last Diamond**, repeat rows 1–2 of Second Diamond.

Row 3: Ch 3, dc in each st across; skip next st on rnd 8, join with sl st in third ch of ch-7 on First Diamond, turn.

Rnd 10: Ch 7, sc in top of ch-3 on First Diamond, ch 4, dc in next dc between Diamonds, (ch 4, sc in top of ch-3 on next Diamond, ch 4, dc in next dc between Diamonds) 8 times, ch 4, sc in top of ch-3 on Last Diamond, ch 4, join with sl st in third ch of ch-7, **turn.** *(20 ch sps, 10 dc, 10 sc)*

Rnd 11: Ch 4, dc in first ch sp, (ch 1, dc in next st, ch 1, dc in next ch sp) around, ch 1, join with sl st in third ch of ch-4, **turn.** *(40 dc)*

Rnd 12: Ch 1, sc in first st, ch 5, skip next st, (sc in next st, ch 5, skip next st) around, join with sl st in first sc, **turn.** *(20 ch sps)*

Rnd 13: Ch 1, 7 sc in each ch sp around, join, **do not turn.** *(140 sc)*

Rnd 14: Sl st in each of first 2 sts, (sc in next st, ch 5, skip next 6 sts) 19 times, sc in next st, ch 5, skip last 3 sts, join, **do not turn.** *(20 ch sps)*

Rnd 15: Ch 1, (2 sc, picot, 2 sc) in each ch sp around, join. Fasten off.

Left Sleeve
Rnds 1–8: With wrong side of work facing you, repeat rnds 1–8 of Right Sleeve. At end of last rnd, **do not turn.**

Rnds 9–15: Repeat rnds 9–15 of Right Sleeve.

Edging
With right side of work facing you, working in remaining lps on opposite side of ch-45 on rnd 1 of Left Sleeve, join with sc in first ch, sc in each of next 3 chs, ch 3, skip next ch, (sc in next 4 chs, ch 3, skip next ch) 8 times; working in remaining lps on opposite side of starting ch on row 1 at top edge of Bib, sc in first 4 chs, (ch 3, skip next ch, sc in next 4 chs) 10 times, ch 3, skip next ch; working in remaining lps on opposite side of ch-45 on rnd 1 of Right Sleeve, skip first ch, sc in next 4 chs, (ch 3, skip next ch, sc in next 4 chs) across. Fasten off.

Finishing
For **Neck Ties,** cut two 10" pieces from ribbon. Sew one end of each ribbon piece to Edging at center back of each Sleeve.

For **Waist Ties,** cut two 10" pieces from ribbon. Sew one end of each ribbon piece to each end of row 23 on Bib.

Crisscross Neck Ties at back and tie to Waist Ties at sides. ✪

Cottontail Cuddlers

Continued from page 33

Row 21: Working in ends of rows across Ribbing, ch 1, sc in each row across, turn. *(20)*

Row 22: Ch 2, hdc in each of next 3 sts, 2 hdc in next st, (hdc in next 4 sts, 2 hdc in next st) across, turn. *(24 hdc)*

Rows 23–27: Ch 2, hdc in each st across, turn.

Row 28: Ch 2, hdc in next st, skip next st, (hdc in each of next 3 sts, skip next st) 5 times, hdc in last st, turn. *(18)*

Row 29: Ch 2, skip next st, (hdc in each of next 2 sts, skip next st) 5 times, hdc in last st. Leaving 12" for sewing, fasten off.

Fold piece in half lengthwise, matching ends of rows and sts; sew folded top and side edges together.

Pad (make 6)
With pink, ch 2, 7 sc in second ch from hook, join with sl st in first sc. Fasten off.

Sew three Pads evenly spaced across top half of one side on each Mitten. ✪

Swaddling Baby

"Bye-bye baby bunting, Daddy's gone a'hunting. To get a baby rabbit skin, to wrap the baby bunting in."

Thus go the lyrics to a traditional lullaby. Though we may no longer go hunting for swaddling clothes, we remain concerned over what baby should wear to stay comfy and cozy.

Medical experts say that maintaining even warmth for baby is most critical during the first two weeks after birth, because it takes time for an infant's own body temperature regulators to adjust to life outside the womb.

After that, babies and toddlers remain vulnerable to loss of body heat primarily through their heads. Young children are also much more sensitive to sunlight and wind exposure than adults.

With these tips in mind, common sense should be a wise parent's guide. Generally, babies and young children should be clothed as an adult would be for the environment. Dress a baby in layers that can easily be adjusted for temperature swings or sudden drafts. Some babies fuss when uncomfortable, while others don't, so touch baby's hands, feet and face to check for chills or overheating, and cover or uncover accordingly. Frequent hugs from loving family members also work well in monitoring youngsters' temperatures!

Bonnets, booties, mittens and blankets, which are comforting essentials for little ones, are especially handy when crocheted from easy-care yarn or long-wearing thread.

Perky Puppy Bib & Pillow

Designed by Peggy Johnston

Finished Sizes: Bib is 8¼" × 11½". Pillow is 8¼" × 11½".

Materials:
- ❏ Worsted yarn:
  - 4 oz. peach
  - 1 oz. white
  - 1 oz. blue
- ❏ Small amount each of tan, white and black sport yarn
- ❏ Small amount variegated blue pompadour baby yarn
- ❏ Black, white and red embroidery floss
- ❏ Polyester fiberfill
- ❏ Tapestry and embroidery needles
- ❏ E, F and G hooks or hooks needed to obtain gauges

Gauges: **E hook and sport yarn,** 5 sc = 1"; 5 sc rows = 1". **F hook and sport yarn,** 9 sc = 2"; 9 sc rows = 2". **G hook and worsted yarn,** 4 sc = 1"; 4 sc rows = 1".

Basic Stitches: Ch, sl st, sc, dc.

Notes: Work in continuous rnds; do not join or turn unless otherwise stated. Mark first st of each rnd.

For Face, Cheeks and Nose, the wrong side of the sts is the right side of the work.

PILLOW
Side (make 2)
Row 1: With G hook and peach, ch 28, sc in second ch from hook, sc in each ch across, turn. *(27 sc made)*

Rows 2–40: Ch 1, sc in each st across, turn. At end of last row, **do not turn.**

Rnd 41: Working around outer edge, ch 1, sc in end of each row and in each st around with 3 sc in each corner st, join with sl st in first sc, **turn.** Fasten off. *(142)*

Rnd 42: Join blue worsted yarn with sc in any st, sc in each st around with 3 sc in center st of each corner, join, **turn.** Fasten off. *(150)*

Rnd 43: Join white worsted yarn with sc in any st, sc in each st around with 3 sc in center st of each corner, join, **turn.** Fasten off. *(158)*

Face
Rnd 1: With F hook and tan, ch 2, 8 sc in second ch from hook. *(8 sc made)*

Rnd 2: 2 sc in each st around. *(16)*

Rnd 3: (2 sc in next st, sc in next st) around. *(24)*

Rnd 4: (2 sc in next st, sc in each of next 2 sts) around. *(32)*

Rnd 5: Sc in each st around.

Rnd 6: (2 sc in next st, sc in each of next 3 sts) around. *(40)*

Rnd 7: (2 sc in next st, sc in next 4 sts) around. *(48)*

Rnd 8: (2 sc in next st, sc in next 5 sts) around. *(56)*

Rnd 9: (2 sc in next st, sc in next 6 sts) around. *(64)*

Rnd 10: (2 sc in next st, sc in next 7 sts) around. *(72)*

Rnd 11: (2 sc in next st, sc in next 8 sts) around. *(80)*

Rnd 12: Sc in each st around, join with sl st in first sc. Fasten off.

Cheek (make 2)
Rnds 1–5: With F hook and white sport yarn, repeat rnds 1–5 of Face. At end of last rnd, join with sl st in first sc. Fasten off.

Sew five sts of each Cheek piece together. Sew Cheek pieces centered over lower half of Face as shown in photo.

Nose
Rnd 1: With F hook and black sport yarn, ch 2, 6 sc in second ch from hook. *(6 sc made)*

Rnd 2: 2 sc in each st around. *(12)*

Rnd 3: Sc in each st around, join with sl st in first sc. Fasten off.

Sew Nose over top of Cheeks and over rnd 1 of Face.

Facial Features
With white and black floss, using satin stitch *(see Stitch Guide)*, embroider Eyes on Face above Cheeks as shown in photo.

With black floss, using outline stitch, embroider around edge of each Eye. With white floss, using French knot, embroider twinkle in each Eye *(see photo)*.

With black sport yarn, using straight stitch, embroider Eyebrows above Eyes and one short vertical line on Cheeks below Nose.

• • • • • • • • • • • • • • • Continued on page 43

Beary Warm Hat & Mittens

Designed by Linda Williams

Finished Size: Fits toddler 2–3.

Materials:
- ❑ Worsted yarn:
  - 4 oz. white
  - 2 oz. contrasting color *(CC)*
  - 1 oz. brown
  - Small amount each of gold and red
- ❑ 3" piece cardboard
- ❑ Tapestry needle
- ❑ G hook or hook needed to obtain gauge

Gauge: 4 dc = 1"; 2 dc rows = 1".

Basic Stitches: Ch, sl st, sc, dc, tr.

HAT
Rnd 1: With white, ch 4, 9 dc in fourth ch from hook, join with sl st in top of ch-3. *(10 dc made)*
Rnd 2: Ch 1, 2 sc in each st around, join with sl st in first sc. *(20 sc)*
Rnd 3: (Ch 3, dc) in first st, dc in next st, (2 dc in next st, dc in next st) around, join. *(30)*
Rnd 4: Ch 1, sc in each of first 2 sts, 2 sc in next st, (sc in each of next 2 sts, 2 sc in next st) around, join. *(40)*
Rnd 5: Ch 3, dc in each of next 2 sts, 2 dc in next st, (dc in next 3 sts, 2 dc in next st) around, join. *(50)*
Rnd 6: Ch 1, sc in first 4 sts, 2 sc in next st, (sc in next 4 sts, 2 sc in next st) around, join. *(60)*
Rnd 7: Ch 3, dc in next 8 sts, 2 dc in next st, (dc in next 9 sts, 2 dc in next st) around, join. *(66)*
Rnd 8: Ch 1, sc in each st around, join.
Rnd 9: Ch 3, dc in each st around, join.
Rnds 10–24: Repeat rnds 8 and 9 alternately, ending with rnd 8. At end of last rnd, fasten off.

Cuff
Rnd 1: Join CC with sc in first st of last rnd on Hat, sc in each st around, join with sl st in first sc. *(66 sc made)*
Rnd 2: Ch 3, dc in each st around, join with sl st in top of ch-3.
Rnd 3: Ch 1, **sc front post (fp**—*see Stitch Guide)* around ch-3 on last rnd, ch 2 *(counts as first dc)*, **dc back post (bp)** around next st, (dc fp around next st, dc bp around next st) around, join with sl st in top of ch-2.

Rnds 4–6: Ch 1, sc fp around ch-2 on last rnd, ch 2, dc bp around next st, (dc fp around next st, dc bp around next st) around, join. At end of last rnd, fasten off.

Ear Flaps & Ties
Row 1: Working on inside of Hat behind Cuff, join white with sc in 11th st of rnd 24, sc in next 9 sts leaving remaining sts unworked, turn. *(10 sc made)*
Row 2: Ch 1, sc in each st across, turn.
Row 3: Ch 1, sc first 2 sts tog, sc in each st across to last 2 sts, sc last 2 sts tog, turn. *(8)*
Rows 4–9: Repeat rows 2 and 3 alternately. At end of last row *(2)*.
Row 10: Ch 1, sc in each st across; ch 60, sl st in second ch from hook, sl st in next 58 chs, sl st in first st on row 10. Fasten off.
For second **Flap**, skip next 25 sts on rnd 24 past first Flap; joining white in next st, repeat rows 1–10.
For **Pom-Pom**, wrap CC yarn around cardboard about 75 to 100 times. Slide loops off cardboard and tie a separate strand of CC yarn around center of all loops. Cut ends of loops. Trim to shape.
Tack Pom-Pom to rnd 1 of Hat.

LEFT MITTEN
Rnd 1: With white, ch 2, 8 sc in second ch from hook, join with sl st in first sc. *(8 sc made)*
Rnd 2: Ch 1, 2 sc in each st around, join. *(16)*
Rnd 3: Ch 1, 2 sc in first st, sc in next st, (2 sc in next st, sc in next st) around, join. *(24)*
Rnd 4: Ch 1, sc in each of first 2 sts, 2 sc in next st, (sc in each of next 2 sts, 2 sc in next st) around, join. *(32)*
Rnds 5–15: Ch 1, sc in each st around, join.
Rnd 16: Ch 1, sc in first 26 sts, ch 4, skip next 4 sts *(thumbhole made)*, sc in each of last 2 sts, join. *(28 sts, 4 chs)*
Rnd 17: Ch 1, sc in each st and in each ch around, join.
Rnd 18: Ch 1, sc in each st around, join.
Rnd 19: Ch 1, sc in first 6 sts, sc next 2 sts tog, (sc in next 6 sts, sc next 2 sts tog) around, join. *(28)*
Rnd 20: Ch 1, sc in first 5 sts, sc next 2 sts tog, (sc in next 5 sts, sc next 2 sts tog) around, join. *(24)*

• • • • • • • • • • • • • • • • Continued on page 42

Beary Warm Hat & Mittens

Continued from page 41

Rnd 21: Ch 1, sc in first 4 sts, sc next 2 sts tog, (sc in next 4 sts, sc next 2 sts tog) around, join. Fasten off. *(20)*

Cuff

Rnd 1: Join CC with sl st in in first st of last rnd on Mitten, ch 3, dc in each st around, join with sl st in top of ch-3. *(20 dc made)*

Rnd 2: Ch 1, sc fp around ch-3 on last rnd, ch 2, dc bp around next st, (dc fp around next st, dc bp around next st) around, join with sl st in top of ch-2.

Rnds 3–4: Ch 1, sc fp around ch-2 on last rnd, ch 2, dc bp around next st, (dc fp around next st, dc bp around next st) around, join. At end of last rnd, fasten off.

Thumb

Rnd 1: Join CC with sc in first ch on thumbhole, sc in each ch, in end of each row, and in each st around, join with sl st in first sc. *(10 sc made)*

Rnds 2–4: Ch 1, sc in each st around, join.

Rnd 5: Ch 1, sc in each of first 3 sts, sc next 2 sts tog, sc in each of next 3 sts, sc last 2 sts tog, join. *(8)*

Rnds 6–7: Ch 1, sc in each st around, join.

Rnd 8: Ch 1, sc first 2 sts tog, (sc next 2 sts tog) around, join. Leaving 6" for sewing, fasten off. Sew opening closed.

RIGHT MITTEN

Rnds 1–15: Repeat rnds 1–15 of Left Mitten.

Rnd 16: Ch 1, sc in each of first 2 sts, ch 4, skip next 4 sts, sc in last 26 sts, join. *(28 sts, 4 chs)*

Rnds 17–21: Repeat rnds 17–21 of Left Mitten.

Cuff & Thumb

Work same as Left Mitten Cuff and Thumb.

LARGE BEAR

Head

Rnd 1: With brown, ch 2, 6 sc in second ch from hook, join with sl st in first sc. *(6 sc made)*

Rnd 2: Ch 1, 2 sc in each st around, join. *(12)*

Rnd 3: Ch 1, 2 sc in first st, sc in next st, (2 sc in next st, sc in next st) around, join. *(18)*

Rnd 4: Ch 1, 2 sc in first st, sc in each of next 2 sts, (2 sc in next st, sc in each of next 2 sts) around, join. *(24)*

Rnd 5: Ch 1, 2 sc in first st, sc in each of next 3 sts, (2 sc in next st, sc in each of next 3 sts) around, join. *(30)*

Rnd 6: Ch 1, 2 sc in first st, sc in next 4 sts, (2 sc in next st, sc in next 4 sts) around, join. **Do not fasten off.** *(36)*

Ears

Skip first 2 sts on last rnd of Bear, 10 tr in next st, skip next 2 sts, sl st in each of next 3 sts, skip next 2 sts, 10 tr in next st, skip next 2 sts, sl st in next st leaving remaining sts unworked. Fasten off.

Muzzle

Rnd 1: With gold, ch 2, 6 sc in second ch from hook, join with sl st in first sc. *(6 sc made)*

Rnds 2–3: Ch 1, sc in each st around, join. At end of last rnd, Fasten off.

Sew to lower half of Head as shown in photo.

With brown, using French knot *(see Stitch Guide)*, embroider nose over rnd 1 on Muzzle.

With red, using outline stitch, embroider mouth over rnd 2 on bottom of Muzzle.

Eye (make 2)

With white, ch 2, 6 sc in second ch from hook, join with sl st in first sc. Fasten off.

With brown, using French knot, embroider pupil to center of each Eye.

Sew Eyes to upper half of Head as shown in photo.

Sew assembled Bear to front of Hat centered between Ear Flaps above turned-up Cuff as shown in photo.

SMALL BEAR (make 2)

Head

Rnds 1–5: Work rnds 1–5 of Large Bear Head. At end of last rnd, **do not fasten off.**

Ears, Muzzle & Eyes

Work same as Large Bear Ears, Muzzle and Eye.

Sew each assembled Bear to top of each Mitten as shown in photo. ✪

Perky Puppy Bib & Pillow

Continued from page 38

With black sport yarn, using French knot, embroider four randomly placed Whisker Spots on each Cheek.

With red floss, using satin stitch, embroider tongue on Face centered below Cheeks.

Sew Face centered over rows 14–31 on one Pillow Side.

Ear (make 2)
Row 1: With F hook and black sport yarn, ch 4, sc in second ch from hook, sc in each of last 2 chs, turn. *(3 sc made)*

Rows 2–8: Ch 1, sc in each st across, turn.

Row 9: (Ch 3, dc) in first st, dc in each of next 2 sts, turn. *(4 dc)*

Row 10: (Ch 3, dc) in first st, dc in each of next 2 sts, 2 dc in last st, turn. *(6)*

Row 11: Ch 1, sc first 2 sts tog, sc in each of next 2 sts, sc last 2 sts tog. Fasten off. *(4)*

Sew Ears to each side of Face as shown in photo.

Bow Tie
Row 1: With F hook and variegated, ch 7, sc in second ch from hook, sc in each ch across, turn. *(6 sc made)*

Rows 2–12: Ch 1, sc in each st across, turn.

Row 13: Ch 1, sc first 2 sts tog, (sc next 2 sts tog) 2 times, turn. *(3)*

Rows 14–15: Ch 1, sc in each st across, turn.

Row 16: Ch 1, 2 sc in each st across, turn. *(6)*

Rows 17–27: Ch 1, sc in each st across, turn.

Rnd 28: Working around outer edge, ch 1, sc in each st and in end of each row around with 3 sc in each corner st, join with sl st in first sc. Fasten off.

Wrap separate strand of variegated yarn around center of Bow Tie ten times. Secure ends of back of Bow Tie. Sew to Pillow Side below Face.

Pillow Assembly
Hold Pillow Sides wrong sides together, matching sts and rows; working in **back lps** *(see illustration),* sew Sides together, stuffing before closing.

BIB
Front & Sides
Rows 1–32: Work rows 1–32 of Pillow Side.

Row 33: For **First Side,** ch 1, sc in first 8 sts leaving last 19 sts unworked, turn. *(8)*

Rows 34–40: Ch 1, sc in each st across, turn. At end of last row, fasten off.

Row 33: For **Second Side,** skip next 11 sts on row 32, join peach with sc in next st, sc in last 7 sts, turn. *(8)*

Rows 34–40: Ch 1, sc in each st across, turn. At end of last row, **do not fasten off.**

Edging
Row 1: Beginning at top left corner of neck edge, sc in each st and in end of each row around outer edge to top right corner of neck edge with 3 sc in each outer corner. Fasten off. **Do not turn.**

Row 2: Join blue worsted yarn with sc in first st of last row, sc in each st across with 3 sc in center st of each outer corner. Fasten off. **Do not turn.**

Row 3: With white worsted yarn, repeat row 2.

Ties & Neck Edging
With G hook and peach, ch 50, sc in end of row 40 at top corner of neck edge, sc in end of each row and in each unworked st on row 32 across to end of row 40 at other top corner, ch 50. Fasten off.

Tie a knot in end of each Tie.

Face, Cheeks & Nose
With E hook work Pillow Face, Cheeks and Nose on page 38.

Facial Features
Work Pillow Facial Features on page 38.

Ears & Bow Tie
With E hook, work Pillow Ears and Bow Tie on this page. ✪

Buckaroo Booties

An Annie Original

Finished Sizes: Small Sole is 3½" long. Medium Sole is 4¼" long. Large Sole is 5" long.

Materials:
- ❑ Worsted yarn:
    1 oz. each of brown and gold
- ❑ Tapestry needle
- ❑ F or G hook or hook needed to obtain gauge for desired size

Gauges: F hook, 9 sc = 2"; 9 sc rows = 2". **G hook,** 4 sc = 1"; 4 sc rows = 1".

Basic Stitches: Ch, sl st, sc, hdc, dc.

Notes: For **small** size, use **F hook** and number in front of brackets [ ]. For **medium** size, use **G hook** and first number inside [ ]. For **large** size, use **G hook** and second number inside [ ].

Work in continuous rnds; do not join or turn unless otherwise stated. Mark first st of each rnd.

SOLE (make 2)

Rnd 1: With brown, ch 12 [12, 14], sc in second ch from hook, sc in next 7 [7, 9] chs, hdc in next ch, 2 hdc in next ch, 5 hdc in last ch; working in remaining lps on opposite side of starting ch, 2 hdc in next ch, hdc in next ch, sc in next 7 [7, 9] chs, 2 sc in last ch. *(28 sts made) [28 sts made, 32 sts made]*

Rnd 2: 2 sc in first st, sc in next 10 [10, 12] sts, (2 sc in next st, sc in next st) 3 times, sc in next 9 [9, 11] sts, 2 sc in next st, sc in last st. *(33 sc) [33 sc, 37 sc]*

Rnd 3: 2 sc in first st, sc in next 11 [11, 13] sts, (2 sc in next st, sc in next st) 2 times, (sc in next st, 2 sc in next st) 2 times, sc in next 11 [11, 13] sts, 2 sc in next st, sc in last st, join with sl st in first sc, **turn.** *(39) [39, 43]*

Rnd 4: Working this rnd in **back lps** *(see Stitch Guide),* ch 1, sc in each st around, join. Fasten off. *(39 sc) [39 sc, 43 sc]*

Heel Edge

Working in **front lps** of center 13 sts on rnd 3 at heel end of Sole, join brown with sl st in first st, sc in next 11 sts, sl st in last st. Fasten off.
Repeat on other Sole.

SIDES

Rnd 1: Working in sts of Heel Edge and in remaining **front lps** of rnd 3 on Sole, join gold with sc in center st of Heel Edge, sc in each st around. *(39 sc made) [39 sc made, 43 sc made]*

Rnd 2: Sc in first 14 [14, 16] sts, skip next st, hdc in next st, skip next st, dc in each of next 2 sts, dc next 2 sts tog, dc in each of next 2 sts, skip next st, hdc in next st, skip next st, sc in last 13 [13, 15] sts. *(34 sts) [34 sts, 38 sts]*

Rnd 3: Sc in first 13 [13, 15] sts, skip next st, sc in next st, skip next st, sc in each of next 3 sts, skip next st, sc in next st, skip next st, sc in last 12 [12, 14] sts. *(30 sc) [30 sc, 34 sc]*

Rnd 4: Sc in first 12 [12, 14] sts, (skip next st, sc in st) 4 times, sc in last 10 [10, 12] sts. *(26) [26, 30]*

Rnd 5: Sc in first 6 [6, 7] sts, sl st in next 5 [5, 6] sts, skip next st, sc in each of next 3 sts, skip next st, sl st in next 5 [5, 6] sts, sc in next 5 [5, 6] sts, sc in first sc of this rnd, join with sl st in next st. Fasten off.

NOTE: *The following rnds may not end or begin where you think they should, but follow the directions as they are written for correct placement of shaping.*

Rnd 6: Working this rnd in **back lps,** join brown with sc in st before joining sl st on last rnd, sc in next 10 [10, 12] sts, skip next st, sc in each of next 2 sts, skip next st, sc in last 9 [9, 11] sts.

Rnd 7: Sc in next 22 [22] sts; for **large size only,** [sc in next 10 sts, skip next st, sc in each of next 2 sts, skip next st, sc in next 12 sts].

Rnds 8–9: Sc in next 22 [22, 24] sts.

Rnd 10: 2 sc in next st, sc in next 11 [11, 12] sts, 2 sc in next st, sc in next 9 [9, 10] sts, sc in next st.

Rnds 11–13: Sc in next 24 [24, 26] sts.

Rnd 14: Sc in next 4 [4, 5] sts, hdc in next st, skip next st, dc in next st, 4 dc in next st, dc in next st, skip next st, hdc in next st, sc in next 5 [5, 6] sts, hdc in next st, skip next st, dc in next st, 4 dc in next st, dc in next st, skip next st, hdc in next st, sc in next st, sl st in next st. Fasten off.

Repeat on other Sole.

TOP EDGE

Rnd 1: Join gold with sc in center back st on last rnd of Sides, sc in each st around with 2 sc in the second dc of each 4-dc group.

Rnd 2: Skip first st, sc in each st around with 2 sc in the second sc of each 2-sc group, join with sl st in first sc. Fasten off.

Repeat on other Sides.

FRONT DECORATION

Row 1: Working in the center front 3 remaining lps of rnd 5 on Sides, join gold in first st, sc in each of next 2 sts, turn. *(3 sc made)*

Rows 2–3: Ch 1, sc in each st across, turn.

Row 4: Ch 1, (sc, hdc) in first st, 3 dc in next st, (hdc, sc) in last st. Fasten off.
Repeat on other Sides.
Tack top edge of each Decoration in place on front of Sides.

SIDE DECORATION (make 4)
With gold, ch 25 [25, 30]. Fasten off.
Arrange one Decoration piece in a loop design on each side of each Bootie as shown in photo and tack in place. ✪

Quackers Please!

Designed by Karin Strom

Finished Sizes: Duck Toy is 6½" tall. Bottle Warmer fits a 12-oz. bottle.

Materials:
- ❏ Worsted yarn:
    - 3 oz. green
    - 2 oz. yellow
    - Small amount each of orange and white
- ❏ Polyester fiberfill
- ❏ Blue embroidery floss
- ❏ 2 blue ⅝" buttons
- ❏ White ribbon:
    - 1 yd. of ¼" wide
    - 8" of ⅝" wide
- ❏ Cardboard
- ❏ White and blue sewing thread
- ❏ Tapestry and sewing needles
- ❏ G hook or hook needed to obtain gauge

Gauge: 4 sc = 1"; 4 sc rows = 1".

Basic Stitches: Ch, sl st, sc, hdc, dc.

Notes: Work in continuous rnds; do not join or turn unless otherwise stated. Mark first st of each rnd.
Wrong side of sts is right side of work.

BOTTLE WARMER
Rnd 1: With green, ch 2, 6 sc in second ch from hook. *(6 sc made)*
Rnd 2: 2 sc in each st around. *(12)*
Rnd 3: (Sc in next st, 2 sc in next st) around. *(18)*
Rnd 4: (Sc in each of next 2 sts, 2 sc in next st) around. *(24)*
Rnds 5–33: Sc in each st around. At end of last rnd, join with sl st in first sc. Fasten off.
Rnd 34: Join white with sc in any st, ch 5, (sc in next st, ch 5) around, join.

Duck Head
Rnds 1–3: With yellow, repeat rnds 1–3 of Bottle Warmer.
Rnd 4: Sc in each st around, join with sl st in first sc. Fasten off.

Duck Bill
Row 1: With orange, ch 2, 3 sc in second ch from hook, turn. *(3 sc made)*
Row 2: Ch 1, 2 sc in each st across. Fasten off.
Sew ends of rows on Bill across center of Head as shown in photo.

Duck Finishing
With blue floss, using satin stitch *(see Stitch Guide)*, embroider Eyes above Bill about ½" apart.
For **pom-pom,** cut a 1¼" piece from cardboard, wrap yellow yarn around cardboard 50 times. Slide loops off cardboard and tie a separate strand of yellow yarn around center of all loops. Cut ends of loops. Trim to shape a 1¼" ball. Sew to top of Head.
Sew assembled Head over rnds 15–22 on Bottle Warmer. Cut an 8" piece from ¼" ribbon and tie in a bow around st at center bottom of Head.
Cut a 15" piece from ¼" ribbon and tie in a bow around top of Bottle Warmer. Tack center of ribbon in place on Bottle Warmer with sewing thread and needle.

BIB
Row 1: With green, ch 15, sc in second ch from hook, sc in each ch across, turn. *(14 sc made)*
Row 2: Ch 1, sc in first st, 2 sc in each of next 6 sts, sc in next st, 2 sc in each of next 5 sts, sc in last st, turn. *(25)*
Row 3: Ch 1, sc in each st across, turn.
Row 4: Ch 1, sc in first 12 sts, sc next 2 sts tog, sc in last 11 sts, turn. *(24)*
Row 5: Ch 1, sc in each st across, turn.
Row 6: Ch 1, sc first 2 sts tog, sc in each st across to last 2 sts, sc last 2 sts tog, turn. *(22)*
Row 7: Ch 1, sc in each st across, turn.
Row 8: Ch 1, sc in first 10 sts, 2 sc in each of next 2 sts, sc in last 10 sts, turn. *(24)*
Row 9: Ch 1, sc in each st across, turn.
Row 10: Ch 1, sc in first 11 sts, 2 sc in each of next 2 sts, sc in last 11 sts, turn. *(26)*
Row 11: Ch 1, sc in each st across, turn.
Row 12: Ch 1, sc in first 12 sts, 2 sc in each of next 2 sts, sc in last 12 sts, turn. *(28)*
Row 13: Ch 1, sc in each st across, turn.
Row 14: Ch 1, sc first 2 sts tog, sc in next 11 sts, 2 sc in each of next 2 sts, sc in next 11 sts, sc last 2 sts tog, turn. *(28)*
Row 15: Ch 1, sc in each st across, turn.
Row 16: Ch 1, sc in first 13 sts, 2 sc in each of next 2 sts, sc in last 13 sts, turn. *(30)*
Row 17: Ch 1, sc first 2 sts tog, sc in each st across to last 2 sts, sc last 2 sts tog, turn. *(28)*
Row 18: Ch 1, sc in each st across, turn.
Rows 19–20: Ch 1, sc first 2 sts tog, sc in each st across to last 2 sts, sc last 2 sts tog, turn. *(26, 24)*
Row 21: Ch 1, sc first 2 sts tog, (sc in next 4 sts, sc next 2 sts tog), sc in next 8 sts, sc next 2 sts tog; repeat between ( ). Fasten off. *(20)*

• • • • • • • • • • • • • • • • • • • Continued on page 48

Quackers Please!

Continued from page 47

Edging & Ties

Row 1: Working in ends of rows and sts across outer edge, join green with sc in end of row 1, sc in same row, sc in next 20 rows, sc in next 20 sts on row 21, sc in next 20 rows, 2 sc in last row. Fasten off. **Do not turn.**

Rnd 2: Join white with sl st in first st of last row; for first **Tie,** ch 51, sc in second ch from hook, sc in next 49 chs, (sc, ch 3, dc) in same st as joining sl st, skip each of next 2 sts, *(sc, ch 3, dc) in next st, skip each of next 2 sts; repeat from * 19 more times, sl st in next st; for second **Tie,** ch 51, sc in second ch from hook, sc in next 49 chs; working in remaining lps of starting ch on row 1, sc in each ch across, join with sl st in first sc. Fasten off.

Duck Head, Bill & Finishing

Work same as Duck instructions on page 47. Sew assembled Duck to center of Bib.

Cut an 8" piece from ¼" ribbon and tie in a bow around st at center bottom of Head.

DUCK TOY
Body

Rnd 1: With yellow, ch 2, 6 sc in second ch from hook. *(6 sc made)*

Rnd 2: 2 sc in each st around.

Rnd 3: (Sc in next st, 2 sc in next st) around. *(18)*

Rnd 4: (Sc in each of next 2 sts, 2 sc in next st) around. *(24)*

Rnds 5–6: Sc in each st around.

Rnd 7: (2 sc in next st, sc in each of next 3 sts) around. *(30)*

Rnds 8–11: Sc in each st around.

Rnd 12: (2 sc in next st, sc in next 4 sts) around. *(36)*

Rnds 13–16: Sc in each st around.

Rnd 17: (Sc next 2 sts tog, sc in next 4 sts) around. *(30)*

Rnd 18: Sc in each st around. Turn piece so correct side of sts are showing on outside of piece. Stuff.

Rnd 19: (Sc next 2 sts tog, sc in each of next 3 sts) around. *(24)*

Rnd 20: (Sc next 2 sts tog, sc in each of next 2 sts) around. Finish stuffing. *(18)*

Rnd 21: (Sc in next st, sc next 2 sts tog) around. *(12)*

Rnd 22: (Sc next 2 sts tog) around, join with sl st in first sc. Fasten off. Sew opening closed.

Wing Side (make 4)

Rnd 1: With yellow, ch 7, 3 sc in second ch from hook, sc in next 4 chs, 3 sc in last ch; working in remaining lps of starting ch, sc in next 4 chs. *(14 sc made)*

Rnd 2: (2 sc in each of next 3 sts, sc in next 4 sts) around. *(20)*

Rnd 3: *(Sc in next st, 2 sc in next st) 3 times, sc in next 4 sts; repeat from *. *(26)*

Rnd 4: Sc in each st around, join with sl st in first sc. Fasten off.

For each **Wing,** sew two Side pieces together.

Sew top and one rounded end of each Wing to each side of Body over rnds 9–11 as shown in photo.

Foot (make 2)

Rnd 1: With orange, ch 2, 6 sc in second ch from hook. *(6 sc made)*

Rnd 2: 2 sc in each st around, join with sl st in first sc. *(12)*

Row 3: Working in rows for **Toes,** (ch 5, hdc in second ch from hook, hdc in each of next 3 chs, sl st in each of next 2 sts on rnd 2), ch 6, hdc in second ch from hook, hdc in each of next 4 chs, sl st in each of next 2 sts on rnd 2; repeat between ( ). **Do not turn.**

Rnd 4: Working around outer edge, ch 1, sc in last 5 sts on rnd 2; working in remaining lps of chs and in sts on Toes, sc in each ch and in each st with sc in end of each Toe and in first sl st of each Toe, join with sl st in first sc. Fasten off.

Sew Feet to bottom of Body as shown in photo.

Bill Top

Row 1: With orange, ch 2, 3 sc in second ch from hook, turn. *(3 sc made)*

Row 2: Ch 1, 2 sc in each st across, turn. *(6)*

Row 3: Ch 1, sc in first st, 2 sc in next st, (sc in next st, 2 sc in next st) across, turn. *(9)*

Row 4: Ch 1, sc in each st across. Fasten off.

Bill Bottom

Rows 1–3: Repeat rows 1–3 of Bill Top. At end of last row, fasten off.

Sew first and last st of row 3 on Bill Bottom together. Sew bottom edge of Bill Bottom over rnds 9–10 on center front of Body.

Curving the bottom edge around Bill Bottom *(see photo),* sew Bill Top over rnds 7–9 of Body.

Finishing

For each **pom-pom** *(make 2),* cut a 3" piece from cardboard, wrap yellow yarn around cardboard 100 times. Slide loops off cardboard and tie a separate strand of yellow yarn around center of all loops. Cut ends of loops. Trim to shape a 3" ball.

Sew one pom-pom to top of Head and one to rnd 17 at center back of Body.

For **Eyes,** with blue sewing thread, sew buttons to rnd 6 on front of Body about ¾" apart.

Tie ⅝" ribbon in a bow around st at center bottom of Bill. ✪

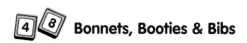

CHAPTER 3

Afghans & More

Matthew, Mark, Luke and John

Matthew, Mark, Luke and John,
Bless the bed that I lie on.
Four corners to my bed,
Four angels round my head.
One to guide, one to pray,
And two to watch my soul today.

This very old prayer, for centuries better known in England than the Lord's Prayer, may have its roots in half-Celtic and half-Christian ritual. Like the popular, "Now I Lay Me Down to Sleep," it was commonly recited by children at bedtime. Another version goes, "One to watch, One to pray, And two to bear my souls away."

Humpty Dumpty Afghan Set

Humpty Dumpty Doll designed by Michele Wilcox
Afghan designed by Deborah Levy-Hamburg

Humpty Dumpty Doll

Finished Size: 15" tall with Hat.

Materials:
- ❏ Worsted yarn:
  - 3½ oz. blue
  - 2 oz. off-white
  - 1 oz. black
  - ½ oz. burgundy
- ❏ 1¼" cardboard circle
- ❏ Polyester fiberfill
- ❏ Tapestry needle
- ❏ F hook or hook needed to obtain gauge

Gauge: 9 sc = 2"; 9 sc rows = 2".

Basic Stitches: Ch, sl st, sc.

Note: Work in continuous rnds; do not join or turn unless otherwise stated. Mark first st of each rnd.

HEAD & BODY
Rnd 1: With off-white, ch 2, 6 sc in second ch from hook. *(6 sc made)*
Rnd 2: 2 sc in each st around. *(12)*
Rnd 3: (Sc in next st, 2 sc in next st) around. *(18)*
Rnd 4: (Sc in each of next 2 sts, 2 sc in next st) around. *(24)*
Rnds 5–6: Sc in each st around.
Rnd 7: (Sc in each of next 3 sts, 2 sc in next st) around. *(30)*
Rnd 8: (Sc in next 4 sts, 2 sc in next st) around. *(36)*
Rnds 9–10: Sc in each st around.
Rnd 11: (Sc in next 5 sts, 2 sc in next st) around. *(42)*
Rnds 12–13: Sc in each st around.
Rnd 14: (Sc in next 6 sts, 2 sc in next st) around. *(48)*
Rnds 15–16: Sc in each st around.
Rnd 17: (Sc in next 7 sts, 2 sc in next st) around. *(54)*
Rnd 18: Sc in each st around.
Rnd 19: Sc in each st around changing to blue *(see Stitch Guide)* in last st made. Fasten off off-white.
Rnds 20–30: Sc in each st around.
Rnd 31: (Sc in next 7 sts, sc next 2 sts tog) around. *(48)*

Rnd 32: (Sc in next 6 sts, sc next 2 sts tog) around. *(42)*
Rnd 33: (Sc in next 5 sts, sc next 2 sts tog) around. *(36)*
Rnd 34: (Sc in next 4 sts, sc next 2 sts tog) around. *(30)*
Rnd 35: (Sc in each of next 3 sts, sc next 2 sts tog) around. *(24)*
Rnd 36: (Sc in each of next 2 sts, sc next 2 sts tog) around. Stuff. *(18)*
Rnd 37: (Sc in next st, sc next 2 sts tog) around. *(12)*
Rnd 38: (Sc next 2 sts tog) around, join with sl st in first sc. Fasten off. Sew opening closed.

NOSE
Rnd 1: With off-white, ch 2, 6 sc in second ch from hook. *(6 sc made)*
Rnd 2: 2 sc in each st around, join with sl st in first sc. Fasten off.
Sew Nose over rnds 13 and 14 on Head & Body.
With blue, using satin stitch *(see Stitch Guide)*, embroider eyes over rnds 11–12 about 1" apart.
With burgundy, using fly and straight stitches *(see Stitch Guide)*, embroider mouth over rnds 15–17 centered below Nose *(see photo)*.

FOOT & LEG (make 2)
Rnds 1–4: With black, repeat rnds 1–4 of Head & Body.
Rnd 5: (Sc in each of next 3 sts, 2 sc in next st) around. *(30)*
Rnds 6–8: Sc in each st around.
Rnd 9: (Sc next 2 sts tog) 6 times, sc in last 18 sts. *(24)*
Rnd 10: (Sc next 2 sts tog) 3 times, (sc in each of next 3 sts, sc next 2 sts tog) 3 times, sc in each of last 3 sts. *(18)*
Rnd 11: (Sc in next st, sc next 2 sts tog) around. Stuff. Continue stuffing as you work. *(12)*
Rnd 12: Sc in each st around changing to off-white in last st made. Fasten off black.
Rnds 13–15: Sc in each st around changing to burgundy in last st of last rnd.
Rnds 16–17: Sc in each st around changing to off-white in last st of last rnd.

• • • • • • • • • • • • • • • • • Continued on page 55

Just Ducky Afghan

Designed by Darla Fanton

Text on page 54

Just Ducky Afghan

Photo on page 52

Finished Size: 36" × 41½".

Materials:
- ❏ Worsted yarn:
  - 12 oz. each of white and med. blue
  - 7 oz. each of lt. blue and yellow
  - 3 oz. each of orange and brown
  - 1 oz. each of red, dk. blue and black
- ❏ Tapestry needle
- ❏ G hook or hook needed to obtain gauge

Gauge: 4 sc = 1"; 5 sc rows = 1".

Basic Stitches: Ch, sl st, sc, dc.

Notes: Wind a separate ball of yarn for each section of color.

When changing colors *(see Stitch Guide)*, drop first color to wrong side of work, pick up when needed. Do not carry dropped color along back of work. Always change to next color in last st of last color used.

BLOCK (make 16)

Row 1: With white, ch 30, sc in second ch from hook, sc in each ch across, turn. *(29 sc made) Front of row 1 is right side of work.*

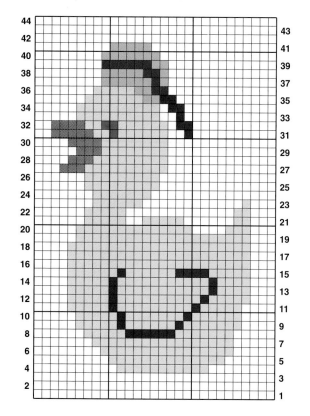

Rows 2–44: Ch 1, sc in each st across changing colors according to corresponding row on graph, turn. At end of last row, fasten off.

Edging

Rnd 1: Working around outer edge, with right side of work facing you, join med. blue with sc in first st of last row, 2 sc in same st *(corner made)*, sc in each st across to last st, 3 sc in last st; working loosely enough to keep edge flat, (skip end of next row, sc in end of next row) across to next corner; working in remaining lps on opposite side of starting ch on row 1, 3 sc in first ch, sc in each ch across to last ch, 3 sc in last ch; working loosely enough to keep edge flat, (skip end of next row, sc in end of next row) across, join with sl st in first sc.

Rnd 2: Ch 3, 3 dc in next st, dc in each st across to center st of next corner, 3 dc in next st, 2 dc in each st across to center st of next corner, 3 dc in next st, dc in each st across to center st of next corner, 3 dc in next st, 2 dc in each st across, dc in same st as ch-3, join with sl st in top of ch-3. Fasten off.

BLOCK ASSEMBLY

Working in **back lps** *(see illustration)*, with med. blue, sew Blocks together in four rows of four Blocks each.

BORDER

Working around outer edge of assembled Blocks, join med. blue with sl st in center st on bottom edge, ch 3, 4 dc in same st as sl st, (skip next 2 sts, sc in next st, skip next 2 sts, 5 dc in next st) around, join with sl st in top of ch-3. Fasten off. ✪

DUCK KEY:
- ☐ = WHITE
- ☐ = YELLOW
- ☐ = LT. BLUE
- ■ = DK. BLUE
- ■ = ORANGE
- ■ = RED
- ■ = BLACK
- ■ = BROWN

Humpty Dumpty Afghan Set

Continued from page 51

Rnds 18–41: Repeat rnds 13–17 consecutively, ending with rnd 16.
Rnd 42: Sc in each st around, join with sl st in first sc. Fasten off both colors.

PANT LEG (make 2)
Rnd 1: With blue, ch 12, sl st in first ch to form ring, ch 1, sc in each ch around. *(12 sc made)*
Rnd 2: (Sc in next st, 2 sc in next st) around. *(18)*
Rnds 3–7: Sc in each st around.
Rnd 8: (Sc in next 5 sts, 2 sc in next st) around. *(21)*
Rnd 9: Sc in each st around, join with sl st in first sc. Fasten off.
Matching rnd 1 of Pant Leg to last rnd of Leg, slip Pant Leg over top of Leg and sew edges together. Flatten top edge and sew to bottom of Body *(see photo)*.

ARM (make 2)
Rnds 1–3: Repeat rnds 1–3 of Head & Body.
Rnds 4–7: Sc in each st around.
Rnd 8: (Sc in next st, sc next 2 sts tog) around. Stuff. *(12)*
Rnd 9: Sc in each st around changing to blue in last st made. Fasten off off-white. Continue stuffing as you work.
Rnds 10–26: Sc in each st around. At end of last rnd, join with sl st in first sc. Fasten off.
Flattening last rnd, sew Arms to each side of Body *(see photo)*.

BOW TIE
Row 1: With burgundy, ch 19, sc in second ch from hook, sc in each ch across, turn. *(18 sc made)*
Rows 2–3: Ch 1, sc in each st across, turn. At end of last row, fasten off.
Sew short edges of piece together.
Place seam at center back of loop; wrap separate strand of burgundy around middle eight times. Secure wraps.
Sew Bow Tie in place on center front of Body *(see photo)*.

HAT
Rnds 1–3: With blue, repeat rnds 1–3 of Head & Body.
Rnd 4: Working this rnd in **back lps** *(see Stitch Guide)*, sc in each st around.
Rnds 5–10: Sc in each st around.
Rnd 11: For **Brim**, working this rnd in **front lps**, 2 sc in each st around. *(36)*
Rnd 12: Sc in each st around, join with sl st in first sc. Fasten off.

Hat Band
Row 1: With burgundy, ch 19, sc in second ch from hook, sc in each ch across, turn. *(18 sc made)*
Row 2: Ch 1, sc in each st across. Fasten off.
Sew short edges of Hat Band together.
Insert cardboard circle inside top of Hat; stuff.
Place Hat Band on Hat above Brim and sew in place.
Sew Hat to top right side of Head *(see photo)*.

Afghan

Finished Size: 36" × 40".

Materials:
❑ Worsted yarn:
    10 oz. burgundy
    8 oz. off-white
    6 oz. blue
❑ G hook or hook needed to obtain gauge

Gauge: 2 shells = 3"; 3 shell rows = 2".

Basic Stitches: Ch, sl st, sc, dc.

Special Stitches:
For **shell**, (3 dc, ch 1, 3 dc) in specified st or ch sp.
For **beginning shell (beg shell)**, ch 3, (2 dc, ch 1, 3 dc) in specified st or ch sp.

FOUNDATION
Row 1: With burgundy, ch 4, (2 dc, ch 1, 3 dc) in fourth ch from hook, turn. *(6 dc, 1 ch sp made)*
Rows 2–50: Ch 1, **shell** *(see Special Stitches)* in ch-1 sp, turn. At end of last row, fasten off.

CENTER
Row 1: Working across one long edge of Foundation, join off-white with sl st in ch-1 sp at end of row 2, **beg shell** *(see Special Stitches)* in end of same row, shell in each ch-1 sp at ends of rows, **do not turn**. Fasten off. *(25 shells made)*
Row 2: Join blue with sl st in ch sp of first shell, beg shell in same ch sp, shell in each ch sp across, **do not turn**. Fasten off.
Rows 3–50: Working in color sequence of off-white, burgundy, off-white, blue, repeat row 2.

EDGING
Row 1: Join off-white with sc in end of row 1 on Center, shell in end of next row, (sc in end of next row, shell in end of next row) across, shell in each ch-1 sp across row 50 of Center, (shell in end of next row, sc in end of next row) across, ending in row 1 of Center, **do not turn**. Fasten off.
Row 2: Join burgundy with sl st in ch at base of row 1 on Foundation, shell in first sc of last row, shell in each ch-1 sp across, sl st in ch-1 sp on last row on Foundation. Fasten off. ✪

Carriage Cover & Pillow

Designed by Ruth Holloway & Deborah Levy-Hamburg

Finished Sizes: Cover is 27½" × 37½". Pillow is 10½" × 13".

Materials:
- ❏ Size 10 crochet cotton thread:
  - 1,250 yds. ecru
  - 1,250 yds. variegated
- ❏ 25" square piece fabric to match variegated thread
- ❏ Sewing thread to match fabric
- ❏ Polyester fiberfill
- ❏ Tapestry and sewing needles
- ❏ No. 7 and No. 8 steel hooks or hooks needed to obtain gauges

Gauges: No. 8 hook, 17 dc = 2"; 9 dc rows = 2". Motif is 2½" square. **No. 7 hook,** 7 mesh = 2"; 4 mesh rows = 1".

Basic Stitches: Ch, sl st, sc, dc.

Special Stitches:
For **double treble crochet cluster (dtr cl),** yo 3 times, insert hook in specified st or sp, yo, pull through, (yo, pull through 2 lps on hook) 3 times, leaving last lps on hook; *yo 3 times, insert hook in same st or sp, yo, pull through, (yo, pull through 2 lps on hook) 3 times, leaving last lps on hook; repeat from * the number of times needed for number of dtr in cluster; yo, pull through all lps on hook.
For **beginning shell (beg shell),** sl st in each of next 2 sts, (sl st, ch 3, 2 dc, ch 1, 3 dc) in next ch sp.
For **shell,** (3 dc, ch 1, 3 dc) in specified st or ch sp.

CARRIAGE COVER
Motif (make 117)
Rnd 1: With No. 8 hook and ecru thread, ch 8, sl st in first ch to form ring, ch 5, **2-dtr cl** (see Special Stitches) in ring, (ch 3, **3-dtr cl** in ring) 7 times, ch 3, join with sl st in top of first cl. Fasten off. (8 cls made)
Rnd 2: Join variegated with sl st in any ch sp, (ch 3, 2 dc, ch 2, 3 dc) in same ch sp, ch 1, 4 dc in next ch sp, ch 1, *(3 dc, ch 2, 3 dc) in next ch sp, ch 1, 4 dc in next ch sp, ch 1; repeat from * around, join with sl st in top of ch-3. (40 dc, 12 ch sps)

Rnd 3: Ch 3, dc in each of next 2 sts; *[for **corner,** (2 dc, ch 2, 2 dc) in next ch sp (corner made), dc in each of next 3 sts, ch 1, dc in next 4 sts, ch 1], dc in each of next 3 sts; repeat from * 2 more times; repeat between [ ], join.
Rnd 4: Ch 3, dc in next 4 sts, *[corner, dc in next 5 sts, ch 1, dc in each of next 2 sts, ch 1, skip next st, 2 dc in next st, ch 1], dc in next 5 sts; repeat from * 2 more times; repeat between [ ], join. Fasten off.

Motif Assembly
Matching sts and working in **back lps** (see illustration on page 54), sew Motifs together nine across and thirteen down.

Border
Rnd 1: With No. 8 hook, join ecru thread with sc in right-hand corner ch sp of one short edge, 2 sc in same ch sp; working in sts and in ch sps, (evenly space 207 sc across to next corner ch sp, 3 sc in corner ch sp), evenly space 313 sc across to next corner ch sp, 3 sc in corner ch sp; repeat between ( ), evenly space 314 sc across, join with sl st in first sc. (1,053 sc made)
Rnd 2: Ch 1, sc in first st, ch 4, skip next 2 sts, (sc in next st, ch 4, skip next 2 sts) around, join. (351 ch sps)
Rnd 3: Ch 1, sc in first ch sp, **shell** (see Special Stitches) in next ch sp, sc in next ch sp, ch 4, (sc in next ch sp, shell in next ch sp, sc in next ch sp, ch 4) around, join. (117 shells)
Rnd 4: Sl st in each of next 3 sts, (sl st, ch 3, 2 dc, ch 3, 3 dc) in next ch sp, ch 4, sc in next ch sp, ch 4, (shell in ch sp of next shell, ch 4, sc in next ch sp, ch 4) around, join with sl st in top of ch-3.
Rnd 5: Beg shell (see Special Stitches), (ch 4, sc in next ch sp) 2 times, ch 4, *shell in next shell, (ch 4, sc in next ch sp) 2 times, ch 4; repeat from * around, join.
Rnd 6: Beg shell, ch 4, skip next ch sp, sc in next ch sp, ch 4, (shell in next shell, ch 4, skip next ch sp, sc in next ch sp, ch 4) around, join.
Rnds 7–10: Repeat rnds 5 and 6 alternately.
Rnd 11: Ch 1, sc in each st, 3 sc in each ch-3 sp and 4 sc in each ch-4 sp around, join with sl st in first sc. Fasten off.

• • • • • • • • • • • • • • • Continued on page 61

Rainbow Puffs Baby Set

Designed by Mae Meats

Finished Sizes: Nap/Changing Pad is 26" × 44". Pillow is 12" across.

Materials:
- ❏ Fuzzy-type worsted yarn:
    - 24 oz. white
    - 10 oz. yellow and green variegated
    - 6 oz. pink variegated
    - 6 oz. blue variegated
    - 6 oz. lilac variegated
    - 3 oz. peach
- ❏ Small amount each of black and brown worsted yarn
- ❏ Polyester fiberfill
- ❏ Pacifier *(optional)*
- ❏ Tapestry needle
- ❏ G hook or hook needed to obtain gauge

Gauge: 4 sc = 1"; 4 sc rows = 1".

Basic Stitches: Ch, sl st, sc, hdc, dc.

Note: Use caution when leaving an infant with a pillow or when placing the infant on its stomach on a puffy surface which may restrict its breathing.

NAP/CHANGING PAD
Block (make 40 white, 10 each of 4 variegated colors)
Row 1: Ch 17, sc in second ch from hook, sc in each ch across, turn. *(16 sc made)*
Rows 2–16: Ch 1, sc in each st across, turn.
Rnd 17: Working around outer edge, ch 1, sc in each st and in end of each row with 3 sc in each corner, join with sl st in first sc. Fasten off. *(72)*

Assembly
To form **Puffy Block,** hold one white Block and one variegated Block wrong sides together; working through both thicknesses, join white with sc in center st at any corner, 2 sc in same st, sc in each st around with 3 sc in center st of each corner stuffing before closing, join with sl st in first sc. Fasten off. Repeat with all remaining Blocks.

With white sew or sc Puffy Blocks together according to Assembly Illustration.

Border
Join white with sl st in center st at any corner of assembled Blocks, (ch 3, 4 dc) in same st as joining sl st, skip next st, sl st in next st, skip next st, (5 dc in next st, skip next st, sl st in next st, skip next st) around, join with sl st in top of ch-3. Fasten off.

BABY FACE PILLOW
Front
Rnd 1: With peach, ch 2, 6 sc in second ch from hook, join with sl st in first sc. *(6 sc made)*
Rnds 2–4: For **Mouth,** ch 1, sc in each st around, join. Turn rnds 1–4 wrong side out.
Rnd 5: With opening of Mouth facing you, ch 1, 2 sc in each st around, join. *(12)*
Rnd 6: Ch 1, sc in first st, 2 sc in next st, (sc in next st, 2 sc in next st) around, join. *(18)*
Rnds 7–24: Ch 1, (sc in each st around to second st of next 2 sc, 2 sc in next st) around, join. At end of last rnd *(126)*.
Rnd 25: Ch 1, sc in each st around, join. Fasten off.

ASSEMBLY ILLUSTRATION

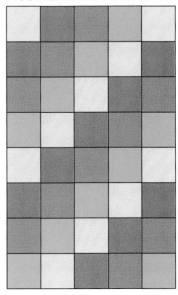

• • • • • • • • • • • • • • • • • • Continued on page 60

Rainbow Puffs Baby Set

Continued from page 59

Back

Rnd 1: With yellow and green variegated, ch 2, 6 sc in second ch from hook, join with sl st in first sc. *(6 sc made)*

Rnds 2–22: Repeat rnds 5–25 of Front. At end of last rnd, **do not fasten off.**

Rnd 23: Hold Front and Back pieces wrong sides together with Front facing you; working through both thicknesses, ch 1, sc in each st around, stuffing before closing, join. *(126)*

Rnd 24: For **Ruffle,** ch 1, skip first st, hdc in each st around, skip ch-1, join with sl st in first hdc. *(125 hdc)*

Rnd 25: Ch 1, skip first st, (sl st in next st, skip next st, 5 dc in next st, skip next st, sl st in next st) around, join with sl st in ch-1. Fasten off.

Nose

Rnd 1: With peach, ch 2, 6 sc in second ch from hook, join with sl st in first sc. *(6 sc made)*

Rnd 2: Ch 1, 2 sc in each st around, join. *(12)*

Rnd 3: Ch 1, sc in each st around, join. Fasten off.

Sew Nose to Front over rnds 7–10 centered above Mouth.

Ear (make 2)

Row 1: With peach, ch 2, 5 sc in second ch from hook, turn. *(5 sc made)*

Row 2: Ch 1, sc in first st, 2 sc in each of next 3 sts, sc in last st, turn. *(8)*

Rows 3–4: Ch 1, 2 sc in first st, sc in each st across to last st, 2 sc in last st, turn. *(10, 12)*

Row 5: Ch 1, sc in first 4 sts, hdc in next 4 sts, sc in last 4 sts. Fasten off.

Cupping Ears as shown in photo, sew ends of rows on edge of Ears to each side of Front over rnds 22–24.

Eyes & Hair

With black, using satin stitch *(see Stitch Guide),* embroider Eyes about 1½" apart centered one rnd above Nose.

For **Hair,** with brown, ch 120, insert hook in 20th ch from hook, (skip next 19 chs, insert hook in next ch) 5 times, yo and pull through all lps on hook, ch 1. Leaving an 8" strand for sewing, fasten off.

Position Hair at center top of Front as shown in photo to form bangs and sew in place.

Bow

Row 1: With yellow and green variegated, ch 6, sc in second ch from hook, sc in each ch across, turn. *(5 sc made)*

Row 2: Ch 1, 3 sc in each st across, turn. *(15)*

Row 3: Ch 1, sc in each st across, turn.

Row 4: Ch 1, sc in first 5 sts, 2 sc in each of next 5 sts, sc in last 5 sts, turn. *(20)*

Rows 5–30: Ch 1, sc in each st across, turn.

Row 31: Ch 1, sc in first 5 sts, (sc next 2 sts tog) 5 times, sc in last 5 sts, turn. *(15)*

Row 32: Ch 1, sc in each st across, turn.

Row 33: Ch 1, sc first 2 sts tog, sc in next st, (sc next 2 sts tog, sc in next st) across, turn. *(10)*

Row 34: Ch 1, sc first 2 sts tog, (sc next 2 sts tog) across, turn. *(5)*

Rows 35–67: Repeat rows 2–34. At end of last row, fasten off.

Fold first and last rows to row 34 at center of piece, forming bow loops; sew edges to center.

Knot

Row 1: With yellow and green variegated, ch 11, sc in second ch from hook, sc in each ch across, turn. *(10 sc made)*

Row 2: Ch 1, sc in each st across. Fasten off.

Wrap Knot around center of Bow, tack ends together at back of Bow. Sew Bow to Front centered 11 rnds below Mouth.

Insert pacifier in Mouth if desired. ✪

Carriage Cover & Pillow

Continued from page 56

PILLOW

Filet Stitches:

For **beginning mesh (beg mesh),** ch 5, skip next 2 chs, dc in next st.

For **mesh,** ch 2, skip next 2 chs or sts, dc in next st.

For **block,** 2 dc in next ch sp, dc in next st, **or** dc in each of next 3 sts.

For **end mesh,** ch 2, skip next 2 chs, dc in third ch of ch-5.

Cover Front

Row 1: With No. 7 hook and ecru thread, ch 110, dc in eighth ch from hook, (ch 2, skip next 2 chs, dc in next ch) across, turn. *(35 mesh made)*

Row 2: Beg mesh *(see Filet Stitches),* **mesh** 33 times, ch 2, dc in third ch of ch-7.

Rows 3–10: Beg mesh, mesh 33 times, **end mesh** *(see Filet Stitches),* turn.

Rows 11–31: Work according to corresponding row of graph below, turn. At end of last row, fasten off.

Cover Back

Row 1: With No. 8 hook and variegated thread, ch 91, dc in fourth ch from hook, dc in each ch across, turn. *(89 dc made)*

Rows 2–34: Ch 3, dc in each st across, turn. At end of last row, fasten off.

Border

Rnd 1: With right side of work facing you, working around outer edge of Cover Front, with No. 8 hook, join variegated with sc in last mesh at end of row 1, (sc, ch 2, 2 sc) in same mesh, *evenly space 59 sc across end of rows to next corner mesh, (2 sc, ch 2, 2 sc) in corner mesh*; working in remaining lps on opposite side of starting ch, sc in each worked ch and in each ch sp across to next corner mesh, (2 sc, ch 2, 2 sc) in corner mesh; repeat between first *, sc in each st and in each ch sp across, join with sl st in first sc. *(268 sc made)*

Rnds 2–3: Ch 1, sc in each st around with (2 sc, ch 1, 2 sc) in each corner ch sp, join. At end of last rnd, fasten off. *(300)*

Rnd 4: Hold Cover Front and Back wrong sides together, with Front facing you; working through both thicknesses, join variegated thread with sc in bottom right-hand corner ch sp, 2 sc in same ch sp, evenly space 70 sc across to next corner ch sp, 3 sc in corner ch sp, evenly space 81 sc across to next corner ch sp, 3 sc in corner ch sp, evenly space 71 sc across to next corner ch sp, 3 sc in corner ch sp; working on Front edge only, evenly sp 81 sc across, join. Fasten off.

Rnd 5: Join ecru with sc in any st, ch 3, skip next 2 sts, (sc in next st, ch 3, skip next 2 sts) around, join. *(105 ch sps)*

Rnds 6–9: Repeat rnds 3–6 of Carriage Cover Border.

Rnd 10: Repeat rnd 11 of Carriage Cover Border.

Pillow Form

From fabric, cut two 9" × 11½" pieces. Allowing ½" for seam, sew pieces right sides together, leaving 4" open for turning. Clip corners. Turn. Stuff. Sew opening closed.

Insert Pillow Form in Pillow Cover. ✪

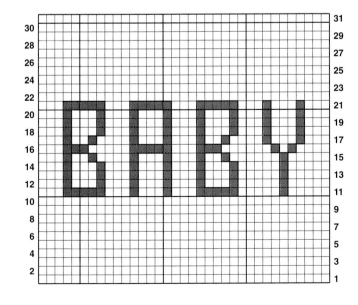

☐ = MESH OR BEGINNING MESH OR END MESH

▦ = BLOCK

Mother's Love Blanket & Cap

Designed by Carol Richter

Finished Sizes: Blanket is 32" × 36". Cap fits newborn to 3 mos.

Materials:
- ❏ 11 oz. white baby yarn
- ❏ ¾ yd. white ½" satin ribbon
- ❏ White sewing thread
- ❏ Sewing needle
- ❏ G hook or hook needed to obtain gauge

Gauge: 1 shell = 1"; 4 pattern rows = 2".

Basic Stitches: Ch, sl st, sc, hdc, dc.

Special Stitches:
For **shell,** (dc, ch 1, dc, ch 1, dc) in specified ch or st.
For **V st,** (dc, ch 1, dc) in specified ch or st.

BLANKET

Row 1: Ch 167, dc in fifth ch from hook, *ch 1, skip each of next 2 chs, sc in next ch, ch 1, skip each of next 2 chs, **shell** (see Special Stitches) in next ch; repeat from * across to last 6 chs, ch 1, skip each of next 2 chs, sc in next ch, ch 1, skip each of next 2 chs, **V st** (see Special Stitches) in last ch, turn. (26 shells, 2 V sts made)

Row 2: (Ch 4, dc) in first dc, *ch 1, dc next 2 dc tog, ch 1, V st in next dc; repeat from * across to ch-4, V st in third ch of ch-4, turn. (83 dc)

Row 3: Ch 1, sc in first dc of V st, sc in ch sp of same V st, (Ch 1, skip next ch sp, shell in next st, ch 1, skip next ch sp, sc in next V st) 27 times, sc in third ch of ch-4, turn.

Row 4: Ch 3, hdc in next dc, (ch 1, V st in next dc, ch 1, dc next 2 dc tog) 26 times, ch 1, V st in next dc, ch 1, dc next dc and last sc tog, turn.

Row 5: (Ch 4, dc) in first st, (ch 1, skip next ch sp, sc in next V st, ch 1, skip next ch sp, shell in next dc) 26 times, ch 1, sc in next V st, ch 1, V st in last dc, turn.

Rows 6–77: Repeat rows 2–5 consecutively. At end of last row, **do not turn.**

Rnd 78: Working around outer edge, (ch 1, sc in end of next row, ch 1, 3 dc in end of next row) across; working across bottom of row 1, ch 1, sc in first ch, (ch 1, 3 dc in next ch sp, ch 1, sc in next ch sp) across, (ch 1, 3 dc in end of next row, ch 1, sc in end of next row) across to last row, ch 1, 3 dc in end of row, ch 1, sc in first V st, (ch 1, 3 dc in next sc, ch 1, sc in center ch sp of next shell) across to last V st, ch 1, sc in last V st, join with sl st in first sc. Fasten off.

CAP

Rnd 1: Ch 2, 6 sc in second ch from hook, **do not join rnds.** (6 sc made)

Rnd 2: 2 sc in each st around. (12)

Rnd 3: (Sc in next st, 2 sc in next st) around. (18)

Rnd 4: (Sc in each of next 2 sts, 2 sc in next st) around. (24)

Rnd 5: (Sc in each of next 3 sts, 2 sc in next st) around. (30)

Rnd 6: (Sc in each of next 2 sts, 2 sc in next st) around. (40)

Rnd 7: Sc in each st around.

Rnd 8: (2 sc in next st, sc in each of next 3 sts) around. (50)

Rnd 9: Sc in each st around.

Row 10: Working this row in **back lps** (see Stitch Guide), (ch 4, dc) in first st, (ch 1, skip next st, sc in next st, ch 1, skip next st, shell in next st) 11 times, ch 1, skip next st, sc in next st, ch 1, skip next st, V st in next st leaving last st unworked, turn. (11 shells)

Row 11: (Ch 4, dc) in first st, *ch 1, dc next 2 sts tog, ch 1, V st in next st; repeat from * across to ch-4, V st in third ch of ch-4, turn.

Row 12: Ch 1, sc in first dc of V st, sc in ch sp of same V st, (ch 1, skip next ch sp, shell in next st, ch 1, skip next ch sp, sc in next V st) 12 times, sc in third ch of ch-4, sc in last dc of last V st, turn.

Row 13: Ch 3, hdc in next dc, (ch 1, V st in next dc, ch 1, dc next 2 dc tog) 11 times, ch 1, V st in next dc, ch 1, dc next dc and last sc tog, turn.

Row 14: (Ch 4, dc) in first st, (ch 1, skip next ch sp, sc in next V st, ch 1, skip next ch sp, shell in next st) 11 times, ch 1, sc in next V st, ch 1, V st in last dc, turn.

Row 15: Repeat row 11.

Row 16: Sl st in each of next 6 dc and chs, sl st in next ch, sl st in next dc, (ch 1, sc in next V st, ch 1, skip next ch sp, shell in next st) 8 times, ch 1, sc in next st leaving remaining sts unworked, turn.

Row 17: Ch 3, dc in next dc, (ch 1, V st in next dc, ch 1, dc next 2 sts tog) 7 times, ch 1, V st in last dc, turn.

Row 18: (Ch 1, sc in next V st, ch 1, skip next ch sp, shell in next st) 7 times, ch 1, sc in next V st. Fasten off.

Rnd 19: Working around outer edge, join with sc in first unworked st on rnd 9, sc in each st, sc in each ch and sc evenly spaced across end of each row, join with sl st in first sc. Fasten off.

Cut ribbon in half. Sew one end of each piece to each bottom front corner of Cap. ✿

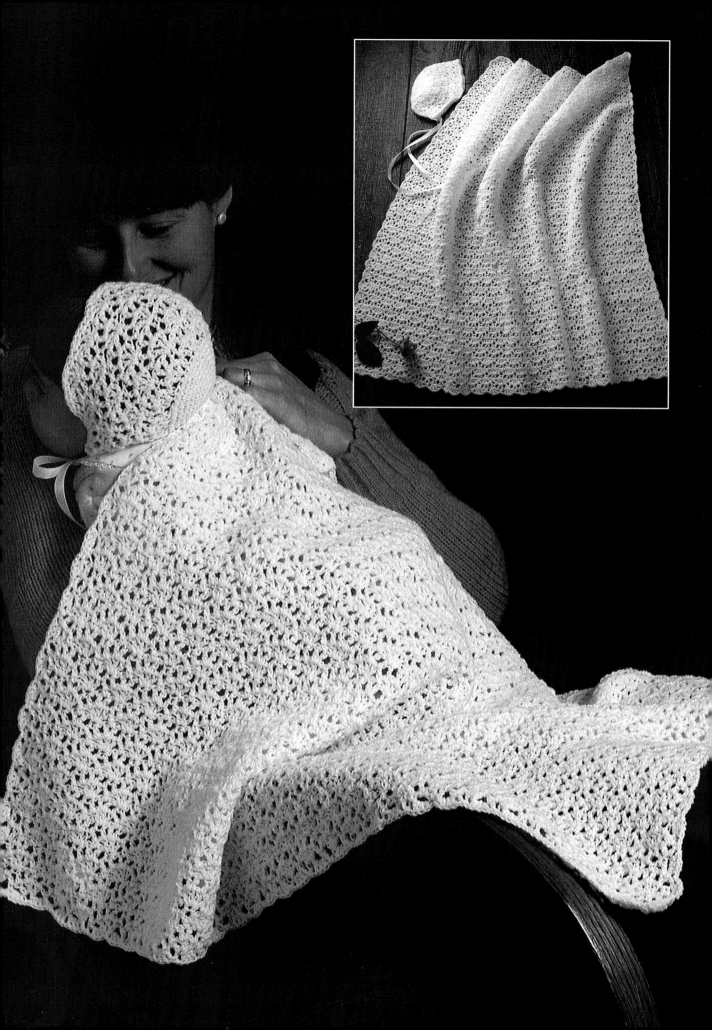

Granny Bear Afghan

Designed by Edna Howell

Finished Size: 41" × 44".

Materials:
- ❏ Worsted yarn:
  - 12 oz. white
  - 3 oz. lt. blue
  - 2 oz. each of lt. brown, med. brown and dk. brown *(for Bears)*
  - 1 oz. each of med. blue, purple, pink, yellow and green *(for Bows)*
  - ½ oz. black
- ❏ Brown sewing thread
- ❏ Tapestry and sewing needles
- ❏ G hook or hook needed to obtain gauge

Gauge: 4 dc = 1"; 2 dc rows = 1". Motif is 4½" across.

Basic Stitches: Ch, sl st, hdc, dc.

Special Stitches:
For **beginning shell (beg shell)**, (ch 3, 2 dc, ch 2, 3 dc) in specified ch sp.
For **shell**, (3 dc, ch 2, 3 dc) in specified st or ch sp.

BEAR MOTIF (make 20 lt. brown, 20 med. brown, 21 dk. brown)
Rnd 1: Ch 4, sl st in first ch to form ring, ch 3, 2 dc in ring, ch 2, (3 dc in ring, ch 2) 3 times, join with sl st in top of ch-3. *(12 dc, 4 ch sps made)*
Rnd 2: Sl st in each of next 2 sts; for **Face,** (sl st, ch 3, 5 dc) in next ch sp, ch 4; for **Arm,** 3 dc in next ch sp, ch 4; for **Legs,** (4 dc, ch 2, 4 dc) in next ch sp, ch 4; for **Arm,** 3 dc in last ch sp, ch 4, join. *(20)*
Row 3: For **Ears,** (ch 1, hdc) in first st, hdc in next st, sl st in each of next 2 sts, hdc in next st, (hdc, sl st) in next st leaving last 14 sts unworked, **do not turn.** Fasten off.
Rnd 4: Working around outer edge of Bear shape, join white with sl st in first ch sp on rnd 2, **beg shell** *(see Special Stitches)* in same ch sp as joining sl st, ch 2, (**shell** in next ch sp, ch 2) 4 times, shell in second sl st of Ears, ch 2, join.
Rnd 5: Sl st in each of next 2 sts, sl st in next ch sp, beg shell in same ch sp, (ch 1, 3 dc in next ch sp, ch 1, shell in ch sp of next shell) 5 times, ch 1, 3 dc in last ch sp, ch 1, join. Fasten off.
With black, using French knot *(see Stitch Guide),* embroider eyes and nose on Face as shown in photo.

Bow (make 61 in desired colors)
Ch 40. Fasten off. Tie in bow around two center sts of rnd 1 below Head.

With brown sewing thread and needle, tack ends and loops of Bow to Bear.

ASSEMBLY
For **joining,** hold two Motifs wrong sides together, matching sts and chs on side edges *(see Motif illustration);* working through both thicknesses in **back lps** *(see Stitch Guide),* join lt. blue with sc in second ch of corner ch sp, sc in each st and ch across to next corner ch sp, sc in first ch of corner ch sp. Fasten off.

MOTIF ILLUSTRATION

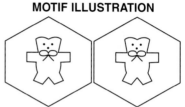

Alternating colors of bears as desired, repeat joining making a strip with a total of nine Motifs.
Make two strips each with five Motifs, six Motifs, seven Motifs and eight Motifs.
Arranging strips as shown in Assembly illustration, work joining across edges of strips.

MOTIF ASSEMBLY ILLUSTRATION

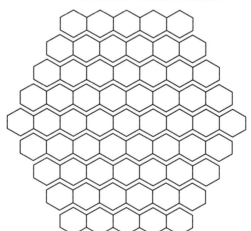

EDGING
Rnd 1: Working this rnd in **back lps,** starting in any outer corner, join lt. blue with sc in first ch of corner, sc in each ch and in each st around outer edge of assembled strips, join with sl st in first sc. Fasten off.
Rnd 2: Working this rnd in **back lps,** join white with sl st in first st, hdc in each of next 2 sts, (sl st in next st, hdc in each of next 3 sts) around to last 3 sts, sl st in next st, hdc in each of last 2 sts, join with sl st in first sl st. Fasten off. ✪

Bright Ribbons Mile-A-Minute Afghan

An Annie Original

Finished Size: 37" × 39" without Tassels.

Materials:
- ❑ Worsted yarn:
    - 28 oz. variegated
    - 3 oz. each of five solid colors to match colors in variegated yarn
- ❑ 6" piece corrugated cardboard
- ❑ Tapestry needle
- ❑ G hook or hook needed to obtain gauge

Gauge: 4 dc = 1"; dc is ¾" tall. Panel is 4¼" wide.

Basic Stitches: Ch, sl st, sc, dc.

Special Stitch: For **shell,** (3 dc, ch 1, 3 dc) in specified st or ch sp.

PANEL (make 7)

Row 1: With variegated, ch 13, shell in fourth ch from hook *(shell made)*, ch 12, skip next 8 chs, shell in last ch, turn. *(2 shells made)*

Row 2: Ch 3, shell in first ch sp, ch 11, shell in last ch-1 sp, turn.

Row 3: Ch 3, shell in first ch-1 sp, ch 10, shell in last ch-1 sp, turn.

Row 4: Repeat row 3.

Row 5: Repeat row 2.

Row 6: Ch 3, shell in first ch-1 sp, ch 6; working over chains of last 5 rows *(see illustration)*, sc around chains, ch 6, shell in last ch-1 sp, turn.

Row 7: Ch 3, shell in first ch-1 sp, ch 7, shell in last ch-1 sp, turn.

Row 8: Ch 3, shell in first ch-1 sp, ch 12, shell in last ch-1 sp, turn.

Rows 9–63: Repeat rows 2–8 consecutively, ending with row 7. At end of last row, ch 3, sl st in top of ch-3 at end of previous row. Fasten off.

JOINING EDGE

For **First Edge,** working around outer edge of one Panel, with variegated, work the following steps to complete the joining:

A: Join with sc in first ch-1 sp of last row on Panel, work 15 dc in ch-7 sp, sc in next ch-1 sp;

B: 6 dc in each ch-3 sp down first side, sc in bottom of next shell;

C: 15 dc in ch-8 sp at end, sc in bottom of next shell, 6 dc in each ch-3 sp down second side, skip sc at beginning of step A, join with sl st in top of first dc. Fasten off.

For **Second Edge,** working around outer edge of another Panel, with variegated, work the following steps to complete the joining:

A: Join with sc in first ch-1 sp of last row on Panel, work 15 dc in ch-7 sp, sc in next ch-1 sp;

B: To join this side to second side of last Panel, *3 dc in next ch-3 sp, sc in sp between center sts of next 6-dc group on last Panel, 3 dc in same ch-3 sp on this Panel; repeat from * down this side, sc in bottom of next shell;

C: 15 dc in ch-8 sp at end, sc in bottom of next shell, 6 dc in each ch-3 sp down second side, skip sc at beginning of step A, join with sl st in top of first dc. Fasten off.

Repeat Second Edge using each remaining Panel.

RIBBON (make 1 each of 3 solid colors & 2 each of 2 solid colors)

Row 1: Ch 4, 5 dc in fourth ch from hook, turn. *(5 dc made)*

Row 2: Ch 2 *(does not count as a st)*, dc in each dc across, turn. *(5 dc)*

Repeat row 2 until piece is long enough to fit along center of Panel.

Last Row: For **5-dc decrease,** (yo, insert hook in next st, yo, pull lp through, yo, pull through 2 lps on hook, leave last 2 lps on hook) 5 times, yo, pull through all lps on hook. Fasten off.

Weave Ribbon through middle of each Panel *(see photo)*.

TASSELS

For **Tassel,** cut 32 strands of yarn each 12" long. Tie separate strand of yarn around center of all strands held together. Fold strands in half at tie. Wrap another separate strand of yarn around all strands 1" from tied end several times and secure end of yarn behind wraps *(see illustration)*.

Make two Tassels to match color of each Ribbon. Tack one to each end of matching Ribbon. Tack each end of Ribbon to center of each end on wrong side of Panel. ✪

An Original by Annie™

Sleepytime Bear

Designed by Dianne Janise

Finished Size: 34½" × 42".

Materials:
- ❑ Sport yarn:
    - 15 oz. white
    - 4½ oz. each of pale green, pale yellow and violet
- ❑ E crochet hook and E afghan hook or hooks needed to obtain gauges

Gauges: E crochet hook, 5 dc = 1"; 3 dc rows = 1".
E afghan hook, 7 afghan sts = 1"; 11 afghan rows = 2".

Basic Stitches: Ch, sl st, sc, dc.

Special Stitches:
Each afghan stitch row is worked in two stages as follows:

For **row 1 of afghan stitch,** ch length needed, insert hook in second ch from hook, yo, pull through ch, (insert hook in next ch, yo, pull through ch) across leaving all lps on hook; to **work lps off hook,** yo, pull through first lp on hook, (yo, pull through 2 lps on hook—*see illustration 1)* across leaving last lp on hook *(this lp is first st of next row).*

For **row 2 of afghan stitch,** skip first vertical bar, (insert hook under next vertical bar, yo, pull through bar—*see illustration 2)* across to last bar, insert hook under last bar and lp directly behind it *(see illustration 3),* yo, pull through bar and lp; work lps off hook. Repeat row 2 until piece is desired size.

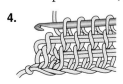   3.

To **change colors** on first half of afghan st row, drop first color; insert hook under vertical bar, yo with second color, pull through bar *(see illustration 4).*

To **change colors** on second half of afghan st row, drop first color; with second color, pull through next 2 lps on hook *(see illustration 5).*

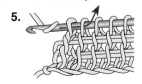   5.

Always drop yarn to wrong side of work. Pick up dropped colors when needed. Fasten off when no longer needed.

For **puff stitch (ps),** yo, insert hook in specified st, yo, pull long lp through st, (yo, insert hook in same st, yo, pull long lp through st) 3 times, yo, pull through all lps on hook, ch 1.

For **slanted shell,** (sl st, ch 3, 3 dc) in specified st.

Note: Wind white into seven balls, violet into five balls and pale green into two balls.

CENTER
Row 1: With E afghan hook and white, ch 95, work **afghan stitch** *(see Special Stitches).*

Rows 2–9: Work **afghan stitch** *(see Special Stitches).*

Rows 10–105: Repeat row 2 changing colors according to corresponding row on graph on page 74.

Rows 106–115: With white, repeat row 2.

Row 116: Sl st in each vertical bar across. Fasten off.
With pale green, using backstitch, satin stitch and straight stitch *(see Stitch Guide),* embroider facial features and paws according to graph.

BORDER
Rnd 1: Working around outer edge, with right side of work facing you, with E crochet hook, join white with sc in end of row 115 on right-hand side of Center, 2 sc in same row, sc in next 95 sts, 3 sc in end of next row, sc in end of each row across to row 1, 3 sc in end of row 1; working in remaining lps on opposite side of starting ch at bottom of row 1, sc in next 95 chs, 3 sc in end of next row, sc in end of each row across, join with sl st in first sc. *(428 sc made)*

Rnd 2: Ch 3, *3 dc in next st *(corner made),* dc in next st, (dc next 2 sts tog, dc in next st) across to center st of next 3-sc group, 3 dc in next st *(corner made),* dc in each st across* to center st of next 3-sc group; repeat between first *, join with sl st in top of ch-3. *(372 dc)*

Rnd 3: Ch 3, dc in each st around with 3 dc in center st of each corner, join. *(380)*

Rnds 4–5: Ch 3, dc in each st around with 5 dc in center st of each corner, join. At end of last rnd, fasten off. *(396, 412)*

Rnd 6: Join pale yellow with sc in first st, **ps** *(see Special Stitches)* in next st, (sc in next st, ps in next st) around, join with sl st in first sc. Fasten off.

• • • • • • • • • • • • • • • • Continued on page 73

Tropical Treasures

Fish Pillow designed by Michele Wilcox
Waves Afghan designed by Deborah Levy-Hamburg

Fish Pillow

Finished Size: 13" × 16" long.

Materials:
- ❑ Worsted yarn:
  - 2 oz. each of lt. blue, dk. blue, lt. coral and dk. coral
  - 1 oz. white
  - Small amount black
- ❑ Polyester fiberfill
- ❑ Tapestry needle
- ❑ F hook or hook needed to obtain gauge

Gauge: 9 sc = 2"; 9 sc rows = 2".

Basic Stitches: Ch, sl st, sc, dc.

PILLOW SIDE (make 2)
Row 1: With dk. coral, ch 6, sc in second ch from hook, sc in each ch across, turn. *(5 sc made) Front of row 1 is right side of work.*

Rows 2–4: Ch 1, 2 sc in first st, sc in each st across to last st, 2 sc in last st, turn. *(7, 9, 11)*

Row 5: Ch 1, sc in each st across, turn.

Rows 6–8: Repeat row 2. *(13, 15, 17)*

Row 9: Ch 1, sc in each st across, turn.

Rows 10–12: Repeat row 2. *(19, 21, 23)*

Row 13: Ch 1, sc in each st across changing to dk. blue in last st *(see Stitch Guide)*, turn. Fasten off dk. coral.

Rows 14–16: Repeat row 2. *(25, 27, 29)*

Rows 17–36: Ch 1, sc in each st across, turn.

Rows 37–39: Ch 1, sc first 2 sts tog, sc in each st across to last 2 sts, sc last 2 sts tog, turn. *(27, 25, 23)*

Row 40: Ch 1, sc in each st across, turn.

Rows 41–43: Repeat row 37. *(21, 19, 17)*

Row 44: Ch 1, sc in each st across, turn.

Row 45: Repeat row 37 changing to lt. coral in last st made. Fasten off dk. blue. *(15)*

Rows 46–47: Repeat row 37. *(13, 11)*

Rows 48–49: Ch 1, sc in each st across, turn.

Rows 50–55: Repeat row 2. At end of last row *(23)*.

Row 56: For **First Tail Fin,** ch 1, sc in first 11 sts leaving last 12 sts unworked, turn. *(11)*

Row 57: Ch 1, sc first 2 sts tog, sc in each st across, turn. *(10)*

Row 58: Ch 1, sc in each st across to last 2 sts, sc last 2 sts tog, turn. *(9)*

Rows 59–64: Repeat rows 57 and 58 alternately. At end of last row *(3)*.

Row 65: Ch 1, sc in first st, sc last 2 sts tog, turn. Fasten off.

Row 56: For **Second Tail Fin,** skip next unworked st on row 55, join lt. coral with sc in next st, sc in each st across, turn. *(11)*

Row 57: Ch 1, sc in each st across to last 2 sts, sc last 2 sts tog, turn. *(10)*

Row 58: Ch 1, sc first 2 sts tog, sc in each st across, turn. *(9)*

Rows 59–64: Repeat rows 57 and 58 alternately. At end of last row *(3)*.

Row 65: Ch 1, sc first 2 sts tog, sc in last st. Fasten off.

•••••••••••••••• Continued on page 72

Tropical Treasures

Continued from page 70

Top Fin

Row 1: Working in ends of rows on one edge of Pillow Side, with right side facing you, join lt. blue with sc in end of row 17, sc in each row across to row 36, turn. *(20 sc made)*

Rows 2–3: Ch 1, sc first 2 sts tog, sc in each st across to last 2 sts, sc last 2 sts tog, turn. *(18, 16)*

Row 4: Ch 1, sc in each st across to last 2 sts, sc last 2 sts tog, turn. *(15)*

Row 5: Ch 1, sc first 2 sts tog, sc in each st across, turn. *(14)*

Rows 6–11: Repeat rows 4 and 5 alternately. At end of last row, **do not turn.**

Row 12: Working in ends of rows, (skip next row, 5 dc in next row, skip next row, sc in next row) 2 times, skip next row, 5 dc in next row, skip next row, sc in end of row 38 on Pillow Side. Fasten off.

Bottom Fin

Row 1: With wrong side of work facing you, repeat row 1 of Top Fin on opposite edge of Pillow Side.

Rows 2–12: Repeat rows 2–12 of Top Fin.

SIDE FIN (make 2)

Row 1: With dk. coral, ch 3, sc in second ch from hook, sc in last ch, turn. *(2 sc made)*

Rows 2–3: Ch 1, 2 sc in first st, sc in each st across to last st, 2 sc in last st, turn. *(4, 6)*

Row 4: Ch 1, sc in each st across, turn.

Rows 5–6: Repeat row 2. *(8, 10)*

Rows 7–13: Ch 1, sc in each st across, turn.

Row 14: Ch 1, sc first 2 sts tog, (sc next 2 sts tog) across, turn. *(5)*

Rnd 15: Working in sts and in ends of rows around outer edge, ch 1, sc first 2 sts tog, sc in next st, sc last 2 sts tog, **do not turn;** sl st in side of last sc made, (ch 3, skip next row, sl st in next row) across to row 1; working in remaining lps on opposite side of starting ch on row 1, (sl st, ch 3, sl st) in next ch, skip next ch, (ch 3, skip next row, sl st in next row) across, join with sl st in first sc. Fasten off.

EDGING

Rnd 1: Hold Pillow Sides wrong sides together, matching edges; working through both thicknesses around outer edges, join white with sc in any st, sc in each st and in end of each row around with 3 sc in tip of each Fin, stuffing before closing *(end with an even number of sts)*, join with sl st in first sc.

Rnd 2: (Ch 3, skip next st, sl st in next st) around, join with sl st in first ch of ch-3. Fasten off.

FINISHING

Sew Side Fins to Pillow Sides centered over rows 21–37 *(see photo).*

With black, using satin stitch *(see Stitch Guide)*, embroider eyes 1" from one edge between rows 8 and 9 on each Pillow Side.

Waves Afghan

Finished Size: 28" × 48".

Materials:
- ❏ Worsted yarn:
  - 11 oz. white
  - 2½ oz. each of lt. blue, dk. blue, lt. coral and dk. coral
- ❏ I hook or hook needed to obtain gauge

Gauge: 4 V sts = 3"; 1 shell row and 1 V st row = 1¼".

Basic Stitches: Ch, sl st, sc, dc.

Special Stitches:
For **V st,** (dc, ch 1, dc) in specified st or ch sp.
For **shell,** (2 dc, ch 1, 2 dc) in specified st or ch sp.

AFGHAN

Row 1: With white, ch 103, **V st** *(see Special Stitches)* in fifth ch from hook *(4 skipped chs count as first dc and ch sp)*, (skip next 2 chs, V st in next ch) across to last 2 chs, skip next ch, dc in last ch, turn. *(2 dc, 33 V sts made)*

Row 2: Ch 3, **shell** *(see Special Stitches)* in next V st, (ch 1, skip next V st, shell in next V st) across to last st, dc in last st, turn. *(2 dc, 33 ch-1 sps)*

Row 3: Ch 3, V st in each ch-1 sp across to last st, dc in last st, turn. *(2 dc, 33 V sts)*

Row 4: (Ch 3, dc) in first st, ch 1, skip next V st, (shell in next V st, ch 1, skip next V st) across to last st, 2 dc in last st, turn. *(4 dc, 33 ch-1 sps)*

Row 5: Ch 3, V st in each ch-1 sp across to last st, dc in last st, turn. Fasten off. *(2 dc, 33 V sts)*

Row 6: Join dk. coral with sl st in first st, ch 3, shell in next V st, (ch 1, skip next V st, shell in next V st) across to last st, dc in last st, turn. Fasten off.

Row 7: Join lt. coral with sl st in first st, ch 3, V st in each ch-1 sp across to last st, dc in last st, turn. Fasten off.

Row 8: Join dk. coral with sl st in first st, (ch 3, dc) in first st, ch 1, skip next V st, (shell in next V st, ch 1, skip next V st) across to last st, 2 dc in last st, turn. Fasten off.

Row 9: Join lt. coral with sl st in first st, ch 3, V st in each ch-1 sp across to last st, dc in last st, turn. Fasten off.

Row 10: Join dk. coral with sl st in first st, ch 3, shell in next V st, (ch 1, skip next V st, shell in next V st) across to last st, dc in last st, turn. Fasten off.

Row 11: Join white with sl st in first st, ch 3, V st in each ch-1 sp across to last st, dc in last st, turn.

Row 12: (Ch 3, dc) in first st, ch 1, skip next V st, (shell in next V st, ch 1, skip next V st) across to last st, 2 dc in last st, turn.

Row 13: Ch 3, V st in each ch-1 sp across to last st, dc in last st, turn.

Row 14: Ch 3, shell in next V st, (ch 1, skip next V st, shell in next V st) across to last st, dc in last st, turn.

Row 15: Ch 3, V st in each ch-1 sp across to last st, dc in last st, turn. Fasten off.

Row 16: Join dk. blue with sl st in first st, (ch 3, dc) in same st as sl st, ch 1, skip next V st, (shell in next V st, ch 1, skip next V st) across to last st, 2 dc in last st, turn. Fasten off.

Row 17: Join lt. blue with sl st in first st, ch 3, V st in each ch-1 sp across to last st, dc in last st, turn. Fasten off.

Row 18: Join dk. blue with sl st in first st, ch 3, shell in next V st, (ch 1, skip next V st, shell in next V st) across to last st, dc in last st, turn. Fasten off.

Row 19: Join lt. blue with sl st in first st, ch 3, V st in each ch-1 sp across to last st, dc in last st, turn. Fasten off.

Row 20: Join dk. blue with sl st in first st, (ch 3, dc) in same st as sl st, ch 1, skip next V st, (shell in next V st, ch 1, skip next V st) across to last st, 2 dc in last st, turn. Fasten off.

Row 21: Join white with sl st in first st, ch 3, V st in each ch-1 sp across to last st, dc in last st, turn.

Row 22: Ch 3, shell in next V st, (ch 1, skip next V st, shell in next V st) across to last st, dc in last st, turn.

Row 23: Ch 3, V st in each ch-1 sp across to last st, dc in last st, turn.

Row 24: (Ch 3, dc) in first st, ch 1, skip next V st, (shell in next V st, ch 1, skip next V st) across to last st, 2 dc in last st, turn.

Row 25: Ch 3, V st in each ch-1 sp across to last st, dc in last st, turn. Fasten off.

Rows 26–75: Repeat rows 6–25 consecutively, ending with row 15. At end of last row, **do not turn or fasten off.**

Border

Rnd 1: Working around outer edge, ch 1, 2 sc in end of each row and in each st around with 3 sc in each corner st, join with sl st in first sc.

Rnds 2–4: Ch 1, sc in each st around with 3 sc in center st of each corner, join. At end of last rnd, fasten off. ✪

Sleepytime Bear

Continued from page 69

Rnd 7: Join white with sl st in first st, ch 3, dc in each st around with 5 dc in center st of each corner, join.

Rnds 8–10: Ch 3, dc in each st around with 5 dc in center st of each corner, join. At end of last rnd, fasten off.

Rnd 11: With pale green, repeat rnd 6.

Rnds 12–15: Repeat rnds 7–10.

Rnd 16: With violet, repeat rnd 6.

Rnds 17–20: Repeat rnds 7–10.

Rnds 21–31: Repeat rnds 6–16. At end of last rnd, **do not fasten off.**

Rnd 32: (Ch 3, 3 dc) in first st, *(skip next 3 sts, **slanted shell**—*see Special Stitches*—in next st) across to one st before next corner st, (skip next st, slanted shell in next st) 2 times; repeat from * 3 more times, skip next 3 sts, (slanted shell in next st, skip next 3 sts) across, join with sl st in first ch of first ch-3. Fasten off.

CENTER TRIM

Holding pale yellow on wrong side of work and working in sts on rnd 1 of Border, insert E crochet hook through any st from front to back, yo, pull lp through to front side of work, *insert hook through next st from front to back, yo, pull lp through to front and through lp on hook; repeat from * around. Fasten off. ✪

Graph on page 74

Sleepytime Bear

Continued from page 73

SLEEPYTIME BEAR KEY:

■ = VIOLET □ = WHITE

▨ = PALE GREEN ◨ = PALE GREEN EMBROIDERY

LAST VERTICAL BAR

FIRST VERTICAL BAR

Afghans & More

CHAPTER 4

Nursery Decor

Twinkle, Twinkle, Little Star

Twinkle, twinkle, little star,
How I wonder what you are!
Up above the moon so high,
Like a diamond in the sky.

What child among us hasn't crept out of bed to gaze into the starry heavens and recite this poem? The author of this familiar rhyme, published in 1806, was Jane Taylor (1783-1824). She and her sister, Ann, were popular writers of nursery poems.

Prancing Pony

Designed by Michele Wilcox

Finished Size: Pony is 10" tall.

Materials:
- ❏ Worsted yarn:
    - 4 oz. white
    - Small amount each of lt. green, pink, yellow and blue
- ❏ Polyester fiberfill
- ❏ Pink acrylic paint
- ❏ Small paintbrush
- ❏ 16" piece of ¼" wooden dowel
- ❏ 4¾"-diameter wooden heart
- ❏ Drill
- ❏ Stiff brush
- ❏ Craft glue
- ❏ Tapestry needle
- ❏ F hook or hook needed to obtain gauge

Gauge: 9 sc = 2"; 9 sc rows = 2".

Basic Stitches: Ch, sl st, sc, hdc.

Note: Work in continuous rnds; do not join or turn unless otherwise stated. Mark first st of each rnd.

HEAD

Rnd 1: Starting at **Muzzle,** with white, ch 2, 6 sc in second ch from hook. *(6 sc made)*
Rnd 2: 2 sc in each st around. *(12)*
Rnd 3: (Sc in next st, 2 sc in next st) around. *(18)*
Rnds 4–6: Sc in each st around.
Rnd 7: (Sc in next st, sc next 2 sts tog) around. *(12)*
Rnd 8: Sc in each st around.
Rnd 9: (Sc in next st, 2 sc in next st) around. *(18)*
Rnd 10: Sc in each st around.
Rnd 11: (Sc in each of next 2 sts, 2 sc in next st) around. *(24)*
Rnd 12: Sc in each st around.
Rnd 13: (Sc in each of next 3 sts, 2 sc in next st) around. *(30)*
Rnds 14–16: Sc in each st around.
Rnd 17: (Sc in each of next 3 sts, sc next 2 sts tog) around. *(24)*
Rnd 18: (Sc in each of next 2 sts, sc next 2 sts tog) around. Stuff. Continue stuffing as you work. *(18)*
Rnd 19: Sc in each st around.
Rnd 20: (Sc in next st, sc next 2 sts tog) around. *(12)*
Rnd 21: (Sc next 2 sts tog) around, join with sl st in first sc. Fasten off. Sew opening closed.

NECK

Rnd 1: Starting at top, with white, ch 18, sl st in first ch to form ring, sc in each ch around. *(18 sc made)*
Rnds 2–3: Sc in each st around.
Rnd 4: (Sc in next 5 sts, 2 sc in next st) around. *(21)*
Rnds 5–7: Sc in each st around.
Rnd 8: (Sc in next 6 sts, 2 sc in next st) around, join with sl st in first sc. Fasten off. *(24)*
Sew top edge of Neck over rnds 12–17 on bottom of Head. Stuff Neck.

EAR (make 2)

Rnd 1: With white, ch 2, 6 sc in second ch from hook. *(6 sc made)*
Rnd 2: Sc in each st around.
Rnds 3–4: 2 sc in first st, sc in each st around. At end of last rnd, join with sl st in first sc. Fasten off.
Flattening last rnd, sew to rnd 16 on top of Head 1" apart.

MANE

For each **fringe,** cut two 6" strands white. Fold strands in half, insert hook in st, pull fold through st, pull ends through fold. Tighten.
Beginning at rnd 15 of Head, fringe the two center sts across top of Head and back of Neck. Brush to separate strands. Trim ends to 1½" long.

BODY

Rnd 1: Starting at rear end, with white, ch 2, 6 sc in second ch from hook. *(6 sc made)*
Rnd 2: 2 sc in each st around. *(12)*
Rnd 3: (Sc in next st, 2 sc in next st) around. *(18)*
Rnd 4: (Sc in each of next 2 sts, 2 sc in next st) around. *(24)*
Rnd 5: (Sc in each of next 3 sts, 2 sc in next st) around. *(30)*
Rnd 6: (Sc in next 4 sts, 2 sc in next st) around. *(36)*
Rnds 7–13: Sc in each st around.
Rnd 14: Sc in first 6 sts; for **Back Shaping,** (sc next 2 sts tog) 8 times; sc in last 14 sts. *(28)*
Rnds 15–27: Sc in each st around. Stuff. Continue stuffing as you work.
Rnd 28: (Sc in next 5 sts, sc next 2 sts tog) around. *(24)*
Rnd 29: (Sc in each of next 2 sts, sc next 2 sts tog) around. *(18)*
Rnd 30: (Sc in next st, sc next 2 sts tog) around. *(12)*
Rnd 31: (Sc next 2 sts tog) around, join with sl st in first sc. Fasten off. Sew opening closed.
Sew bottom edge of Neck over rnds 22–29 on top of Body.

Continued on page 78

Prancing Pony

Continued from page 76

BRIDLE

For **Mouthpiece,** with lt. green, ch 18, sl st in first ch to form ring; for **Headpiece,** ch 26, skip next 9 chs of ch-18, sl st in next ch; for **Reins,** ch 46, sl st in joining sl st on ch-18, **turn;** (ch 3, skip next ch, sl st in next ch) across ch-46. Fasten off.

SADDLE

Rnd 1: With pink, ch 9, sc in second ch from hook, sc in next 6 chs, 3 sc in last ch; working in remaining lps on opposite side of starting ch, sc in next 6 chs, 2 sc in last ch. *(18 sc made)*

Rnd 2: 2 sc in first st, sc in next 6 sts, 2 sc in each of next 3 sts, sc in next 6 sts, 2 sc in each of last 2 sts. *(24)*

Rnd 3: Sc in first st, 2 sc in next st, sc in next 6 sts, (sc in next st, 2 sc in next st) 3 times, sc in next 6 sts; repeat between ( ) 2 more times. *(30)*

Rnd 4: Sc in each of first 2 sts, 2 sc in next st, sc in next 6 sts, (sc in each of next 2 sts, 2 sc in next st) 3 times, sc in next 6 sts; repeat between ( ) 2 more times, join with sl st in first sc. Fasten off. *(36)*

Rnd 5: Join lt. green with sc in first st, sc in each st around, join. Fasten off.

Rnd 6: Join yellow with sl st in first st, ch 3, skip next st, (sl st in next st, ch 3, skip next st) around, join with sl st in first sl st. Fasten off.

Sew Saddle to center back of Body at base of Mane *(see photo).*

FRONT LEG (make 2)

Rnd 1: Starting at **Hoof,** with white, ch 2, 6 sc in second ch from hook. *(6 sc made)*

Rnd 2: 2 sc in each st around. *(12)*

Rnd 3: Working this rnd in **back lps** *(see Stitch Guide),* sc in each st around.

Rnd 4: Working in **both lps,** sc in each st around.

Rnd 5: (Sc next 2 sts tog) 4 times, sc in last 4 sts. *(8)*

Rnds 6–11: Sc in each st around. Stuff. Continue stuffing as you work.

Rnd 12: Sc in each of first 2 sts; for **Knee,** 2 sc in each of next 4 sts; sc in each of last 2 sts. *(12)*

Rnds 13–14: Sc in each st around.

Rnd 15: Sc in first 4 sts, (sc next 2 sts tog) 2 times, sc in last 4 sts. *(10)*

Rnds 16–19: Sc in each st around.

Rnd 20: (Sc in next 4 sts, 2 sc in next st) around. *(12)*

Rnd 21: (Sc in each of next 2 sts, 2 sc in next st) around. *(16)*

Rnds 22–25: Sc in each st around.

Rnd 26: (Sc in each of next 2 sts, sc next 2 sts tog) around. *(12)*

Rnd 27: (Sc next 2 sts tog) around, join with sl st in first sc. Fasten off. Sew opening closed.

To shape Leg, tack rnd 3 to rnd 7 at back of Leg. Tack rnd 11 to rnd 15 at back of Knee.

Sew rnds 23–27 of each Leg over rnds 22–28 on each side of Body 1¾" apart across front of Body.

BACK LEG (make 2)

Rnds 1–21: Repeat rnds 1–21 of Front Leg.

Rnd 22: (Sc in each of next 3 sts, 2 sc in next st) around. *(20)*

Rnds 23–27: Sc in each st around.

Rnd 28: (Sc in each of next 2 sts, sc next 2 sts tog) around. *(15)*

Rnd 29: (Sc in next st, sc next 2 sts tog) around. *(10)*

Rnd 30: (Sc next 2 sts tog) around, join with sl st in first sc. Fasten off. Sew opening closed.

To shape Leg, tack rnd 3 to rnd 7 at back of Leg. Tack rnd 11 to rnd 15 at front of Leg.

Sew rnds 23–30 of each Leg over rnds 2–12 on each side of Body 2" apart across rear of Body.

TAIL

Cut fifty 8" strands of white. Tie separate 8" strand white around center of all strands held together, leaving ends of strand for sewing.

Sew centered on top half of rnd 4 at rear end of Body. Brush strands of Tail to separate. Trim ends evenly.

HEART SIDE (make 2)

Row 1: Starting at **Tip,** with lt. green, ch 2, 3 sc in second ch from hook, turn. *(3 sc made)*

Row 2: Ch 1, sc in first st, 2 sc in next st, sc in last st, turn. *(4)*

Rows 3–5: Ch 1, 2 sc in first st, sc in each st across to last st, 2 sc in last st, turn. At end of last row *(10).*

Row 6: Ch 1, sc in each st across, turn.

Rnd 7: Working in sts and in ends of rows around outer edge, (ch 2, sc, hdc) in first st, dc in next st, 2 dc in next st, hdc in next st, sl st in each of next 2 sts, hdc in next st, 2 dc in next st, dc in next st, (hdc, sc) in last st, sc in each row across to Tip, 3 sc in bottom of row 1; sc in each row across, join with sl st in first sc. Fasten off.

Hold Heart Sides wrong sides together, matching sts; working through **back lps** *(see illustration),* sew edges together, stuffing before closing.

FINISHING

With blue, using French knot *(see Stitch Guide)*, embroider eyes over rnd 12 of Head 1¾" apart.

With pink, using straight stitch, embroider mouth from rnd 4 on one side of Head around end of Muzzle to rnd 4 at same point on opposite side of Head, pulling stitch tightly to indent. Secure stitch.

Place Bridal on Pony's Head *(see photo)*.

Drill ¼" hole in center of wooden heart. Paint heart and dowel. Let Dry.

Apply glue and insert one end of dowel in Tip of crochet Heart.

Insert other end of dowel through center of Body, going in through middle of Saddle and out at bottom of Body. Position Horse as desired on dowel and apply small amount of glue at exit point on bottom of Body to secure in place.

Apply glue and insert other end of dowel in hole of wooden heart. ✪

Naming Baby

"Monday's child is fair of face, Tuesday's child is full of grace. Wednesday's child is full of woe, Thursday's child has far to go. Friday's child is loving and giving, Saturday's child works hard for his living. But the child that is born on the Sabbath day, is bonny and blithe, and good and gay."

This old English poem, especially popular during the Victorian era, holds that a child's character is determined by the day on which he or she is born, a mere gift of chance.

While as modern parents we might dismiss this saying as an amusing superstition, most of us still agonize over the meaning and power of the names we give our offspring.

For some of us, family succession dictates our choice, with little junior sharing father's or grandfather's name, or a baby daughter given mom's, aunt's, grandma's, or even dad's name, in a feminine form of course!

For others of us, it's not so easy. So parents have been known to turn to many sources for inspiration, including national leaders, novels, folkloric heroes and distant branches of the family tree.

In the Middle Ages, Christian law decreed that a child's name must include the name of a saint or martyr, or the child could not be baptized.

Only biblical names, such as Faith, Hope, Charity, Comfort, Mercy and Sarah, or Matthew, Mark, Luke, John, James and Nathan, were considered proper by early American Puritans. Even now the Bible remains a rich source of possible names for children.

While some children have become the namesake of Hollywood stars, including Marilyn Monroe, Judy Garland, Charlton Heston and Cary Grant, the irony is that many actors and actresses change their names. For example, Cary Grant was originally Archibald Leach and Judy Garland was Frances Gumm.

While we may not believe, as some cultures do, that names affect a child's soul and fortunes, it's interesting to check the meaning of names you're considering for your child. Thus, you might choose Aileen (light), Carissa (loving), Dallas (wise) or Emily (industrious) instead of Ursula (little she-bear), Thera (unmastered one), Brunhilda (armored warrior woman) or Almira (clothes basket).

And if you favor a meaning, but don't like the name, remember there are usually lots of derivations. If you want your little prince of a son to have an appropriate name, you could choose from Rick, Richard, Ulric, Rex, Roy, Regan, Ryan, or Basil, all of which mean "king."

There are other considerations in picking a name that will be a pleasing legacy for your child. To illustrate with notable personalities: Tennis great Bjorn Borg (regard for family nationality); Senator Birch Bayh (alliteration and rhythm); Beau Bridges (whether or not to use a nickname); and George Beverly Shea (crossing accepted gender lines).

A few final thoughts about the art of nomenclature. Try not to make your child's name trendy, obscure or anything that might end up an embarrassment. To that end, even if you are the governor of Texas, please don't name your daughter Ima Hogg!

Cottage Cushions

Designed by Joanna Dominick

Finished Sizes: House Cushion is 10" × 13". Lawn Cushion is 9" × 11½".

Materials:
- ❑ Worsted yarn:
    - 5 oz. green
    - 4 oz. yellow
    - 2 oz. gray
    - 1 oz. each of dk. blue and lt. blue
    - Small amount each of pink, red, white and brown
- ❑ Polyester fiberfill
- ❑ Tapestry needle
- ❑ G hook or hook needed to obtain gauge

Gauge: 4 sc = 1"; 4 sc rows = 1".

Basic Stitches: Ch, sl st, sc, hdc, dc, tr.

Special Stitch:
For **sc loop stitch (lp st),** insert hook in st, wrap yarn around finger, insert hook from left to right through all lps on finger, pull lps through st, drop lps from finger, yo, pull through all lps on hook.

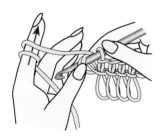

HOUSE CUSHION
Side (make 2)
Row 1: With gray, ch 10, sc in third ch from hook, sc in next 6 chs, (sc, hdc) in last ch, turn. *(8 sc, 2 hdc made)*

Rows 2–16: Ch 2 *(counts as first hdc),* sc in same st, sc in each st across to last st, (sc, hdc) in last st, turn. At end of last row *(40 sts).*

Row 17: Ch 1, sc in each st across, turn. Fasten off.

Row 18: Working this row in **back lps** *(see Stitch Guide),* skip first 2 sts, join yellow with sc in next st, sc in next 35 sts leaving last 2 sts unworked, turn. *(36 sc)*

Rows 19–51: Ch 1, sc in each st across, turn. At end of last row, fasten off.

Working in **front lps** of row 17, join brown with sc in first st, sc in each st across. Fasten off.

Door
Row 1: With dk. blue, ch 15, sc in second ch from hook, sc in each ch across, turn. *(14 sc made)*

Rows 2–8: Ch 1, sc in each st across, turn.

Row 9: Ch 1, sc in first 13 sts, 2 sc in next st, **do not turn;** sc in end of next 9 rows; working in remaining lps on opposite side of starting ch, 2 sc in next ch, sc in next 13 chs. Fasten off.

Doorknob
With lt. blue, ch 3, sl st in third ch from hook. Leaving 6" for sewing, fasten off.

Sew Knob to center st of row 1 on Door. Sew Door to center of one Side over rows 36–51.

Window (make 2)
Row 1: With lt. blue, ch 12, dc in fourth ch from hook, dc in each ch across, turn. *(10 dc made)*

Rows 2–4: Ch 3, dc in each st across, turn. At end of last row, fasten off.

Sew Windows over rows 21–30 of Side 3" apart *(see photo).*

With dk. blue, using straight stitch *(see Stitch Guide),* embroider lines on each Window to form panes *(see photo).*

Shutter (make 4)
Row 1: With dk. blue, ch 10, sc in second ch from hook, sc in each ch across, turn. *(9 sc made)*

Row 2: Ch 1, sc in each st across. Fasten off.

Sew Shutters to each side of each Window.

Window Box (make 2)
Row 1: With dk. blue, ch 13, sc in third ch from hook, sc in next 9 chs, (sc, hdc) in last ch, turn. *(10 sc, 2 hdc made)*

Row 2: (Ch 2, sc) in first st, sc in next 11 sts, (sc, hdc) in last st. Fasten off.

Sew each Box to bottom edge of each Window.

Fence Post (make 4)
With white, ch 10, sc in second ch from hook, sc in each ch across. Fasten off.

Fence Rail (make 4)
With white, ch 13, sc in second ch from hook, sc in each ch across. Fasten off.

Sew two Rails horizontally across bottom edge of Side ¾" from each side edge of Door *(see photo).* Sew remaining Rails ¾" above first Rails.

Sew two Posts at each end of each set of Rails.

• • • • • • • • • • • • • • • • • • Continued on page 85

Carousel Filet

Designed by Rose Beckett

Finished Size: 33¾" × 34¾".

Materials:
- ❏ 1,600 yds. size 8 crochet cotton thread
- ❏ 18 plastic 1" rings
- ❏ 4 round flat 10mm crystal beads
- ❏ Sewing thread to match crochet cotton
- ❏ Tapestry and sewing needles
- ❏ No. 8 steel hook or hook needed to obtain gauge

Gauge: 9 dc = 1"; 4 dc rows = 1".

Basic Stitches: Ch, dc.

Filet Stitches:
For **beginning block (beg block)**, ch 3, dc in each of next 3 sts.

For **block**, dc in each of next 3 sts, or, 2 dc in next ch sp, dc in next st.

For **mesh**, ch 2, skip next 2 chs or sts, dc in next st.

For **beginning decrease (beg dec)**, sl st in first 4 sts.

For **end decrease (end dec)**, leave last 3 sts unworked.

CURTAIN
Row 1: Starting at top, ch 315, dc in fourth ch from hook, dc in each ch across, turn. *(313 dc made)*

Rows 2–3: Ch 3, dc in each st across, turn.

Row 4: Beg block—*see Notes above*, **block** 2 times, (**mesh**, block, mesh, block 3 times) 8 times, mesh 2 times, block 3 times; repeat between ( ) across, turn.

Rows 5–135: Work according to corresponding row of graph on page 84, turn. At end of last row, fasten off.

Sew beads to Curtain according to placements on graph.

Sew plastic rings evenly spaced across top edge. ✪

●●●●●●●●●●●●●●●●●●●●●●●● Graph on page 84

Carousel Filet

Instructions on page 82

CAROUSEL HORSE KEY:
- ☐ = BLOCK OR BEG BLOCK
- ☐ = MESH
- ● = BEAD PLACEMENT
- ◉ = BEG OR END DEC

Cottage Cushions

Continued from page 81

Bush (make 2)
Row 1: With green, ch 5, sc in second ch from hook, sc in each ch across, turn. *(4 sc made)*
Row 2: Ch 1, **sc loop st** *(see Special Stitch)* in each st across, turn.
Row 3: Ch 1, sc in each st across, turn.
Row 4: Repeat row 2.
Row 5: Ch 1, sc first 2 sts tog, sc last 2 sts tog, turn. *(2)*
Row 6: Repeat row 2. Fasten off.
Positioning row 1 at bottom edge of Side, sew one Bush on each side of Door.

Flower (make 7 pink, 2 yellow, 2 red)
Work same as Doorknob.

Leaf (make 11)
With green, ch 3, sl st in third ch from hook, (ch 3, sl st in same ch as last sl st) 2 times. Leaving 6" end for sewing, fasten off.
Pull 6" end on one Flower through center of one Leaf, tack in place. Repeat with all Flowers and Leaves.
Arrange and sew three Flowers across each Window Box as shown in photo. Arrange and sew remaining pink Flowers across bottom Fence Rails as shown in photo.

Chimney (make 2)
Row 1: With one strand red and one strand gray held together as one, ch 9, tr in fifth ch from hook, dc in next ch, hdc in next ch, sc in next ch, sl st in last ch, turn. *(6 sts made)*
Row 2: Ch 1, skip first sl st, sl st in next st, sc in each of next 2 sts, hdc in each of last 2 sts, turn. *(5 sts)*
Row 3: Ch 1, sc in each st across. Fasten off.
Sew row 1 of one Chimney to ends of rows 4–8 on right-hand edge of roof on front Side. Sew row 1 of second Chimney in same position on left-hand edge of roof on back Side.

Tie (make 4)
With brown, ch 70. Fasten off.

Finishing
Hold front and back Sides wrong sides together, with front facing you and matching Chimneys; working through both thicknesses, join brown in any st with sc, sc in each st and in end of each row around with 2 sc in each corner, join with sl st in first sc. Fasten off.
Pull one Tie through space between corner sts at each bottom and top corner of Cushion.

LAWN CUSHION
Top
Row 1: With green, ch 46, sc in second ch from hook, sc in each ch across, turn. *(45 sc made)*
Row 2: Ch 1, sc loop st in each st across, turn.
Row 3: Ch 1, sc in each st across, turn.
Rows 4–40: Repeat rows 2 and 3 alternately, ending with row 2. At end of last row, fasten off.

Bottom
Row 1: With green, ch 46, sc in second ch from hook, sc in each ch across, turn. *(45 sc made)*
Rows 2–40: Ch 1, sc in each st across, turn. At end of last row, fasten off.

Tie (make 2)
With green, ch 70. Fasten off.

Finishing
Hold front and back Sides wrong sides together, with front facing you; working through both thicknesses, join green in any st with sc, sc in each st and in end of each row around with 2 sc in each corner stuffing before closing, join with sl st in first sc. Fasten off.
Pull one Tie through space between corner sts at each back corner of Cushion. ✪

Putting Baby to Bed

"Hush-a-bye, baby, on the tree top, When the wind blows, the cradle will rock; When the bough breaks, the cradle will fall, Down will come baby, cradle and all."
Legend suggests that this popular lullaby came about after a Pilgrim lad saw Indians rocking their children in birch bark cradles hung in saplings.
Nowadays, although there are many contrivances, including mechanical swings and motorized cradles, there's no better way to soothe baby to sleep than old-fashioned rocking.
Creativity in suiting each baby's individual needs is the key. Some children like to hear a lullaby, while others respond to soft-spoken stories; some want to be held over the shoulder and patted, while others like to lie face down over the knees. Regardless of their baby's particular preferences, most parents and grandparents find that a rocking chair is an invaluable addition to the nursery.

Bear Family Pillows

Designed by Michele Wilcox

Father Bear Pillow

Finished Size: 12" square.

Materials:
- ❏ Worsted yarn:
  - 5 oz. gray
  - 1½ oz. each of dk. brown and fuzzy beige
  - ½ oz. each of red and green
- ❏ Polyester fiberfill

- ❏ Tapestry needle
- ❏ F hook or hook needed to obtain gauge

Gauge: 9 sc = 2"; 9 sc rows = 2".

Basic Stitches: Ch, sl st, sc.

Notes:
Wind a separate ball of yarn for each section of color.

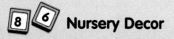

When changing colors *(see Stitch Guide),* drop first color to wrong side of work, pick up when needed. Do not carry dropped color along back of work. Always change to next color in last st of last color used. Fasten off color when no longer needed.

PILLOW FRONT
Row 1: With gray, ch 48, sc in second ch from hook, sc in each ch across, turn. *(47 sc made)*

Rows 2–4: Ch 1, sc in each st across, turn.

Rows 5–46: Ch 1, sc in each st across changing colors according to corresponding row of graph on page 88, turn.

Rows 47–50: Ch 1, sc in each st across, turn.

Rnd 51: Working around outer edge, ch 1, sc in each st and in end of each row around with 3 sc in each corner, join with sl st in first sc. Fasten off.

Facial Features
With dk. brown, using French knot, satin stitch and straight stitch *(see Stitch Guide),* embroider eyes, nose and mouth according to graph.

PILLOW BACK
Row 1: With gray, ch 48, sc in second ch from hook, sc in each ch across, turn. *(47 sc made)*

Rows 2–50: Ch 1, sc in each st across, turn.

Rnd 51: Working around outer edge, ch 1, sc in each st and in end of each row around with 3 sc in each corner, join with sl st in first sc. Fasten off.

Continued on page 88

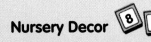

Bear Family Pillows

Continued from page 87

EDGING

Rnd 1: Hold Pillow Front and Back wrong sides together; working through both thicknesses in **back lps** *(see Stitch Guide),* join gray with sc in any st, sc in each st around stuffing before closing, join with sl st in first sc.

Rnd 2: Working in **both lps,** (ch 3, skip next st, sl st in next st) around to last 2 sts, ch 3, skip last 2 sts, join with sl st in first sl st. Fasten off.

Mama Bear Pillow

Finished Size: 12" square.

Materials:
❑ Worsted yarn:
    5 oz. off-white
    1½ oz. each of lt. brown and yellow
    ½ oz. green
    Small amount dk. brown
❑ Polyester fiberfill
❑ Tapestry needle
❑ F hook or hook needed to obtain gauge

Gauge: 9 sc = 2"; 9 sc rows = 2".

Basic Stitches: Ch, sl st, sc.

Notes: See Father Bear Pillow Notes on page 86.

PILLOW FRONT
Starting with off-white, work same as Father Bear Pillow Front according to graph on page 89.

Facial Features
Work same as Father Bear Pillow Facial Features. With yellow, using French knot, embroider dots on Pillow Front according to graph.

PILLOW BACK & EDGING
With off-white, work same as Father Bear Pillow Back and Edging.

Baby Bear Pillow

Finished Size: 9" square.

Materials:
❑ Worsted yarn:
    4 oz. lt. blue
    1½ oz. lt. brown
    1 oz. each of dk. blue and red
    Small amount dk. brown
❑ Polyester fiberfill
❑ Tapestry needle
❑ F hook or hook needed to obtain gauge

FATHER BEAR KEY:
☐ = GRAY
▨ = BEIGE
■ = DK. BROWN
▨ = GREEN
■ = RED
▧ = DK. BROWN EMBROIDERY

FATHER BEAR

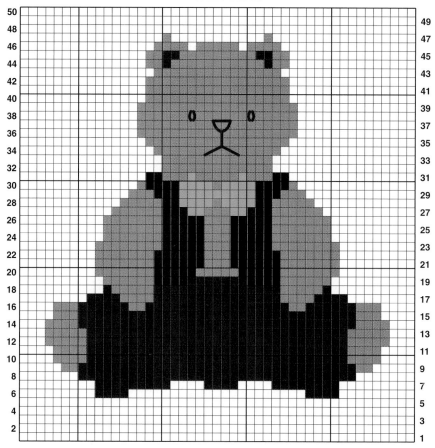

BABY BEAR

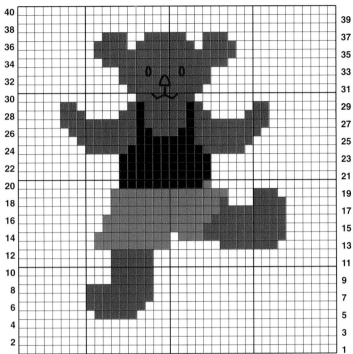

Gauge: 9 sc = 2"; 9 sc rows = 2".

Basic Stitches: Ch, sl st, sc.

Notes: See Father Bear Pillow Notes on page 86.

PILLOW FRONT
Starting with lt. blue, work same as Father Bear Pillow Front according to graph on this page.

Facial Features
Work same as Father Bear Pillow Facial Features.

PILLOW BACK & EDGING
With lt. blue, work same as Father Bear Pillow Back and Edging. ✪

MAMA BEAR

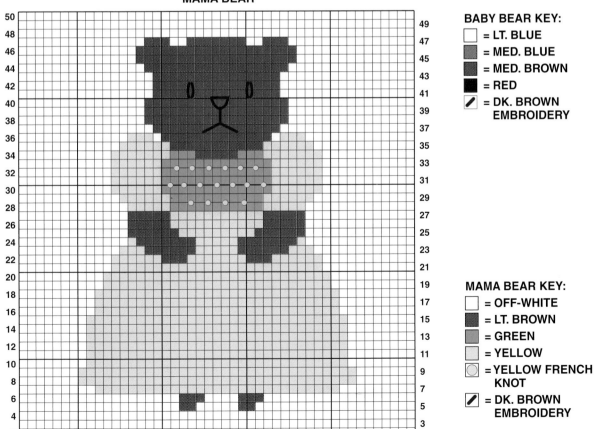

BABY BEAR KEY:

☐ = LT. BLUE

▨ = MED. BLUE

▨ = MED. BROWN

■ = RED

✎ = DK. BROWN EMBROIDERY

MAMA BEAR KEY:

☐ = OFF-WHITE

■ = LT. BROWN

▨ = GREEN

▨ = YELLOW

◎ = YELLOW FRENCH KNOT

✎ = DK. BROWN EMBROIDERY

Cow & Moon Mobile

Designed by Michele Wilcox

Finished Sizes: Moon is 9" across. Star is 4½" across.

Materials:
- ❏ Worsted yarn:
    - 4 oz. each of yellow and off-white
    - 1 oz. each of red, blue and green
    - ½ oz. each of black, coral and pink
- ❏ ¹⁄₁₆" satin ribbon:
    - 18" of yellow
    - 11" of blue
    - 8" of red
    - 4" of green
- ❏ Polyester fiberfill
- ❏ Tapestry needle
- ❏ F and G hooks or hooks needed to obtain gauges

Gauges: **F hook,** 9 sc = 2"; 9 sc rows = 2". **G hook,** 4 sc = 1"; 4 sc rows = 1".

Basic Stitches: Ch, sl st, sc, hdc.

Special Stitches:
For **increase (inc),** 2 sc in next st.
For **decrease (dec),** sc next 2 sts tog.

Notes: Work in continuous rnds; do not join or turn unless otherwise stated. Mark first st of each rnd.
Use F hook unless otherwise stated.

MOON SIDE (make 2)
Row 1: With G hook and yellow, ch 2, 6 sc in second ch from hook, turn. *(6 sc made)*
Row 2: Ch 1, 2 sc in each st across, turn. *(12)*
Row 3: Ch 1, sc in each st across, turn.
Row 4: Ch 1, sc in first st, **inc** *(see Special Stitches),* (sc in next st, inc) across, turn. *(18)*
Row 5: Ch 1, sc in each of first 2 sts, inc, (sc in each of next 2 sts, inc) across, turn. *(24)*
Row 6: Ch 1, sc in each st across, turn.
Row 7: Ch 1, sc in each of first 3 sts, inc, (sc in each of next 3 sts, inc) across, turn. *(30)*
Row 8: Ch 1, sc in first 4 sts, inc, (sc in next 4 sts, inc) across, turn. *(36)*
Row 9: Ch 1, sc in each st across, turn.
Row 10: Ch 1, sc in first 5 sts, inc, (sc in next 5 sts, inc) across, turn. *(42)*
Row 11: Ch 1, sc in first 6 sts, inc, (sc in next 6 sts, inc) across, turn. *(48)*
Row 12: Ch 1, sc in each st across, turn.

Row 13: Ch 1, sc in first 7 sts, inc, (sc in next 7 sts, inc) across, turn. *(54)*
Row 14: Ch 1, sc in first 8 sts, inc, (sc in next 8 sts, inc) across, turn. *(60)*
Row 15: Ch 1, sc in each st across, turn.
Row 16: Ch 1, sc in first 9 sts, inc, (sc in next 9 sts, inc) across, turn. *(66)*
Row 17: Ch 1, sc in first 10 sts, inc, (sc in next 10 sts, inc) across, turn. *(72)*
Row 18: Ch 1, sc in each st across. Fasten off.
Hold Moon Sides together, matching sts and ends of rows; working through **back lps** *(see illustration on page 78),* sew edges of Moon Sides together, stuffing before closing.

STAR SIDE (make 2 each of red, blue, green)
Rnd 1: Ch 2, 5 sc in second ch from hook. *(5 sc made)*
Rnd 2: Inc in each st around. *(10)*
Rnd 3: (Sc in next st, inc) around. *(15)*
Rnd 4: (Sc in each of next 2 sts, inc) around. *(20)*
Rnd 5: (Sc in each of next 3 sts, inc) around. *(25)*
Rnd 6: (Sc in next 4 sts, inc) around. *(30)*
Row 7: Working in rows, for **First Point,** sc in first 6 sts leaving last 24 sts unworked, turn. *(6)*
Row 8: Ch 1, sc in each st across, turn.
Row 9: Ch 1, **dec** *(see Special Stitches),* sc in each of next 2 sts, dec, turn. *(4)*
Row 10: Ch 1, sc in each st across, turn.
Row 11: Ch 1, dec 2 times, turn. *(2)*
Row 12: Ch 1, dec, turn. *(1)*
Row 13: Skip st and end of last row, sl st in end of next 5 rows, **do not turn.**
Row 7: For **Second Point,** sc in next 6 unworked sts on rnd 6, turn. *(6)*
Row 8: Ch 1, sc in each st across, turn.
Row 9: Ch 1, dec, sc in each of next 2 sts, dec, turn. *(4)*
Row 10: Ch 1, sc in each st across, turn.
Row 11: Ch 1, dec 2 times, turn. *(2)*
Row 12: Ch 1, dec, turn. *(1)*
Row 13: Skip st and end of last row, sl st in end of next 5 rows, **do not turn.**
For remaining **Points,** repeat rows 7–13 of Second Point three more times. At end of last Point, join with sl st in first st of row 7 on First Point. Fasten off.
Hold Star Sides wrong sides together, matching Points; working through **back lps,** sew edges of Star Sides together, stuffing before closing.

• • • • • • • • • • • • • • • Continued on page 95

Tissue Train

Designed by Maryann Larkin

Finished Size: Entire Train is 24" long.

Materials:
- ❑ 2 oz. each of yellow, blue pink, and green worsted yarn
- ❑ Cotton balls
- ❑ Cotton swabs
- ❑ Diaper pins
- ❑ 4 packages of pocket-size tissues
- ❑ Polyester fiberfill
- ❑ Tapestry needle
- ❑ G hook or hook needed to obtain gauge

Gauge: 4 dc = 1"; 2 dc rows = 1".

Basic Stitches: Ch, sl st, sc, hdc, dc.

Note: Each Car of Train holds a package of pocket-size tissues.

ENGINE
Car Top
Row 1: With blue, ch 21, dc in fourth ch from hook, dc in each ch across, turn. *(19 dc made)*
Row 2: Ch 3, dc in each st across, turn.
Row 3: Ch 2 *(counts as first hdc)*, hdc in next 5 sts, ch 7, skip next 7 sts, hdc in last 6 sts, turn.
Row 4: Ch 3, dc in each st and in each ch across, turn.
Row 5: Ch 3, dc in each st across, turn.
Rnd 6: Working around outer edge, ch 1, sc in each st, sc in end of each hdc row and 2 sc in end of each dc row around, join with sl st in first sc.
Rnd 7: Working this rnd in **back lps** *(see Stitch Guide)*, ch 3, dc in each st around, join with sl st in top of ch-3.
Rnd 8: Working in **both lps**, ch 3, dc in each st around, join. Fasten off.

Car Bottom
Row 1: With blue, ch 21, dc in fourth ch from hook, dc in each ch across, turn. *(19 dc made)*

Row 2: Ch 3, dc in each st across, turn.
Row 3: Ch 2, hdc in each st across, turn.
Rows 4–5: Ch 3, dc in each st across, turn.
Rnd 6: Working around outer edge, ch 1, sc in each st, sc in end of each hdc row and 2 sc in end of each dc row around, join with sl st in first sc. Fasten off.

Sew Car Bottom to Car Top around one short and two long edges, leaving last short edge open for inserting tissue package.

Cab
Row 1: With pink, ch 8, dc in fourth ch from hook, dc in each ch across, turn. *(6 dc made)*
Rows 2–4: Ch 3, dc in each st across, turn.
Rnd 5: Working around outer edge, ch 1, sc in each st and 2 sc in end of each dc row around, join with sl st in first sc.
Rnd 6: Working this rnd in **back lps**, ch 3, dc in each st around, join with sl st in top of ch-3.

Continued on page 94

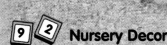

Tissue Train

Continued from page 92

Rnds 7–8: Working in **both lps,** ch 3, dc in each st around, join. At end of last rnd, fasten off. Stuff.
Sew bottom edge of Cab to Car Top just behind center opening, being careful to not cover opening.

Smokestack
Row 1: With green, ch 9, dc in fourth ch from hook, dc in each ch across, turn. *(7 dc made)*
Rows 2–3: Ch 3, dc in each st across, turn.
Rnd 4: Working around outer edge, ch 1, sc in each st and 2 sc in end of each dc row around, join with sl st in first sc.
*NOTE: Work rnds 5–8 in **back lps.***
Rnd 5: Ch 3, dc in each st around, join with sl st in top of ch-3.
Rnd 6: Ch 3, (dc next 2 sts tog, dc in next st) 8 times, dc in each of last 2 sts, join. Stuff lightly. *(18)*
Rnd 7: Ch 1, (sc in each of next 2 sts, sc next 2 sts tog) 4 times, sc in each of last 2 sts, join. *(14 sc)*
Rnd 8: Ch 3, dc in each st around, join. Fasten off. Finish stuffing.
Sew bottom edge of Smokestack to front of Car Top, being careful to not cover center opening.

Cowcatcher
Row 1: With yellow, ch 14, dc in fourth ch from hook, dc in each ch across, **do not turn.** *(12 dc made)*
Row 2: Ch 1, 2 sc in end of last row, turn. *(2 sc)*
Row 3: Working this row in **front lps,** ch 1, (sc, hdc) in first st, dc in next st, turn. *(3 sts)*
Row 4: Ch 1, sc in each st across, **do not turn;** sc in ch-1 at end of row 2; working in remaining lps on opposite side of starting ch, sc in each ch across, (2 sc, sl st) in end of row 1, turn. *(18 sc, 1 sl st)*
Row 5: Working this row in **front lps,** (ch 3, dc) in first st, hdc in next st, sc in next st, sl st in next st leaving remaining sts unworked, turn. *(5 sts)*
Row 6: Working in **both lps,** skip sl st, sc in each of next 3 sts. Fasten off.
Sew Cowcatcher to front of Car Top between rnds 6 and 7 *(see photo).*

Small Wheel Piece (make 4)
Rnd 1: With pink, ch 4, sl st in first ch to form ring, 8 sc in ring, **do not join rnd.** *(8 sc made)*
Rnd 2: 2 sc in each st around, join with sl st in first sc. Fasten off.
For each **Wheel,** hold two Pieces wrong sides together; working through both thicknesses in **back lps,** join pink with sl st in any st of last rnd, sl st in each st around, join with sl st in first sl st. Fasten off.

Large Wheel Piece (make 4)
Rnd 1: With green, ch 4, sl st in first ch to form ring, 8 sc in ring, **do not join rnds.** *(8 sc made)*
Rnd 2: 2 sc in each st around. *(16)*
Rnd 3: (Sc in next st, 2 sc in next st) around. *(24)*
Rnd 4: (Sc in each of next 2 sts, 2 sc in next st) around, join with sl st in first sc. Fasten off.
Assemble each Wheel in same manner as Small Wheels.
Sew center of Small Wheels to each side at front end of Car Top *(see photo).* Sew center of Large Wheels to each side at back end.

CARGO CARS
Car Top (make 1 yellow, 1 green)
Row 1: Ch 21, dc in fourth ch from hook, dc in each ch across, turn. *(19 dc made)*
Row 2: Ch 3, dc in each st across, turn.
Row 3: Ch 2, hdc in each st across, turn.
Rows 4–5: Ch 3, dc in each st across, turn.
Rnd 6: Working around outer edge, ch 1, sc in each st, sc in end of each hdc row and 2 sc in end of each dc row around, join with sl st in first sc. Fasten off.
Rnd 7: Working this rnd in **back lps,** ch 3, dc in each st around, join with sl st in top of ch-3.
Rnd 8: Working in **both lps,** ch 3, dc in each st around, join. Fasten off.

Car Bottom (make 1 yellow, 1 green)
Work same as Car Bottom instructions for Engine on page 92.

Cargo Hold (make 1 pink, 1 yellow)
Rnd 1: Ch 57, sl st in first ch to form ring, ch 3, dc in each ch around, join with sl st in top of ch-3. *(57 sc made)*
Rnd 2: Working this rnd in **back lps,** ch 3, dc next 2 sts tog, dc in next 13 sts, (dc next 2 sts tog) 2 times, dc in next 7 sts, (dc next 2 sts tog) 2 times, dc in next 13 sts, (dc next 2 sts tog) 2 times, dc in next 7 sts, dc last 2 sts tog, join. *(49 dc)*
Rnd 3: Working this rnd in **back lps,** ch 1, sc in first st, sc next 2 sts tog, sc in next 11 sts, (sc next 2 sts tog) 2 times, sc in next 5 sts, (sc next 2 sts tog) 2 times, sc in next 11 sts, (sc next 2 sts tog) 2 times, sc in next 5 sts, sc last 2 sts tog, join. Fasten off.
Matching pink to yellow and yellow to green, sew last rnd of each Cargo Hold to top of each Cargo Car Top.

Wheel (make 2 green, 2 pink, 4 blue)
Work same as Small Wheel Piece instructions for Engine on this page.
Sew center of each Wheel to each side of Cargo Car Top as shown in photo.

CABOOSE
Car Top & Car Bottom
With pink, work same as for Cargo Car Top and Car Bottom on page 92.

Cab
Row 1: With blue, ch 10, dc in fourth ch from hook, dc in each ch across, turn. *(8 dc made)*
Rows 2–6: Ch 3, dc in each st across, turn.
Rnds 7–9: Repeat rnds 6–8 of Engine Car Bottom on page 92. At end of last rnd, **do not fasten off.**
Rnd 10: Ch 3, dc in each st around, join. Fasten off.

Stuff Caboose Cab lightly with fiberfill. Sew bottom edge of Cab to Caboose Car Top.

Wheel (make 2 yellow, 2 green)
Work same as Small Wheel Piece instructions for Engine on page 94.

CAR COUPLING (make 1 each of blue, green, pink)
Ch 8, sl st in second ch from hook, sl st in each ch across. Fasten off.
Sew to center bottom of ends on Cars, connecting them end to end. ✪

Cow & Moon Mobile

Continued from page 91

COW
Body
Rnd 1: With off-white, ch 2, 6 sc in second ch from hook. *(6 sc made)*
Rnd 2: Inc in each st around. *(12)*
Rnd 3: (Sc in next st, inc) around. *(18)*
Rnd 4: (Sc in each of next 2 sts, inc) around. *(24)*
Rnd 5: (Sc in each of next 3 sts, inc) around. *(30)*
Rnds 6–10: Sc in each st around.
Rnd 11: For **Top of Body,** (dec, sc in next st) 6 times; sc in last 12 sts. *(24)*
Rnds 12–17: Sc in each st around.
Rnd 18: (Sc in each of next 2 sts, dec) around. *(18)*
Rnd 19: (Sc in next st, sc next 2 sts tog) around. Stuff. *(12)*
Rnd 20: Dec around, join with sl st in first sc. Fasten off. Sew opening closed.

Body Spot
Rnd 1: With black, ch 9, sc in second ch from hook, sc in next 6 chs, 3 sc in last ch; working in remaining lps on opposite side of starting ch, sc in next 6 chs, 2 sc in next ch. *(18 sc made)*
Rnd 2: Inc, sc in next 6 sts, inc 3 times, sc in next 6 sts, inc 2 times. *(24)*
Rnd 3: Sc in first st, inc, sc in each of next 2 sts, hdc in each of next 3 sts, sc in each of next 2 sts, (inc, sc in next st) 3 times, sc in each of next 2 sts, hdc in each of next 3 sts, (sc in next st, inc) 2 times, join with sl st in first sc. Fasten off.
Sew Spot over rnds 7–14 on top of Body.

Head
Rnd 1: With off-white, ch 2, 6 sc in second ch from hook. *(6 sc made)*
Rnd 2: Inc in each st around. *(12)*
Rnd 3: (Sc in next st, inc) around. *(18)*
Rnd 4: (Sc in each of next 2 sts, inc) around. *(24)*
Rnds 5–7: Sc in each st around.
Rnd 8: (Sc in each of next 2 sts, dec) around. *(18)*

Rnd 9: (Sc in next st, dec) around. Stuff. *(12)*
Rnd 10: Sc in each st around.
Rnd 11: Dec around, join with sl st in first sc. Fasten off. Sew opening closed.
With Head turned to left side of Body *(see photo),* sew rnds 8–11 of Head to rnds 17–19 of Body.

Muzzle
Rnd 1: With coral, ch 2, 6 sc in second ch from hook. *(6 sc made)*
Rnd 2: Inc in each st around. *(12)*
Rnd 3: Sc in each st around.
Rnd 4: (Dec, sc in next st) around, join with sl st in first sc. Fasten off. Stuff.
Sew last rnd of Muzzle over rnds 1–3 on lower half of Head.

Ear Side (make 2 black, 2 coral)
Ch 4, sc in second ch from hook, sc in next ch, 3 sc in last ch; working in remaining lps on opposite side of starting ch, sc in each of next 2 chs. Fasten off.
Hold one black and one coral Ear Side wrong sides together with coral Side facing you; working through both thicknesses in **back lps,** join black with sc in first st, sc in each of next 2 sts, 3 sc in next st, sc in each st across. Fasten off. Repeat with remaining Ear Sides.
Sew straight edge at bottom of Ears to rnd 5 on top of Head 1¾" apart.

Horn (make 2)
Row 1: With pink, ch 2, 3 sc in second ch from hook, turn. *(3 sc made)*
Row 2: Ch 1, sc in first st, inc, sc in last st, turn. *(4)*
Row 3: Ch 1, sc in each st across. Fasten off.
Fold Horn piece in half; sew ends of rows together.
Sew bottom edge of Horn to rnd 4 on top of Head 1" apart.

Continued on page 96

Cow & Moon Mobile

Continued from page 95

Head Spot

With black, ch 5, sc in second ch from hook, hdc in each of last 3 chs. Fasten off.

With sc at front, sew Spot over rnds 2–5 on Head between Horns.

Facial Features

With black, using French knot *(see Stitch Guide)*, embroider eyes between rnds 2 and 3 on Head centered above Muzzle 1" apart, and embroider nostrils on each side of rnd 1 on Muzzle.

With black, using fly stitch, embroider mouth centered below nostrils between rnds 2 and 3 of Muzzle.

Leg (make 4)

Rnd 1: With off-white, ch 2, 8 sc in second ch from hook. *(8 sc made)*

Rnd 2: Working this rnd in **back lps,** sc in each st around.

Rnds 3–8: Sc in each st around.

Rnd 9: (Sc in next st, inc) around. *(12)*

Rnd 10: Sc in each st around, join with sl st in first sc. Fasten off. Stuff.

Sew two Legs over rnds 13–16 on bottom of Body 1" apart. Sew two Legs over rnds 3–6 on bottom of Body ¾" apart.

Leg Spot (make 4)

With black, ch 2, 6 sc in second ch from hook, join with sl st in first sc. Fasten off.

Sew each Spot over rnds 5–7 on side of each Leg *(see photo).*

Tail

With off-white, ch 5, sl st in second ch from hook, sl st in each ch across. Fasten off.

Cut two 1½" strands of black yarn. Hold both strands together and fold in half, insert hook in one end of Tail, pull fold through, pull ends of strands through fold, tighten.

Sew other end of Tail to rnd 6 at center top of Body.

Finishing

Sew Cow to straight edge of Moon as shown in photo. Tack one end of matching color ribbon to one Point on each Star. Sew other end of each ribbon to bottom edge of Moon centered below Cow.

For **Hanger,** tack one end of yellow ribbon to top point on Moon, tie other end of ribbon in bow. ✪

Keeping Playtime Safe

An old nursery song from the 17th century urges: "Boys and girls, come out to play, The moon doth shine as bright as day, Leave your supper, and leave your sleep, And come with your playfellows into the street. Come with a whoop, come with a call, Come with a good will, or come not at all."

Nowadays, not only we would not urge our children to play in the street, we prefer that they sleep at night, and play during the day. But it is during playtime that parents and other caretakers have to be most watchful about potential risks to their youngsters.

Most of us know the necessity of childproofing our homes. More than one expert suggests getting down at baby level, on hands and knees, to see the need for covering unused electrical outlets, putting away breakables, keeping medicines and household chemicals locked up, padding sharp corners and blocking off stairways.

But with older babies and active toddlers, watching for outdoor dangers is a must, too. Swimming pools and busy streets are obvious; often overlooked are heavy garage and screen doors, overly friendly pets, rough-hewn landscape timbers, pesticide residues on garden plants and storm drain openings.

Children are naturally curious about the world—it is up to us to guide them safely through their exploratory learning.

CHAPTER 5

Lovely Layettes

Diddle, Diddle, Dumpling, My Son John

Diddle, diddle, dumpling, my son John,
Went to bed with his trousers on;
One shoe off, one shoe on,
Diddle, diddle, dumpling, my son John.

"Diddle, diddle, dumpling, " the cry of hot dumpling sellers in the streets of London in the 18th and 19th centuries, became immortalized in this nursery rhyme which represents the challenge of mothers everywhere in keeping socks and covers on their sleeping babies.

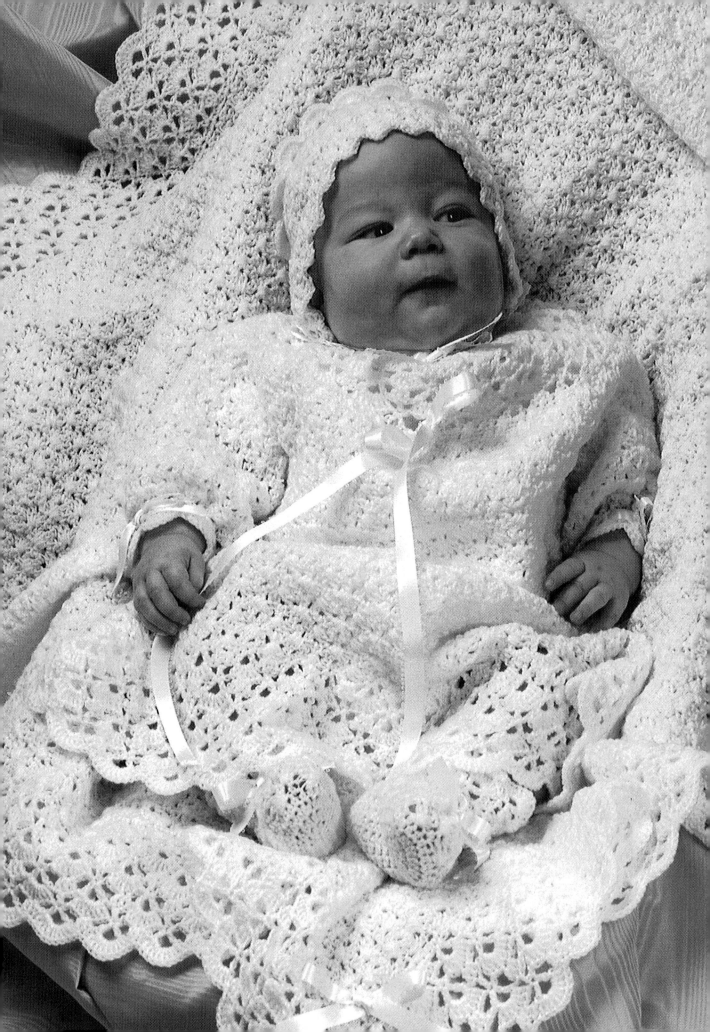

First Portrait

Designed by Ann Parnell

Finished Sizes: Shawl is 38" × 42". Gown fits infant's 0–6 mos. Bonnet fits up to 16" head. Bootie Sole is 4" long.

Materials:
- ❑ White fingering yarn:
  - 16 oz. for Shawl
  - 8 oz. for Gown, Bonnet and Booties
- ❑ 1 white ⅜" button
- ❑ 6½ yds. of white ⅜" ribbon
- ❑ Tapestry needle
- ❑ E and G hooks or hook needed to obtain gauge

Gauge: G hook, 4 cross shells = 3½"; 3 cross shell rows = 1".

Basic Stitches: Ch, sl st, sc, hdc, dc.

Special Stitches:
For **cross shell (cr shell),** skip next ch or st, 2 dc in next ch or st; ch 2, working around last 2 sts made, 2 dc in skipped ch or st.

For **2-skip cross shell (2-skip cr shell),** skip next 2 chs or sts, 2 dc in next ch or st, ch 2; working around last 2 sts made, 2 dc in second skipped ch or st.

For **3-skip cross shell (3-skip cr shell),** skip next 3 chs or sts, 2 dc in next ch or st, ch 2; working around last 2 sts made, 2 dc in second skipped ch or st.

For **V st,** (dc, ch 2, dc) in next st or ch sp.

For **beginning half shell (beg half shell),** (ch 3, 2 dc) in first st.

For **end half shell,** 3 dc in last st.

SHAWL

Row 1: With G hook, ch 218, sc in second ch from hook, *skip next ch, **2-skip cr shell** (see Special Stitches), skip next ch, sc in next ch; repeat from * across, turn. (36 shells, 37 sc made)

Row 2: Beg half shell (see Special Stitches), sc in next ch sp, *3-skip cr shell, sc in next ch sp; repeat from * across to last st, **end half shell,** turn.

Row 3: Ch 1, sc in first st, 3-skip cr shell, (sc in next ch sp, 3-skip cr shell) across to ch-3, sc in top of ch-3, turn.

Rows 4–105: Repeat rows 2 and 3 alternately.

Row 106: (Ch 2, hdc) in first st, 2 sc in next ch sp, (skip next st, hdc in next st, dc in next st, hdc in next st, skip next st, 2 sc in next ch sp) across to last 3 sts, skip next st, hdc in last 2 sts, **do not turn or fasten off.** (181 sts)

Border

Rnd 1: With E hook, working in ends of rows, ch 1, 2 sc in first row, evenly space 208 sc across next 104 rows, 3 sc in next row; working in remaining lps on opposite side of starting ch, evenly space 181 sc across, 3 sc in next row, evenly space 208 sc across next 104 rows, 3 sc in next row, sc in next 180 sts, 2 sc in last st, join with sl st in first sc. (790 sc made)

Rnd 2: Ch 3, dc in next st, (ch 1, **V st**—see Special Stitches—in next st, ch 1, 3 dc in next st) 3 times, *(ch 1, skip next 2 sts, V st in next st, ch 1, skip next 2 sts, 3 dc in next st) 34 times, (ch 1, V st in next st, ch 1, 3 dc in next st) 5 times, (ch 1, skip next 2 sts, V st in next st, ch 1, skip next 2 sts, 3 dc in next st) 28 times, ch 1, skip next 2 sts, V st in next st, (ch 1, 3 dc in next st, ch 1, V st in next st*) 4 times, ch 1, 3 dc in next st; repeat between first *, ch 1, dc in last st, join with sl st in third ch of ch-3. (144 V sts, 144 3-dc groups)

Rnd 3: Ch 4 (counts as first dc and ch-1), 7 dc in ch sp of first V st, (ch 1, dc in center st of next 3-dc group, ch 1, 7 dc in ch sp of next V st) around, ch 1, join with sl st in third ch of ch-4.

Rnd 4: (Ch 5, dc) in first st (counts as first V st), ch 1, skip next 3 sts, 3 dc in next st, ch 1, skip next 3 sts, (V st in next st, ch 1, skip next 3 sts, 3 dc in next st, ch 1, skip next 3 sts) around, join with sl st in third ch of ch-5.

Rnd 5: (2 sl sts, ch 3, 3 dc) in ch sp of first V st, ch 1, dc in center st of next 3-dc group, ch 1, (7 dc in ch sp of next V st, ch 1, dc in center st of next 3-dc group, ch 1) around, 3 dc in same ch sp as first sl st of this rnd, join with sl st in top of ch-3.

Rnd 6: (Ch 3, dc) in first st, ch 1, skip next 3 sts, V st in next st, (ch 1, skip next 3 sts, 3 dc in next st, ch 1, skip next 3 sts, V st in next st) around to last 3 sts, ch 1, skip last 3 sts, dc in same st as joining sl st of last rnd, join.

Rnds 7–8: Repeat rnds 3 and 4.

Rnd 9: (Sl st, ch 3, 8 dc) in ch sp of first V st, sc in center st of next 3-dc group, (9 dc in ch sp of next V st, sc in center st of next 3-dc group) around, join with sl st in top of ch-3. Fasten off.

Cut four 16" pieces from ribbon. Tie each piece in a bow at each corner of rnd 1 on Border.

GOWN

Row 1: With E hook, ch 74, (dc, ch 1, dc) in fourth ch from hook, *skip next ch, (dc, ch 1, dc) in next

Continued on page 100

First Portrait

Continued from page 99

ch; repeat from * across to last 2 chs, skip next ch, dc in last ch, turn. *(35 ch sps, 72 dc made)*

Row 2: Ch 4 *(counts as first dc and ch-1)*, 3 dc in first ch sp, (V st in next ch sp, 3 dc in next ch sp) across, dc in third ch of ch-4, turn. *(17 V sts, 18 3-dc groups, 2 dc)*

Row 3: Ch 4, dc in center st of next 3-dc group, (ch 1, 5 dc in ch sp of next V st, ch 1, dc in center st of next 3-dc group) across to last st, ch 1, dc in third ch of ch-4, turn. *(17 5-dc groups) Front of row 3 is right side of work.*

Row 4: Ch 3, V st in next st, ch 1, (skip next 2 sts, 3 dc in next st, ch 1, skip next 2 sts, V st in next st, ch 1) across to last st, dc in third ch of ch-4, turn.

Row 5: Ch 4, 5 dc in ch sp of first V st, ch 1, (dc in center st of next 3-dc group, ch 1, 5 dc in ch sp of next V st, ch 1) across to last st, dc in third ch of ch-4, turn.

Row 6: Ch 4, skip next 2 sts, 3 dc in next st, ch 1, skip next 2 sts, (V st in next st, ch 1, skip next 2 sts, 3 dc in next st, ch 1, skip next 2 sts) across to last st, dc in third ch of ch-4, turn.

Row 7: Ch 4, dc in center st of next 3-dc group, ch 1, (7 dc in ch sp of next V st, ch 1, dc in center st of next 3-dc group, ch 1) across to last st, dc in third ch of ch-4, turn.

Row 8: Ch 4, V st in next st, ch 1, skip next 3 sts, (3 dc in next st, ch 1, skip next 3 sts, V st in next st, ch 1) across to last st, dc in third ch of ch-4, turn.

Row 9: Working in sts and in ch sps, beg half shell, skip next ch sp and next sc, *sc in next ch sp, skip next st and next ch sp, 2 dc in next st, ch 2, work 2 dc in last skipped st *(cr shell made)*, sc in next st, skip next st and next ch sp, 2 dc in next st, ch 2, 2 dc in last skipped st *(cr shell made)*; repeat from * across to last 4 sts and ch sps, sc in next ch sp, skip next st and ch sp, end half shell in last st, turn.

Row 10: With G hook, ch 1, sc in first st, 3-skip cr shell, (sc in next ch sp, 3-skip cr shell) across to last st, sc in top of ch-3, turn.

Row 11: Beg half shell, sc in next ch sp, (3-skip cr shell, sc in next ch sp) across to last st, end half shell, turn.

Rows 12–13: Repeat rows 10 and 11.

Row 14: Ch 1, sc in first st, (3-skip cr shell, sc in next ch sp) 6 times; for **Underarm,** ch 15, skip next 5 cr shells; sc in next ch sp, (3-skip cr shell, sc in next ch sp) 11 times; for **Underarm,** ch 15, skip next 5 cr shells; (sc in next ch sp, 3-skip cr shell) 6 times, sc in third ch of ch-4, turn. *(23 cr shells)*

Row 15: Beg half shell, sc in next ch sp, (3-skip cr shell, sc in next ch sp) 5 times; *working in sts and in chs, 3-skip cr shell, (sc in next ch sp, 2-skip cr shell) 4 times, sc in next ch sp*, (3-skip cr shell, sc in next ch sp) 10 times; repeat between first *,

(3-skip cr shell, sc in next ch sp) 5 times, end half shell, turn.

Rows 16–45: Repeat rows 10 and 11 alternately.

Row 46: For **Bottom Border,** with E hook, (ch 3, dc) in first st, skip next 2 sts, V st in next sc, (3 dc in next ch sp, V st in next sc) across to last st, 2 dc in last st, turn. *(31 V sts, 30 3-dc groups)*

Row 47: Ch 3, 5 dc in ch sp of first V st, ch 1, (dc in center st of next 3-dc group, ch 1, 5 dc in ch sp of next V st, ch 1) across to last st, dc in last st, turn.

Row 48: Ch 3, skip next 2 sts, 3 dc in next st, ch 1, skip next 2 sts, (V st in next st, ch 1, skip next 2 sts, 3 dc in next st, ch 1, skip next 2 sts) across to last st, dc in last st, turn.

Row 49: Ch 3, dc in center st of next 3-dc group, ch 1, (7 dc in ch sp of next V st, ch 1, dc in center st of next 3-dc group, ch 1) across to last st, dc in last st, turn.

Row 50: Ch 3, V st in next st, ch 1, skip next 3 sts, (3 dc in next st, ch 1, skip next 3 sts, V st in next st, ch 1) across to last st, dc in last st, turn.

Row 51: Ch 3, 7 dc in first ch sp of first V st, (ch 1, dc in center st of next 3-dc group, ch 1, 7 dc in ch sp of next V st) across to last st, dc in last st, turn.

Row 52: Ch 3, skip next 3 sts, 3 dc in next st, ch 1, skip next 3 sts, (V st in next st, ch 1, skip next 3 sts, 3 dc in next st, ch 1, skip next 3 sts) across to last st, dc in last st, turn.

Row 53: Ch 3, dc in center st of next 3-dc group, ch 1, (7 dc in ch sp of next V st, ch 1, dc in center st of next 3-dc group, ch 1) across to last st, dc in last st, turn.

Row 54: Ch 3, V st in next st, ch 1, skip next 3 sts, (3 dc in next st, ch 1, skip next 3 sts, V st in next st, ch 1) across to last st, dc in last st, turn.

Row 55: Ch 1, sc in first st, 9 dc in ch sp of first V st, (sc in center st of next 3-dc group, 9 dc in ch sp of next V st) across to last st, sc in last st. Fasten off.

Leaving rows 1–7 loose for back opening, match and sew ends of rows 8–55 together.

Sleeves

Rnd 1: Hold Gown with wrong side of work facing you; working in remaining lps of ch-15 on Underarm, with G hook, skip first 7 chs, join with sc in next ch, 2-skip cr shell, sc in next ch, 2-skip cr shell, sc in next worked ch sp; working in skipped sts and ch sps on row 13, (3-skip cr shell, sc in next ch sp) 5 times, 3-skip cr shell, sc in next worked ch sp; working in remaining lps of ch-15, (2-skip cr shell, sc in next ch) 2 times, join with sl st in first sc, **turn.** *(10 cr shells made)*

Rnd 2: Beg half shell, sc in next ch sp, (3-skip cr shell, sc in next ch sp) around to last st, end half shell, join with sl st in top of ch-3, **turn.** *(9 cr shells, 2 half shells)*

Rnd 3: Ch 1, sc in first st, 3-skip cr shell, (sc in next ch sp, 3-skip cr shell) around to last st, join with sl st in last st, **turn.** *(10 cr shells)*

Rnds 4–11: Repeat rnds 2 and 3 alternately.

Rnd 12: With E hook, sl st across to first ch sp, 3 sc in each ch sp around, join, **turn.** *(30 sc)*

Rnd 13: Ch 3, (skip next 2 sts, V st in next st, skip next 2 sts, 3 dc in next st) 4 times, skip next 2 sts, V st in next st, skip next st, 2 dc in last st, join, **turn.** *(5 V sts)*

Rnd 14: Ch 1, sc in first st, 7 dc in ch sp of first V st, (sc in center st to next 3-dc group, 7 dc in ch sp of next V st) around to last st, sc in last st, join. Fasten off.

Repeat on other Underarm.

Neck Edging

Hold right side of Gown facing you; with E hook, working in remaining lps on opposite side of starting ch on row 1, join with sc in first ch, skip next ch, dc in next ch, skip next 2 chs, 7 dc in next ch sp, (skip next 3 chs, sc in next ch sp, skip next 3 chs, 7 dc in next ch sp) 8 times, skip next ch, sc in last ch, 2 sc in end of each row across both edges of back opening, join with sl st in first sc. Fasten off.

Sew button at top corners of neckline.

Cut 36" piece from ribbon and tie in a bow at center front of Gown on row 8.

Cut two 17" pieces from ribbon. Weave one piece through sts on row 13 of each Sleeve. Tie ends of each ribbon in bow.

BONNET

Rnd 1: With E hook, ch 4, sl st in first ch to form ring, ch 4 *(counts as first dc and ch-1)*, (dc, ch 1) 7 times in ring, join with sl st in third ch of ch-4. *(8 dc, 8 ch sps made)*

Rnd 2: Ch 3, V st in first ch sp, (dc in next st, V st in next ch sp) around, join with sl st in top of ch-3. *(8 dc, 8 V sts)*

Rnd 3: Ch 4, 3 dc in ch sp of first V st, ch 1, skip next st on same V st, (dc in next st, ch 1, 3 dc in ch sp of next V st, ch 1, skip next st on same V st) around, join with sl st in third ch of ch-4. *(32 dc)*

Rnd 4: (Ch 3, 2 dc) in first st, ch 1, skip next st, V st in next st, ch 1, skip next st, (3 dc in next st, ch 1, skip next st, V st in next st, ch 1, skip next st) around, join. *(8 V sts, 8 3-dc groups)*

Rnd 5: (Sl st, ch 4) in next st, 5 dc in ch sp of next V st, ch 1, (dc in center st of next 3-dc group, ch 1, 5 dc in ch sp of next V st, ch 1) around, join with sl st in third ch of ch-4.

Rnd 6: (Ch 5, dc) in first st *(counts as first V st)*, ch 1, skip next 2 sts, 3 dc in next st, ch 1, skip next 2 sts, (V st in next st, ch 1, skip next 2 sts, 3 dc in next st, ch 1, skip next 2 sts) around, join with sl st in third ch of ch-5.

Rnd 7: (2 sl sts, ch 3, 3 dc) in ch sp of first V st, ch 1, V st in center st of next 3-dc group, ch 1, (7 dc in ch sp of next V st, ch 1, V st in center st of next 3-dc group, ch 1) around, 3 dc in same ch sp as first sl st, join with sl st in top of ch-3.

Rnd 8: (Ch 5, dc) in first st, ch 1, 7 dc in ch sp of next V st, ch 1, (V st in center st of next 7-dc group, ch 1, 7 dc in ch sp of next V st) around, join with sl st in third ch of ch-5. *(56 dc, 8 V sts)*

Row 9: Working in rows, for **Brim**, with G hook, (sl st, ch 1, sc) in ch sp of first V st, *cr shell *(see Special Stitches),* skip next 2 sts, sc in next st, skip next 2 sts, cr shell, sc in ch sp of next V st; repeat from * 6 more times leaving remaining sts unworked, turn. *(14 cr shells) Front of row 9 is right side of work.*

Row 10: Beg half shell, sc in next ch sp, (3-skip cr shell, sc in next ch sp) across to last sc, end half shell in last sc, turn. *(13 cr shells, 2 half shells)*

Row 11: Ch 1, sc in first st, 3-skip cr shell, (sc in next ch sp, 3-skip cr shell) across to last st, end half shell in last st, turn. *(14 cr shells)*

Rows 12–17: Repeat rows 10 and 11 alternately.

Row 18: With E hook, beg half shell, sc in next ch sp, (3-skip cr shell, sc in next ch sp) across to last st, end half shell in last st, turn. *(13 cr shells, 2 half shells)*

Rnd 19: Ch 1, sc in first st, 3-skip cr shell, (sc in next ch sp, 3-skip cr shell) across to last st, sc in last st, **do not turn;** working in ends of rows and remaining unworked sts of rnd 8, evenly space 32 hdc around, join with sl st in first sc. Fasten off.

Edging

Rnd 1: Working in sts on rnd 8, with E hook and right side of Bonnet facing you, join with sc in first st on V st at edge of Brim, ch 2, (*sc in second st of same V st, ch 2, sc in sp between second an third st of next 7-dc group, ch 2, sc in sp between sixth and seventh st of same 7-dc group, ch 2*, sc in first st on next V st, ch 2) 6 times; repeat between first *, join with sl st in first sc. *(28 ch sps made)*

Rnd 2: Ch 1, sc in first ch sp, 9 dc in next ch sp, (sc in next ch sp, 9 dc in next ch sp) around, join. Fasten off.

Cut 24" piece from ribbon. Tie in a bow around st at center of rnd 1 on Bonnet.

Cut two 15" pieces from ribbon. Tie a bow at one end of each piece. Sew each bow to each end of rows 18 and 19 on Brim leaving long ends for ties.

BOOTIE (make 2)

Rnd 1: With E hook, ch 13, 2 hdc in second ch from hook, hdc in next 10 chs, 5 hdc in last ch; working in remaining lps on opposite side of starting ch, hdc in next 10 chs, 2 hdc in last ch, join with sl st in first hdc. *(29 hdc made)*

Rnd 2: (Ch 1, 2 hdc) in first st, 2 hdc in next st, hdc in next 10 sts, 2 hdc in each of next 5 sts, hdc in next 10 sts, 2 hdc in each of last 2 sts, hdc in joining sl st, join. *(39 hdc)*

• • • • • • • • • • • • • • • • • • • Continued on page 107

His & Hers Finery

Designed by Catherine Yunke

Baby Girl's Dress

Sizes: Small fits infant's 0–3 mos. Large fits 3–6 mos.

Materials:
- ❑ Size 10 crochet cotton thread:
     500 yds. for Small
     750 yds. for Large
- ❑ 2 small snaps
- ❑ ⅔ yd. of ¼" satin ribbon
- ❑ Sewing thread to match crochet cotton
- ❑ Tapestry and sewing needles
- ❑ No. 2 steel hook for Small or No. 1 steel hook for Large

Gauges: For **Small,** with **No. 2 hook,** 6 dc = 1"; one tr shell = 1"; 5 pattern rows = 2". For **Large,** with **No. 1 hook,** 11 dc = 2"; (sc, tr shell) 4 times = 5"; 4 pattern rows = 2".

Basic Stitches: Ch, sl st, sc, hdc, dc, tr.

SKIRT
Rnd 1: Ch 102, sl st in first ch to form ring, ch 1, sc in each ch around, join with sl st in first sc. *(102 sc made)*

Rnd 2: Ch 1, sc in first st, skip next 2 sts; for **tr shell,** 7 tr in next st *(shell made),* skip next 2 sts, (sc in next st, skip next 2 sts, tr shell in next st, skip next 2 sts) around, join. *(17 shells)*

Rnd 3: (Ch 4, 3 tr) in first st, sc in center st of next shell, (tr shell in next sc, sc in center st of next shell) around, 3 tr in same st as joining sl st of last rnd, join with sl st in top of ch-4.

Rnd 4: Ch 1, sc in first st, tr shell in next sc, (sc in center st of next shell, tr shell in next sc) around, join.

Rnds 5–20: Repeat rnds 3 and 4 alternately.

Rnd 21: (Ch 5, 3 **dtr**—*see Stitch Guide*) in first st, sc in center st of next shell; *for **dtr shell,** 7 dtr in next sc *(shell made),* sc in center st of next shell; repeat from * around, 3 dtr in same st as joining sl st of last rnd, join with sl st in top of ch-5.

Rnd 22: Ch 1, sc in first st, dtr shell in next sc, (sc in center st of next shell, dtr shell in next sc) around, join.

Rnds 23–25: Or to desired length; repeat rnds 21 and 22 alternately.

Rnd 26: Ch 1, sc in first st, ch 3, (sc, ch 3) in each st around, join. Fasten off. *(136 sc)*

BODICE
Row 1: Working in remaining lps on opposite side of starting ch on Skirt, join with sl st in third ch, ch 2, hdc in next 98 chs leaving last ch unworked, turn. *(99 hdc made)*

Row 2: Ch 3, dc in each st across, turn.

Row 3: Ch 2, hdc in each st across, turn.

• • • • • • • • • • • • • • • • Continued on page 104

His & Hers Finery

Continued from page 103

Row 4: For **Right Back,** ch 3, dc in next 21 sts leaving remaining sts unworked, turn. *(22 dc)*

Rows 5–9: Repeat rows 3 and 2 alternately, ending with row 3.

Row 10: For **Shoulder Shaping,** sl st in first 9 sts, ch 3, dc in next 13 sts, turn. *(14)*

Rows 11–12: Repeat rows 3 and 2. At end of last row, fasten off.

Row 4: For **Front,** skip next 6 unworked sts on row 3, join with sl st in next st, ch 3, dc in next 42 sts leaving remaining sts unworked, turn. *(43)*

Rows 5–9: Repeat rows 3 and 2 alternately, ending with row 3.

Row 10: For **Right Shoulder,** ch 3, dc in next 13 sts leaving remaining sts unworked, turn. *(14)*

Rows 11–12: Repeat rows 3 and 2. At end of last row, fasten off.

Row 10: For **Left Shoulder,** skip next 15 unworked sts on row 9 of Front, join with sl st in next st, ch 3, dc in each st across, turn. *(14)*

Rows 11–12: Repeat rows 3 and 2. At end of last row, fasten off.

Row 4: For **Left Back,** skip next 6 unworked sts on row 3, join with sl st in next st, ch 3, dc in each st across, turn. *(22)*

Rows 5–9: Repeat rows 3 and 2 alternately, ending with row 3.

Row 10: For **Shoulder Shaping,** ch 3, dc in next 13 sts leaving remaining sts unworked, turn. *(14)*

Rows 11–12: Repeat rows 3 and 2. At end of last row, fasten off.

Matching sts, sew edges of Shoulders on Front and Backs together.

FRONT TRIM

Working around post *(see illustration)* of hdc sts on row 3 of Bodice, join with sl st around 29th st, (ch 3, skip next st, sl st around next st) 21 times. Fasten off.

Joining around first st, repeat on rows 5, 7 and 9 of Bodice Front.

SLEEVE (make 2)

Rnd 1: Working in sts and in ends of rows around armhole, join with sc in center st at bottom of armhole, evenly space 41 sc around armhole, join with sl st in first sc. *(42 sc made)*

Rnds 2–5: Repeat rnds 2–5 of Skirt. *(7 shells)*

Rnd 6: Ch 1, sc in each of first 2 sts, (*hdc in each of next 2 sts, dc in next st, hdc in each of next 2 sts*, sc in each of next 3 sts) 6 times; repeat between first *, sc in last st, join with sl st in first sc. *(56 sc)*

Rnd 7: Ch 1, sc in each of first 2 sts, sc next 2 sts tog, (sc in each of next 2 sts, sc next 2 sts tog) around, join. *(42 sc)*

Rnd 8: Ch 1, sc in each of first 2 sts, (sc next 2 sts tog, sc in each of next 2 sts) around, join. *(32)*

Rnd 9: Ch 1, sc in each of first 2 sts, sc next 2 sts tog, (sc in each of next 2 sts, sc next 2 sts tog) around, join. *(24)*

Rnd 10: Ch 1, sc in each st around, join. Fasten off. Repeat on other armhole.

NECK EDGING & BACK PLACKETS

Row 1: Working around outer edge in sts and in ends of rows on Bodice, join with sc in row 1 of Left Back, (2 sc in next row, sc in next row) 4 times, 3 sc in next st, sc in next 7 sts; *working in ends of rows and in seam; repeat between ( ) 3 times, 2 sc in next row*, sc in next 15 sts; repeat between first *, sc in next 7 sts, 3 sc in next st, sc in next row; repeat between ( ) 4 times, turn. *(83 sc made)*

Row 2: Ch 1, sc in each st across with 3 sc in center st of each back corner, turn. *(87)*

Row 3: Ch 1, sc in first 15 sts, 3 sc in next st, sc in next st, (ch 3, skip next st, sc in next st) across to center st of next corner, 3 sc in corner st, sc in last 15 sts. Fasten off.

With left Back Placket lapped over right Back Placket, sew ends of rows on Skirt together.

Sew snaps evenly spaced to Back Plackets.

Cut ribbon in half. Tie one piece in a bow around center front st of row 2 on Neck Edging and other piece around center front st of row 1 on Bodice.

Baby Boy's Suit

Sizes: Small fits newborn. Large fits 3 mos.

Materials:
- ❑ Size 10 crochet cotton thread:
  - 500 yds. for Small
  - 600 yds. for Large
- ❑ 5 small snaps
- ❑ ¼ yd. of ¼" satin ribbon
- ❑ Sewing thread to match crochet cotton
- ❑ Tapestry and sewing needles
- ❑ No. 4 steel hook for Small or No. 3 steel hook for Large

Gauges: For **Small,** with **No. 4 hook,** 7 sts = 1"; 6 sc ribbing rows = 1"; 5 hdc rows = 1". For **Large,** with **No. 3 hook,** 13 sts = 2"; 11 sc ribbing rows = 2"; 9 hdc rows = 2".

Basic Stitches: Ch, sl st, sc, hdc.

WAISTBAND

Row 1: Ch 5, sc in second ch from hook, sc in each ch across, turn. *(4 sc made)*

NOTE: *Rows 2–101 are worked in* **back lps** *(see Stitch Guide).*

Rows 2–36: Ch 1, sc in each st across, turn.

Row 37: (Ch 2, hdc) in first st, hdc in each of next 2 sts, 2 hdc in last st, turn. *(6 hdc)*

Rows 38–66: Ch 2, hdc in each st across, turn.

Row 67: Ch 2, hdc next 2 sts tog, hdc in next st, hdc last 2 sts tog, turn. *(4)*

Rows 68–101: Ch 1, sc in each st across, turn.

Row 102: Matching sts, hold opposite side of starting ch and row 101 together; working through both thicknesses, ch 1, sl st in each st across. **Do not turn or fasten off.**

PANTS

Rnd 1: Working in ends of rows around edge of Waistband, ch 1, sc in each of first 2 rows, 2 sc in next row, (sc in each of next 2 rows, 2 sc in next row) around, join with sl st in first sc, **turn.** *(136 sc made)*

Rnds 2–3: Ch 1, sc in each st around, join, **turn.**

Rnds 4–24: Ch 2, hdc in each st around, join with sl st in top of ch-2, **turn.** At end of last rnd, fasten off. Mark 36th st of last rnd.

Row 25: Working in rows for **Front Shaping**, join with sl st in marked st, ch 2, (hdc next 2 sts tog) 2 times, hdc in next 56 sts, (hdc next 2 sts tog) 2 times, hdc in next st leaving remaining sts unworked, turn. *(62)*

Rows 26–36: Ch 2, (hdc next 2 sts tog) 2 times, hdc in each st across to last 5 sts, (hdc next 2 sts tog) 2 times, hdc in last st, turn. At end of last row *(18)*.

Rows 37–40: For **Crotch**, ch 2, hdc in each st across, turn. At end of last row, fasten off.

Row 25: For **Back Shaping**, skip next 2 unworked sts of rnd 24, join with sl st in next st, ch 2, (hdc next 2 sts tog) 2 times, hdc in next 56 sts, (hdc next 2 sts tog) 2 times, hdc in next st leaving last 2 sts unworked, turn. *(62)*

Rows 26–36: Ch 2, (hdc next 2 sts tog) 2 times, hdc in each st across to last 5 sts, (hdc next 2 sts tog) 2 times, hdc in last st, turn. At end of last row *(18)*.

Rows 37–40: For **Crotch**, ch 2, hdc in each st across, turn. At end of last row, fasten off.

Pants Edging

Rnd 1: Working in sts and in ends of rows around outer edge of Pants, join with sc in first skipped st on rnd 24, sc in next st, (sc in next row, 2 sc in each of next 14 rows, sc in next row, 3 sc in next st—*corner made,* sc in next 16 sts, 3 sc in next st—*corner made,* sc in next row, 2 sc in each of next 14 rows, sc in next row), sc in each of next 2 skipped sts on rnd 24; repeat between ( ), join with sl st in first sc, **turn.** *(168 sc made)*

Rnds 2–3: Ch 1, sc in each st around with 3 sc in center st of each corner, join, **turn.** At end of last row, fasten off. *(176, 184)*

Sew two snaps evenly spaced across Crotch sections of Pants Edging.

BODICE

Row 1: Working in ends of rows around opposite edge of Waistband, join with sl st in row 2, ch 2, hdc in each of next 3 rows, (2 hdc in next row, hdc in next 5 rows, 2 hdc in next row, hdc in next 4 rows) 8 times, hdc in next 6 rows, 2 hdc in next row leaving last 2 rows unworked, turn. *(116 hdc made)*

Rows 2–13: Ch 2, hdc in each st across, turn.

Row 14: For **Right Back**, ch 2, hdc in next 25 sts leaving remaining sts unworked, turn. *(26)*

Rows 15–24: Ch 2, hdc in each st across, turn.

Row 25: For **Shoulder**, ch 2, hdc in next 11 sts leaving remaining sts unworked, turn. *(12)*

Row 26: Ch 2, hdc in each st across. Fasten off.

Row 14: For **Front**, skip next 6 unworked sts on row 13, join with sl st in next st, ch 2, hdc in next 51 sts leaving remaining sts unworked, turn. *(52)*

Rows 15–24: Ch 2, hdc in each st across, turn.

Row 25: For **Left Front Shoulder**, ch 2, hdc in next 11 sts leaving remaining sts unworked, turn. *(12)*

Row 26: Ch 2, hdc in each st across. Fasten off.

Row 25: For **Right Front Shoulder**, skip next 28 unworked sts on row 24 of Front, join with sl st in next st, ch 2, hdc in last 11 sts, turn. *(12)*

Row 26: Ch 2, hdc in each st across. Fasten off.

Row 14: For **Left Back**, skip next 6 unworked sts on row 13, join with sl st in next st, ch 2, hdc in last 25 sts, turn. *(26)*

Rows 15–24: Ch 2, hdc in each st across, turn.

Row 25: For **Shoulder**, sl st in first 15 sts, ch 2, hdc in last 11 sts, turn. *(12)*

Row 26: Ch 2, hdc in each st across. Fasten off.

Matching sts, sew edges of Shoulders on Front and Backs together.

SLEEVES

Rnd 1: Working in sts and in ends of rows around armhole, join with sl st in fourth skipped st of row 13 on Bodice, ch 2, hdc in each of next 2 sts, *(2 hdc in next row, hdc in each of next 3 rows) 3 times, 2 hdc in next row; repeat from * once, hdc in each of last 3 sts, join with sl st in top of ch-2, **turn.** *(40 hdc made)*

Rnds 2–6: Ch 2, hdc in each st around, join, **turn.**

Rnd 7: Ch 2, hdc in each st around, join, **do not turn.**

Rnd 8: Ch 1, sc in each st around, join with sl st in first sc. Fasten off.

Repeat on other armhole.

COLLAR

Row 1: Working in ends of rows and in sts across neck edge of Bodice, join with sl st in first st of row 24 on Left Back, ch 2, hdc in each of next 3 sts, hdc next 2 sts tog, hdc in each of next 2 sts, hdc next 2 sts tog, hdc in next 4 sts, *hdc in next row, hdc next 2 rows tog, hdc in next row*, (hdc in next 4 sts, hdc next 2 sts tog) 4 times, hdc in next 4 sts; repeat between first *, hdc in next 4 sts,

• • • • • • • • • • • • • • • • • • • Continued on page 106

His & Hers Finery

Continued from page 105

hdc next 2 sts tog, hdc in each of next 2 sts, hdc next 2 sts tog, hdc in last 4 sts, turn. *(54 hdc made)*

Row 2: For **Right Half,** ch 1, sc in first 27 sts leaving remaining sts unworked, turn. *(27)*

Rows 3–4: Ch 1, sc in each st across, turn.

Row 5: Ch 1, sc in first st, sc next 2 sts tog, sc in each st across to last 3 sts, sc next 2 sts tog, sc in last st, turn. *(25)*

Row 6: Ch 1, sc in first st, sc next 2 sts tog, sc in next 4 sts, 2 sc in next st, sc in next 9 sts, 2 sc in next st, sc in next 4 sts, sc next 2 sts tog, sc in last st, turn. *(25)*

Row 7: Ch 1, sc in first st, sc next 2 sts tog, sc in next 5 sts, (sc in next st, 2 sc in next st) 5 times, sc in next 4 sts, sc next 2 sts tog, sc in last st, turn. *(28)*

Row 8: Ch 1, sc in first st, sc next 2 sts tog, sc in each st across to last 3 sts, sc next 2 sts tog, sc in last st, turn. *(26)*

Row 9: Ch 1, sc in first st, sc next 2 sts tog, sc in next 8 sts, (2 sc in next st, sc in next st) 2 times, sc in next 8 sts, sc next 2 sts tog, sc in last st, turn. *(26)*

Row 10: Ch 1, sc in first st, sc next 2 sts tog, sc in each st across to last 3 sts, sc next 2 sts tog, sc in last st, turn. *(24)*

Row 11: Ch 1, sc in first st, sc next 2 sts tog, sc in next 6 sts, (2 sc in next st, sc in next st) 3 times, sc in next 6 sts, sc next 2 sts tog, sc in last st. Fasten off. *(25)*

Row 2: For **Left Half,** join with sc in next unworked st on row 1, sc in last 26 sts, turn. *(27)*

Rows 3–11: Repeat rows 3–11 of Right Half.

COLLAR EDGING & BACK PLACKETS

Row 1: Working in ends of rows and in sts, join with sl st in row 1 on left edge of Bodice, ch 1, (2 sc in next row, sc in next row) across Bodice, sc in each row and in each st across both Halves of Collar; repeat between ( ) across right edge of Bodice, turn. *(166 sc made)*

Row 2: Ch 1, sc in each st across, turn.

Row 3: For **Left Placket,** ch 1, sc in first 36 sts leaving remaining sts unworked, turn.

Row 4: Ch 1, sc in each st across. Fasten off.

Row 3: For **Right Placket,** skip next 94 unworked sts on row 2, join with sc in next sc, sc in last 35 sts, turn.

Row 4: Ch 1, sc in each st across. Fasten off.

Lap Right Placket over Left Placket; working through both thicknesses, sew ends of Plackets to edge of Waistband.

Sew three snaps evenly spaced across Plackets.

VEST SIDE (make 2)

Row 1: Starting at shoulder edge, ch 13, hdc in third ch from hook, hdc in each ch across, turn. *(12 hdc made)*

Rows 2–8: Ch 2, hdc in each st across, turn.

Row 9: (Ch 2, hdc) in first st, hdc in each st across to last st, 2 hdc in last st, turn. *(14)*

Rows 10–12: Ch 2, hdc in each st across, turn.

Row 13: Repeat row 9. *(16)*

Row 14: Ch 2, hdc in each st across, turn.

Row 15: Repeat row 9. *(18)*

Row 16: Ch 2, hdc in each st across to last st, 2 hdc in last st, turn. *(19)*

Rows 17–19: Ch 2, hdc in each st across, turn.

Row 20: Ch 2, hdc in each st across to last 2 sts, hdc last 2 sts tog, turn. *(18)*

Row 21: Ch 2, hdc next 2 sts tog, hdc in each st across, turn. *(17)*

Row 22: Ch 2, hdc in each st across to last 4 sts, (hdc next 2 sts tog) 2 times, turn. *(15)*

Row 23: Ch 2, (hdc next 2 sts tog) 2 times, hdc in each st across, turn. *(13)*

Rows 24–25: Repeat rows 22 and 23. At end of last row on first Side, **turn.** At end of last row on second Side, **do not turn.**

Row 26: For **first Side only,** working in sts and in ends of rows around outer edge, ch 1, sc in first 9 sts, sc in next row, (2 sc in next row, sc in next row) 12 times, 2 sc in next row, sc in next 10 sts, 2 sc in next st, 2 sc in each of next 25 rows, join with sl st in first sc. Fasten off.

Row 26: For **second Side only,** working in ends of rows and in sts around outer edge, 2 sc in next 25 rows, 2 sc in next st, sc in next 10 sts, 2 sc in next st, (2 sc in next row, sc in next row) 12 times, 2 sc in next row, sc in last 9 sts, join. Fasten off.

Sew sts along shoulder edge of each Side to each shoulder seam on Bodice. Sew edge of each Side from row 15 to row 25 to each side of Bodice below underarm of Sleeve *(see photo).*

Tie ribbon in small bow and tack to Bodice Front between Collar Halves.

Bonnet

Size: Fits newborn.

Materials:
- ❑ 150 yds. size 10 crochet cotton thread
- ❑ 30" of matching color ¼" ribbon
- ❑ No. 5 steel hook or hook needed to obtain gauge

Gauge: 8 dc = 1"; 3 dc rows = 1".

Basic Stitches: Ch, sl st, sc, dc.

BONNET

Rnd 1: Ch 4, 9 dc in fourth ch from hook, join with sl st in top of ch-4. *(10 dc made)*

Rnd 2: (Ch 3, 2 dc) in first st, 2 dc in each of next 4

sts, 3 dc in next st, 2 dc in each of next 4 sts, join with sl st in top of ch-3. *(22)*

Rnd 3: (Ch 3, dc) in first st, 2 dc in each st around, join. *(44)*

Rnd 4: Ch 4, skip next st, (dc in next st, ch 1, skip next st) around, join with sl st in third ch of ch-4. *(22 dc, 22 ch sps)*

Rnd 5: (Ch 3, 2 dc) in first st; skipping ch sps, 3 dc in each dc around, join. *(66)*

Rnd 6: Ch 2, dc next 2 sts tog, ch 3, (dc next 3 sts tog, ch 3) around, join with sl st in top of first decrease. *(22 dc, 22 ch sps)*

Rnd 7: Sl st in next ch, (sl st, ch 3, 2 dc) in next ch, (ch 1, 3 dc) in center ch of each ch-3 around, ch 1, join with sl st in top of ch-3. *(66 dc, 22 ch sps)*

Rnd 8: Ch 3, dc in each of next 2 sts, 2 dc in next ch sp, (dc in each of next 3 sts, 2 dc in next ch sp) around, join. *(110)*

Row 9: Working this row in **back lps** *(see Stitch Guide),* ch 3, dc in next 85 sts leaving remaining sts unworked, turn. *(86)*

Row 10: Ch 3, dc in each st across, turn.

Row 11: Ch 3, (skip next 2 sts, 3 dc in next st) across to last st, dc in last st, turn. *(86)*

Row 12: Ch 4 *(counts as first dc and ch-1)*, (dc next 3 sts tog, ch 1) across to last st, dc in last st, turn. *(30 dc, 29 ch sps)*

Row 13: Ch 3, dc in next ch sp, 3 dc in each of next 27 ch sps, dc in next ch sp, dc in last st, turn. *(85)*

Row 14: Ch 3, dc in next st, (dc next 3 sts tog, ch 1) 27 times, dc in each of last 2 sts, turn. *(31 dc, 27 ch sps)*

Row 15: Ch 3, skip next st, 3 dc in each ch sp across to last 2 sts, 2 dc in next st, dc in last st, turn. *(85)*

Row 16: Ch 4, skip next st, dc in next st, (ch 1, skip next st, dc in next st) across, turn. *(43 dc, 42 chs)*

Row 17: Ch 3, dc in each st and in each ch across, **do not turn.** *(85)*

Row 18: For **Neck Edge,** working in ends of rows and in unworked sts on rnd 8, 2 sc in each of next 9 rows, (sc in next st, sc next 2 sts tog) 8 times, 2 sc in each of next 9 rows, **do not turn.**

Row 19: Working this row in **back lps** of row 17, ch 1, sc in first st, (ch 3, skip next st, sc in next st) across, turn.

Row 20: Working this row in remaining **front lps** of row 17, ch 1, sc in first st, (ch 3, skip next st, sc in next st) across. Fasten off.

Weave ribbon through sts of row 16 on Bonnet, leaving ends long for tying in bow. ✪

First Portrait

Continued from page 101

Rnd 3: (Ch 1, hdc) in first st, 2 hdc in next st, hdc in next 14 sts, 2 hdc in each of next 6 sts, hdc in next 14 sts, 2 hdc in each of last 3 sts, hdc in joining sl st, join. *(50 hdc)*

Rnd 4: Ch 1, hdc in each st around, join with sl st in first hdc, **do not work hdc in joining sl st.**

Rnd 5: With G hook, ch 1, sc in first st, 2-skip cr shell, (skip next st, sc in next st, 2-skip cr shell) around to last st, skip last st, join with sl st in first sc, **turn.** *(10 cr shells)*

Rnd 6: Beg half shell, sc in next ch sp, (3-skip cr shell, sc in next ch sp) 9 times, 2 dc in same ch sp as beg half shell, join with sl st in top of ch-3, **turn.**

Rnd 7: Ch 1, sc in first st, 3-skip cr shell, (sc in next ch sp, 3-skip cr shell) 9 times, join with sl st in first sc, **turn.**

Rnd 8: With E hook, (ch 5, dc) in first st, (3 sc in next ch sp, skip next 2 sts, V st in next st) 3 times, sc in next 4 ch sps, skip next 2 sts, dc in next st, ch 1, sc in ch sp of last V st made, ch 1, dc in same st where last dc was made; for **center,** dc in first on last V st made; (3 sc in next ch sp, skip next 2 sts, V st in next st) 2 times, 3 sc in last ch sp, join with sl st in third ch of ch-5, **turn.** *(6 ch sps)*

Rnd 9: Beg half shell, dc in center st of next 3-sc group, (7 dc in next ch sp, dc in center st of next 3-sc group) 2 times, 7 dc around next st at center, (dc in center st of next 3-sc group, 7 dc in next ch sp) 2 times, dc in center st of next 3-sc group, 3 dc in same ch sp where first 3 dc were made, join with sl st in top of ch-3, **turn.**

Rnd 10: (Ch 3, dc) in first st, (skip next 3 sts, V st in next st, skip next 3 sts, 3 dc in next st) 5 times, skip next 3 sts, V st in next st, join, sl st in next st, **turn.**

Rnd 11: Ch 3, 7 dc in next ch sp, (dc in center st of next 3-dc group, 7 dc in next ch sp) around, join, **turn.**

Rnd 12: (Ch 5, dc) in first st, skip next 3 sts, 3 dc in next st, (skip next 3 sts, V st in next st, skip next 3 sts, 3 dc in next st) around, join with sl st in third ch of ch-5, **turn.**

Rnd 13: Ch 1, sc in next st, 7 dc in next ch sp, (sc in center st of next 3-dc group, 7 dc in next ch sp) around, join with sl st in first sc. Fasten off.

Cut two 17" pieces from ribbon. Beginning and ending at center front, weave ribbon through row 8 of each Bootie, going over sc sts and under V sts. Tie ends of each ribbon in bow. ✪

Antique Elegance

Designed by Emma Jones

Finished Sizes: Infant's 0–3 mos. has 17" chest; 3–6 mos. has 20½" chest.

Materials:
- ❏ 3,500 yds. white size 30 crochet cotton thread
- ❏ 4 yds. white ⅛" satin ribbon
- ❏ White sewing thread
- ❏ Tapestry and sewing needles
- ❏ No. 10 steel hook or hook needed to obtain gauge

Gauge: 5 mesh = 1"; 5 mesh rows = 1".

Basic Stitches: Ch, sl st, sc, dc, tr.

Special Stitches:
For **shell,** (3 dc, ch 2, 3 dc) in specified ch sp.

For **love knot (lk),** *pull up a lp on hook ¼" long, yo and pull lp through, sc in back strand of long lp *(see illustration 1 below).*

For **double love knot (dlk),** *pull up a lp on hook ¼" long, yo and pull lp through, sc in back strand of long lp *(see illustration 1);* repeat from * *(see illustration 2).*

When working into previous row or rnd of love knots and double love knots, insert hook in side of sc between lps *(see illustration 3).*

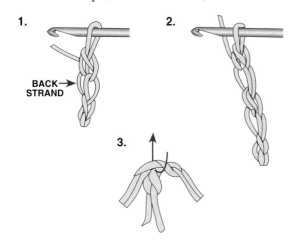

1.   **2.**

BACK→ STRAND

3.

Filet Stitches:
For **beginning mesh (beg mesh),** ch 5, skip next 2 sts or chs, dc in next st.

For **mesh,** ch 2, skip next 2 sts or chs, dc in next st.

For **block,** dc in each of next 3 sts, or, 2 dc in next ch sp, dc in next st.

For **end mesh,** ch 2, dc in third ch of ch-5.

Note:
Instructions are for 0–3 mos. Changes for 3–6 mos. are in [ ].

FRONT YOKE

Row 1: Ch 68 [74], dc in eighth ch from hook, (ch 2, skip next 2 chs, dc in next ch) 4 [6] times, dc in each of next 3 chs, (ch 2, skip next 2 chs, dc in next ch) 7 times, dc in each of next 3 chs, (ch 2, skip next 2 chs, dc in next ch) 7 times, turn. *(19 ch sps, 26 dc) [21 ch sps, 28 dc]*

Row 2: Beg mesh *(see Filet Stitches),* **mesh** 5 times, **block,** mesh, block, mesh 5 times, block, mesh, block, mesh 3 [5] times, ch 2, dc in fifth ch of ch-7, turn. *(17 mesh, 4 blocks) [19 mesh, 4 blocks]*

Row 3: Beg mesh, mesh 2 [4] times, (block, ch 5, skip next 3 dc, tr in next ch sp, ch 5, skip next 3 dc, dc in next st, block), mesh 3 times; repeat between ( ), mesh 4 times, end mesh, turn.

Row 4: Beg mesh, mesh 3 times, (block, ch 5, skip next 3 dc, sc in next ch sp, sc in next tr, sc in next ch sp, ch 5, skip next 3 dc, dc in next st, block), mesh; repeat between ( ), mesh 1 [3] times, end mesh, turn.

Row 5: Beg mesh, mesh 0 [2] times, block, (ch 5, skip next 3 dc, sc in next ch sp, sc in each of next 3 sts, sc in next ch sp, ch 5, skip next 3 dc, dc in next st, block) 2 times, mesh 2 times, end mesh, turn.

Row 6: Beg mesh, mesh 3 times, (3 dc in next ch sp, ch 5, skip next st, sc in each of next 3 sts, ch 5, skip next st, 3 dc in next ch sp, dc in next st), mesh; repeat between ( ), mesh 1 [3] times, end mesh, turn.

Row 7: Beg mesh, mesh 2 [4] times, (3 dc in next ch sp, ch 4, skip next st, tr in next st, ch 4, skip next st, 3 dc in next ch sp, dc in next st), mesh 3 times; repeat between ( ), mesh 4 times, end mesh, turn.

Row 8: Beg mesh, mesh 5 times, (3 dc in next ch sp, ch 2, 3 dc in next ch sp, dc in next st), mesh 5 times; repeat between ( ), mesh 3 [5] times, end mesh, turn.

Row [9]: For **3–6 mos. only,** beg mesh, mesh 6 times, block, mesh 7 times, block, mesh 6 times, end mesh, turn.

Rows [10–16]: Repeat rows 2–8.

Row 9 [17]: For **both sizes,** beg mesh, mesh 4 [6] times, block, mesh 7 times, block, mesh 1 [3] times; for **Neck Opening,** skip next 2 chs, tr in next st leaving last 5 [3] mesh unworked, turn. *(13 mesh, 2 blocks) [17 mesh, 2 blocks]*

• • • • • • • • • • • • • • • • • • • Continued on page 110

Antique Elegance

Continued from page 108

Row 10 [18]: Ch 3, skip next dc and next ch-2 sp, dc in next st, mesh 7 [9] times, block, mesh, block, mesh 3 [5] times, end mesh, turn.

Row 11 [19]: Beg mesh, mesh 2 [4] times, block, ch 5, skip next 3 dc, tr in next ch sp, ch 5, skip next 3 dc, dc in next st, block, mesh 5 [7] times, skip next 2 chs, tr in next st leaving last ch-3 sp unworked, turn.

Row 12 [20]: Ch 3, skip next dc and next ch-2 sp, dc in next st, mesh 3 [5] times, block, ch 5, skip next 3 dc, sc in next ch sp, sc in next tr, sc in next ch sp, ch 5, skip next 3 dc, dc in next st, block, mesh 1 [3] times, end mesh, turn.

Row 13 [21]: Beg mesh, mesh 0 [2] times, block, ch 5, skip next 3 dc, sc in next ch sp, sc in each of next 3 sts, sc in next ch sp, ch 5, skip next 3 dc, dc in next st, block, mesh 2 [4] times leaving last ch-3 sp unworked, turn.

Row 14 [22]: Beg mesh, mesh 2 [4] times, 3 dc in next ch sp, ch 5, skip next st, sc in each of next 3 sts, ch 5, skip next st, 3 dc in next ch sp, dc in next st, mesh 1 [3] times, end mesh, turn.

Row 15 [23]: Beg mesh 2 [4] times, 3 dc in next ch sp, ch 4, skip next st, tr in next st, ch 4, skip next st, 3 dc in next ch sp, dc in next st, mesh 3 [5] times, end mesh, turn.

Row 16 [24]: Beg mesh, mesh 4 [6] times, 3 dc in next ch sp, ch 2, 3 dc in next ch sp, dc in next st, mesh 3 [5] times, end mesh, turn.

Row 17 [25]: Beg mesh, mesh 4 [6] times, block, mesh 5 [7] times, end mesh, turn.

Row 18 [26]: Beg mesh, mesh 4 [6] times, block, mesh, block, mesh 3 [5] times, end mesh, turn.

Row 19 [27]: Beg mesh, mesh 2 [4] times, block, ch 5, skip next 3 dc, tr in next ch sp, ch 5, skip next 3 dc, dc in next st, block, mesh 3 [5] times, end mesh, turn.

Row 20 [28]: Beg mesh, mesh 2 [4] times, block, ch 5, skip next 3 dc, sc in next ch sp, sc in next tr, sc in next ch sp, ch 5, skip next 3 dc, dc in next st, block, mesh 1 [3] times, end mesh, turn.

Row 21 [29]: Beg mesh, mesh 0 [2] times, block, ch 5, skip next 3 dc, sc in next ch sp, sc in each of next 3 sts, sc in next ch sp, ch 5, skip next 3 dc, dc in next st, block mesh 1 [3] times, end mesh, turn.

Row 22 [30]: Ch 5, dc in first st, mesh 3 [5] times, 3 dc in next ch sp, ch 5, skip next st, sc in each of next 3 sts, ch 5, skip next st, 3 dc in next ch sp, dc in next st, mesh 1 [3] times, end mesh, turn.

Row 23 [31]: Beg mesh, mesh 2 [4] times, 3 dc in next ch sp, ch 4, skip next st, tr in next st, ch 4, skip next st, 3 dc in next ch sp, dc in next st, mesh 4 [6] times, end, ch 2, tr in same st as last st made, turn.

Row 24 [32]: Ch 5, dc in first st, mesh 7 [9] times, 3 dc in next ch sp, ch 2, 3 dc in next ch sp, dc in next st, mesh 3 [5] times, end mesh, turn.

Row 25 [33]: Beg mesh, mesh 4 [6] times, block, mesh 7 times, block, mesh 1 [2] times, end mesh, ch 2, tr in same st as last st made, turn.

Row 26 [34]: Ch 19 [13], dc in eighth ch from hook, (ch 2, skip next 2 chs, dc in next ch) 3 [1] times, ch 2, skip last 2 chs, dc in next st, mesh 1 [3] times, block, mesh, block, mesh 5 times, block, mesh, block, mesh 3 [5] times, end mesh, turn.

Rows 27–32 [35–40]: Repeat rows 3–8.

Row [41]: For **3–6 mos. only,** repeat row [9].

Rows [42–48]: Repeat rows 2–8.

Row 33 [49]: For **both sizes,** beg mesh, mesh 4 [6] times, block, mesh 7 times, block, mesh 6 times, end mesh. Fasten off.

BACK YOKE (make 2)

Rows 1–17 [1–25]: Repeat rows 1–17 [1–25] of Front Yoke.

Rows 18–19 [26–27]: Beg mesh, mesh 10 [14] times, end mesh, turn. At end of last row, fasten off.

Matching ends of rows and edges on each Back Yoke to each end of Front Yoke, sew shoulder seams.

Armhole Trim

With right side of work facing you, working in sts across one end of Yoke, join with sl st in first st, beg mesh, mesh 40 [44] times, end mesh. Fasten off. *(42 mesh) [46 mesh]*

Repeat on opposite end of Yoke.

YOKE RUFFLE

Row 1: Working around entire outer edge of Yoke in mesh and in ends of rows, join with sl st in in first mesh at bottom corner of right Back Yoke, **dlk** *(see Special Stitches),* sl st in same mesh as joining sl st, *dlk, (sl st, dlk, sl st) in next mesh; repeat from * around to top corner on right Back Yoke, turn.

Rows 2–4: Lk *(see Special Stitches)* 3 times, sc in center of next dlk, (dlk, sc in center of next dlk) across, turn. At end of last row, fasten off.

SLEEVE CAPS

Row 1: With right side facing you for left Sleeve or wrong side facing you for right Sleeve, working in sts of Armhole Trim behind Yoke Ruffle, join with sl st in sixth dc from corner, beg mesh, mesh 14 [16] times, block, mesh 14 [16] times, tr in next st leaving last 6 mesh unworked, turn. *(29 mesh, 1 block, 1 tr made) [33 mesh, 1 block, 1 tr made]*

Row 2: Ch 5, skip next st and next ch sp, dc in next st, mesh 3 times, block, mesh 8 [10] times, block, mesh, block, mesh 8 [10] times, block, mesh 4 times, tr in third ch of ch-5, turn.

Row 3: Ch 5, skip next st and next ch sp, dc in next st, mesh 2 times, block, mesh, block, mesh 6 [8] times, block, ch 5, skip next 3 dc, tr in next ch sp, ch 5, skip next 3 dc, dc in next st, block, mesh 6 [8] times, block, mesh, block, mesh 2 times, tr in third ch of ch-5, turn.

Row 4: Ch 5, skip next st and next ch sp, dc in next st, (block, mesh) 3 times, mesh 3 [5] times, block, ch 5, skip next 3 dc, sc in next ch sp, sc in next tr, sc in next ch sp, ch 5, skip next 3 dc, dc in next st, block, mesh 4 [6] times, (block, mesh) 3 times, tr in third ch of ch-5, turn.

Row 5: Ch 3, skip next st, (block, mesh) 4 times, mesh 1 [3] times, block, ch 5, skip next 3 dc, sc in next ch sp, sc in each of next 3 sts, sc in next ch sp, ch 5, skip next 3 dc, dc in next st, block, mesh 2 [4] times, (block, mesh) 3 times, 2 dc in next ch sp, dc in third ch of ch-5, turn.

Row 6: Ch 3, skip next 2 sts, dc in next st, (block, mesh) 3 times, mesh 3 [5] times, 3 dc in next ch sp, ch 5, skip next st, sc in each of next 3 sts, ch 5, skip next st, 3 dc in next ch sp, dc in next st, mesh 4 [6] times, (block, mesh) 2 times, block, skip next 2 sts, tr in top of next ch-3, turn.

Row 7: Ch 3, skip next 3 dc, dc in next st, (block, mesh) 2 times, mesh 5 [7] times, 3 dc in next ch sp, ch 4, skip next st, tr in next st, ch 4, skip next st, 3 dc in next ch sp, dc in next st, mesh 6 [8] times, block, mesh, block, ch 3, skip next 3 dc, tr in top of next ch-3, turn.

Row 8: Ch 3, skip next 3 dc, dc in next st, block, mesh 8 [10] times, 3 dc in next ch sp, ch 2, skip next tr, 3 dc in next ch sp, dc in next st, mesh 8 [10] times, block, skip next 3 dc, tr in top of next ch-3, turn.

Row 9: Ch 5, skip next 3 dc, dc in next st, mesh 9 [11] times, block, mesh 10 [12] times leaving last ch-3 unworked. Fasten off.
Repeat on other side of Yoke.

Sleeve Ruffles
Row 1: Join with sc in end of row 1 on one Sleeve Cap, (dlk, sc in next mesh, next block or next row) across to opposite end of row 1, turn.

Rows 2–4: Repeat rows 2–4 of Yoke Ruffle on this page.
Tack ends of rows on Sleeve Ruffle to Yoke behind Yoke Ruffle.
Repeat on other Sleeve Cap.

SKIRT
Row 1: Ch 226, dc in fourth ch from hook, dc in next ch, (ch 2, skip next 2 chs, dc in next ch) 15 times, dc in each of next 3 chs; repeat between ( ) 19 times, dc in each of next 3 chs; repeat between ( ) 19 times, dc in each of next 3 chs; repeat between ( ) 15 times; for **Bottom Edge,** sl st in next 7 chs, (3 dc, ch 2, 3 dc) in last ch, turn. *(86 dc, 69 ch sps)*

Row 2: Ch 3, **shell** *(see Notes)* in next ch sp, ch 7, skip next 7 sl sts or sc, dc in next dc, mesh 5

times, block, (mesh 8 times, block, mesh, block, mesh 8 times, block) 3 times, mesh 5 times, dc in each of last 2 sts, turn. *(61 mesh, 10 blocks, 1 shell, 4 dc)*

Row 3: Ch 3, dc in each of next 2 sts, mesh 4 times, (block, mesh, block, mesh 6 times, block, ch 5, skip next 3 dc, tr in next ch sp, ch 5, skip next 3 dc, dc in next st, block, mesh 6 times) 3 times, block, mesh, block, mesh 4 times, ch 6, skip next ch sp, shell in ch sp of next shell, turn.

Row 4: Ch 3, shell in next shell, ch 6, skip next ch sp, dc in next dc, mesh 3 times, *(block, mesh) 3 times, mesh 3 times, block, ch 5, skip next 3 dc, sc in next ch sp, sc in next tr, sc in next ch sp, ch 5, skip next 3 dc, dc in next st, block, mesh 4 times; repeat from * 2 more times, (block, mesh) 3 times, mesh 2 times, dc in each of last 2 sts, turn.

Row 5: Ch 3, dc in each of next 2 sts, *mesh 2 times, (block, mesh) 4 times, mesh, block, ch 5, skip next 3 dc, sc in next ch sp, sc in each of next 3 sts, sc in next ch sp, ch 5, skip next 3 dc, dc in next st, block; repeat from * 2 more times, mesh 2 times, (block, mesh) 4 times, mesh, ch 3; working over chains of last two rows *(see illustration)*, sc in fourth ch of ch-7 three rows below, ch 3, shell in next shell, turn.

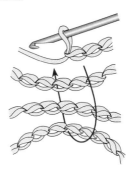

Row 6: Ch 3, shell in next shell, ch 7, skip next sc, dc in next dc, mesh 3 times, *(block, mesh) 3 times, mesh, block, mesh, 3 dc in next ch sp, ch 5, skip next st, sc in each of next 3 sts, ch 5, skip next st, 3 dc in next ch sp, dc in next st, mesh, block, mesh 2 times; repeat from * 2 more times, (block, mesh) 3 times, mesh 2 times, dc in each of last 2 sts, turn.

Row 7: Ch 3, dc in each of next 2 sts, mesh 4 times, *(block, mesh) 2 times, mesh, block, ch 5, skip next 3 dc, tr in next ch sp, ch 5, skip next 3 dc, dc in next st, 3 dc in next ch sp, ch 4, skip next st, tr in next st, ch 4, skip next st, 3 dc in next ch sp, dc in next st, ch 5, skip next 3 dc, tr in next ch sp, ch 5, skip next 3 dc, dc in next st, block, mesh 2 times; repeat from * 2 more times, (block, mesh) 2 times, mesh 3 times, ch 6, skip next ch sp, shell in next shell, turn.

Row 8: Ch 3, shell in next shell, ch 6, skip next ch sp, dc in next dc, mesh 5 times, *block, mesh 2

Continued on page 112

Antique Elegance

Continued from page 111

times, block, ch 5, sc in next ch sp, sc in next tr, sc in next ch sp, ch 5, skip next 3 dc, dc in next st, 3 dc in next ch sp, ch 2, 3 dc in next ch sp, dc in next st, ch 5, skip next 3 dc, sc in next ch sp, sc in next tr, sc in next ch sp, ch 5, skip next 3 dc, dc in next st, block, mesh 2 times; repeat from * 2 more times, block, mesh 5 times, dc in each of last 2 sts, turn.

Row 9: Ch 3, dc in each of next 2 sts, mesh 7 times, *(block, ch 5, skip next 3 dc, sc in next ch sp, sc in each of next 3 sts, sc in next ch sp, ch 5, skip next 3 dc, dc in next st) 2 times, block, mesh 3 times; repeat from * 2 more times, mesh 4 times, ch 3; working over chains of last two rows, sc in fourth ch of ch-7 three rows below, ch 3, shell in next shell, turn.

Row 10: Ch 3, shell in next shell, ch 7, skip next sc, dc in next dc, mesh 5 times, *block, mesh 2 times, (3 dc in next ch sp, ch 5, skip next st, sc in each of next 3 sts, ch 5, skip next st, 3 dc in next ch sp, dc in next st, mesh) 2 times, mesh; repeat from * 2 more times, block, mesh 5 times, dc in each of last 2 sts, turn.

Row 11: Ch 3, dc in each of next 2 sts, mesh 4 times, *(block, mesh) 2 times, mesh, 3 dc in next ch sp, ch 4, skip next st, tr in next st, ch 4, skip next st, 3 dc in next ch sp, dc in next st, ch 5, skip next 3 dc, tr in next ch sp, ch 5, skip next 3 dc, dc in next st, 3 dc in next ch sp, ch 4, skip next st, tr in next st, ch 4, skip next st, 3 dc in next ch sp, dc in next st, mesh 2 times; repeat from * 2 more times, (block, mesh) 2 times, mesh 3 times, ch 6, skip next ch sp, shell in next shell, turn.

Row 12: Ch 3, shell in next shell, ch 6, skip next ch sp, dc in next dc, mesh 3 times, *(block, mesh) 3 times, mesh, 3 dc in next ch sp, ch 2, 3 dc in next ch sp, dc in next st, ch 5, skip next 3 dc, sc in next ch sp, sc in next tr, sc in next ch sp, ch 5, skip next 3 dc, dc in next st, 3 dc in next ch sp, ch 2, 3 dc in next ch sp, dc in next st, mesh 2 times; repeat from * 2 more times, (block, mesh) 3 times, mesh 2 times, dc in each of last 2 sts, turn.

Row 13: Ch 3, dc in each of next 2 sts, *mesh 2 times, (block, mesh) 4 times, mesh, block, ch 5, skip next 3 dc, sc in next ch sp, sc in each of next 3 sts, sc in next ch sp, ch 5, skip next 3 dc, dc in next st, block; repeat from * 2 more times, mesh 2 times, (block, mesh) 4 times, mesh, ch 3; working over chains of last two rows, sc in fourth ch of ch-7 three rows below, ch 3, shell in next shell, turn.

Row 14: Ch 3, shell in next shell, ch 7, skip next sc, dc in next dc, mesh 3 times, *(block, mesh) 3 times, mesh 3 times, 3 dc in next ch sp, ch 5, skip next st, sc in each of next 3 sts, ch 5, skip next st, 3 dc in next ch sp, dc in next st, mesh 4 times; repeat from * 2 more times, (block, mesh) 3 times,

mesh 2 times, dc in each of last 2 sts, turn.

Row 15: Ch 3, dc in each of next 2 sts, mesh 4 times, (block, mesh, block, mesh 6 times, 3 dc in next ch sp, ch 4, skip next st, tr in next st, ch 4, skip next st, 3 dc in next ch sp, dc in next st, mesh 6 times) 3 times, block, mesh, block, mesh 4 times, ch 6, skip next ch sp, shell in next shell, turn.

Row 16: Ch 3, shell in next shell, ch 6, skip next ch sp, dc in next dc, mesh 5 times, (block, mesh 8 times, 3 dc in next ch sp, ch 2, 3 dc in next ch sp, dc in next st, mesh 8 times) 3 times, block, mesh 5 times, dc in each of last 2 sts, turn.

Row 17: Ch 3, dc in each of next 2 sts, mesh 15 times, (block, mesh 19 times) 2 times, block, mesh 15 times, ch 3; working over chains of last two rows, sc in fourth ch of ch-7 three rows below, ch 3, shell in next shell, turn.

Rows 18–175 [18–207]: Repeat rows 2–17 consecutively, ending with row 15.

Row 176 [208]: Ch 3, shell in next shell, ch 3; working over chain of last row, sc in fourth ch of ch-7 two rows below, ch 3, dc in next dc, mesh 5 times, (block, mesh 8 times, 3 dc in next ch sp, ch 2, 3 dc in next ch sp, dc in next st, mesh 8 times) 3 times, block, mesh 5 times, dc in each of last 2 sts. Fasten off.

Sew first and last rows together leaving 6" at top unsewn.

With right sides out, starting at center back, sew Skirt to Yoke as follows:

Gathering Skirt to fit, sew ends of 40 [50] rows at right top edge of Skirt to ends of rows on bottom edge of right Back Yoke. Repeat on left top edge of Skirt and left Back Yoke. Leave next eight rows unsewn on each side of Skirt forming underarms. Gathering to fit, sew remaining rows on front of Skirt across Front Yoke.

SKIRT RUFFLE

Row 1: Ch 119, dc in eighth ch from hook, dc in each of next 3 chs, (ch 2, skip next 2 chs, dc in next ch) 15 times, dc in each of next 3 chs, (ch 2, skip next 2 chs, dc in next ch) 19 times, dc in each of last 3 chs, turn. *(35 ch sps, 45 dc made)*

Row 2: For **Bottom Edge,** ch 9, dc in seventh ch from hook, dc in each of next 2 chs, dc in next st, mesh, (block, mesh 8 times) 2 times, block, mesh, block, mesh 8 times, block, mesh 5 times, block, ch 2, dc in fifth ch of ch-7, turn.

Row 3: Beg mesh, block, mesh 4 times, (block, mesh, block, mesh 6 times, block, ch 5, skip next 3 dc, tr in next ch sp, ch 5, skip next 3 dc, dc in next st), block, mesh 6 times; repeat between ( ), 2 dc in next ch sp, dc in third ch of ch-6, turn.

Row 4: Ch 9, dc in seventh ch from hook, dc in each of next 2 chs, dc in next st, *ch 5, skip next 3 dc,

Lovely Layettes

sc in next ch sp, sc in next tr, sc in next ch sp, ch 5, skip next 3 dc, dc in next st, block, mesh 4 times, (block, mesh) 3 times*, mesh 3 times, block; repeat between first *, mesh 2 times, block, end mesh, turn.

Row 5: Beg mesh, block, mesh 2 times, *(block, mesh) 4 times, mesh, block, ch 5, skip next 3 dc, sc in next ch sp, sc in each of next 3 sts, sc in next ch sp, ch 5, skip next 3 dc, dc in next st*, block, mesh 2 times; repeat between first *, 2 dc in next ch sp, dc in third ch of ch-6, turn.

Row 6: Ch 9, dc in seventh ch from hook, dc in each of next 2 chs, dc in next st, *mesh, 3 dc in next ch sp, ch 5, skip next st, sc in each of next 3 sts, ch 5, skip next st, 3 dc in next ch sp, dc in next st, mesh, block, mesh 2 times, (block, mesh) 3 times*, mesh, block; repeat between first *, mesh 2 times, block, end mesh, turn.

Row 7: Beg mesh, block, mesh 4 times, *(block, mesh) 2 times, mesh, block, ch 5, skip next 3 dc, tr in next ch sp, ch 5, skip next 3 dc, dc in next st, 3 dc in next ch sp, ch 4, skip next st, tr in next st, ch 4, skip next st, 3 dc in next ch sp, dc in next st, ch 5, skip next 3 dc, tr in next ch sp, ch 5, skip next 3 dc, dc in next st*, block, mesh 2 times; repeat between first *, 2 dc in next ch sp, dc in third ch of ch-6, turn.

Row 8: Ch 9, dc in seventh ch from hook, dc in each of next 2 chs, dc in next st, (ch 5, skip next 3 dc, sc in next ch sp, sc in next tr, sc in next ch sp, ch 5, skip next 3 dc, dc in next st, 3 dc in next ch sp, ch 2, 3 dc in next ch sp, dc in next st, ch 5, skip next 3 dc, sc in next ch sp, sc in next st, sc in next ch sp, ch 5, skip next 3 dc, dc in next st, block, mesh 2 times, block), mesh 2 times, block; repeat between ( ), mesh 5 times, block, end mesh, turn.

Row 9: Beg mesh, block, mesh 7 times, (block, ch 5, skip next 3 dc, sc in next ch sp, sc in each of next 3 sts, sc in next ch sp, ch 5, skip next 3 dc, dc in next st) 2 times, block, mesh 3 times; repeat between ( ) 2 times, 2 dc in next ch sp, dc in third ch of ch-6, turn.

Row 10: Beg mesh, *(3 dc in next ch sp, ch 5, skip next st, sc in each of next 3 sts, ch 5, skip next st, 3 dc in next ch sp, dc in next st, mesh) 2 times, mesh, block, mesh 2 times; repeat from *, mesh 3 times, block, end mesh, turn.

Row 11: Beg mesh, block, mesh 4 times, (block, mesh, block, mesh 2 times, 3 dc in next ch sp, ch 4, skip next st, tr in next st, ch 4, skip next st, 3 dc in next ch sp, dc in next st, ch 5, skip next 3 dc, tr in next ch sp, ch 5, skip next 3 dc, dc in next st, 3 dc in next ch sp, ch 4, skip next st, tr in next st, ch 4, skip next st, 3 dc in next ch sp, dc in next st), mesh 2 times; repeat between ( ) leaving last 3 dc and last mesh unworked, turn.

Row 12: Beg mesh, *3 dc in next ch sp, ch 2, 3 dc in next ch sp, dc in next st, ch 5, skip next 3 dc, sc in next ch sp, sc in next tr, sc in next ch sp, ch 5, skip next 3 dc, dc in next st, 3 dc in next ch sp, ch 2, 3 dc in next ch sp, dc in next st, mesh 2 times, (block, mesh) 3 times, mesh; repeat from *, mesh 2 times, block, end mesh, turn.

Row 13: Beg mesh, block, *mesh 2 times, (block, mesh) 4 times, mesh, block, ch 5, skip next 3 dc, sc in next ch sp, sc in each of next 3 sts, sc in next ch sp, ch 5, skip next 3 dc, dc in next st, block; repeat from * leaving last 3 dc and last mesh unworked, turn.

Row 14: Beg mesh, *3 dc in next ch sp, ch 5, skip next st, sc in each of next 3 sts, ch 5, skip next st, 3 dc in next ch sp, dc in next st, mesh 4 times, (block, mesh) 3 times*, mesh 3 times; repeat between first *, mesh 2 times, block, end mesh, turn.

Row 15: Beg mesh, block, mesh 4 times, (block, mesh, block, mesh 6 times, 3 dc in next ch sp, ch 4, skip next st, tr in next st, ch 4, skip next st, 3 dc in next ch sp, dc in next st), mesh 6 times; repeat between ( ) leaving last 3 dc and last mesh unworked, turn.

Row 16: Beg mesh, (3 dc in next ch sp, ch 2, 3 dc in next ch sp, dc in next st, mesh 8 times, block), mesh 8 times; repeat between ( ), mesh 5 times, block, end mesh, turn.

Row 17: Beg mesh, block, mesh 15 times, block, mesh 19 times, block leaving last 3 dc and last mesh unworked, turn.

Row 18: Ch 9, dc in seventh ch from hook, dc in each of next 2 chs, dc in next st, mesh, (block, mesh 8 times) 2 times, block, mesh, block, mesh 8 times, block, mesh 5 times, block, end mesh, turn. *(33 mesh, 7 blocks)*

Rows 19–256 [19–288]: Repeat rows 3–18 consecutively, ending with row 16. At end of last row, fasten off.

Sew first and last rows together.

Matching seams, sew top edge of Ruffle to bottom edge of Skirt, gathering three [seven] rows on Ruffle to every two [five] shells at ends of rows on Skirt.

Leaving 8" at each end for ties, weave 50" piece of ribbon through mesh above Ruffle around bottom edge of Yoke and weave 32" piece of ribbon through mesh below Ruffle around neckline of Yoke. Tack in place at all corners and at center back edges.

Weave 38" piece of ribbon through mesh above shells around bottom of Skirt. Tack in place.

Cut remaining ribbon in half. Tie each piece in a bow around mesh at each bottom corner of Front Yoke *(see photo)*. ✪

Winter Wonder Ensemble

Designed by Michele Maks

Cape

Sizes: Infant's 0–3 mos. is 20" long without Hood. Infant's 3–6 mos. is 21" long without Hood. Infant's 6–9 mos. is 22½" long without Hood.

Materials:
- ❑ White chunky worsted yarn:
  - 30 oz. for 0–3 mos.
  - 33 oz. for 3–6 mos.
  - 36 oz. for 6–9 mos.
- ❑ White satin ribbon:
  - 28 yds. of ⅜"-wide
  - 10 yds. of ¼"-wide
  - 2 yds. of ⅞"-wide
- ❑ White sewing thread
- ❑ Tapestry and sewing needles
- ❑ I hook or hook needed to obtain gauge

Gauge: 7 sts = 2" ; (2 sc, 1 dc, 3 sc) row pattern = 2".

Basic Stitches: Ch, sl st, sc, dc.

Special Stitch: For **decrease (dec),** insert hook in next st or ch, yo, pull lp through, skip next st or ch, insert hook in next st or ch, yo, pull lp through, yo, pull through all lps on hook.

Note: Instructions are for Infant's 0–3 mos. Changes for 3–6 mos. and 6–9 mos. are in [ ].

SKIRT

Row 1: Ch 120 [140, 160], sc in second ch from hook, sc next 2 chs tog, sc in next 6 chs, 3 sc in next ch, (sc in next 8 chs, **dec**—*see Special Stitch,* sc in next 8 chs, 3 sc in next ch) across to last 9 chs, sc in next 6 chs, sc next 2 chs tog, sc in last ch, turn. *(119 sc made) [139 sc made, 159 sc made] Front of row 1 is right side of work.*

Rows 2–3: Ch 1, sc in first st, sc next 2 sts tog, sc in next 6 sts, 3 sc in next st, (sc in next 8 sts, dec, sc in next 8 sts, 3 sc in next st) across to last 9 sts, sc in next 6 sts, sc next 2 sts tog, sc in last st, turn.

NOTE: *When working three sts in same st, second st is point st.*

Row 4: For **beading row,** ch 4, skip next st, dc in next st, (ch 1, skip next st, dc in next st) 3 times, dc in point st, *dc in next st, (ch 1, skip next st, dc in next st) 4 times, skip next st, dc in next st, (ch 1, skip next st, dc in next st) 4 times, dc in point st; repeat from * across to last 9 sts, dc in next st, (ch 1, skip next st, dc in next st) 4 times, turn. *(114 sts and chs) [133 sts and chs, 152 sts and chs]*

Row 5: Working in sts and in ch sps, ch 1, sc in first st, sc next ch sp and next st tog, sc in next 6 ch sps and sts, 3 sc in next point st, (sc in next 8 sts and ch sps, sc next 2 sts tog, sc in next 8 ch sps and sts, 3 sc in next point st) across to last 9 sts and ch sps, sc in next 6 sts and ch sps, sc next st and ch sp tog, sc in last st, turn. *(119 sc) [139 sc, 159 sc]*

Rows 6–53 [6–57, 6–61]: Repeat rows 2–5 consecutively. At end of last row, **do not fasten off.**

First Fill-In Triangle

Row 1: Ch 1, sc in first st, sc next 2 sts tog, sc in next 4 sts, sc next 2 sts tog leaving remaining sts unworked, turn. *(7 sc made)*

Row 2: Ch 1, sc first 2 sts tog, sc in each of next 2 sts, sc next 2 sts tog, sc in last st, turn. *(5)*

Row 3: Ch 1, sc in first st, (sc next 2 sts tog) 2 times, turn. *(3)*

Row 4: Ch 1, sc 3 sts tog, turn. Fasten off. *(1)*

Second Fill-In Triangle

Row 1: Join with sl st in next unworked point st, ch 1, sc next 2 sts tog, sc in next 6 sts, dec, sc in next 6 sts, sc next 2 sts tog leaving remaining sts unworked, turn. *(16 sc made)*

Row 2: Ch 1, sc first 2 sts tog, sc in next 4 sts, dec, sc in next 4 sts, sc last 2 sts tog leaving sl st unworked, turn. *(11)*

Row 3: Ch 1, sc first 2 sts tog, sc in each of next 2 sts, dec, sc in each of next 2 sts, sc last 2 sts tog, turn. *(7)*

Row 4: Ch 1, sc first 2 sts tog, dec, sc last 2 sts tog, turn. *(3)*

Row 5: Ch 1, sc 3 sts tog. Fasten off. **Do not turn.**

Repeat Second Fill-In Triangle 4 [5, 6] more times.

Last Fill-In Triangle

Row 1: Join with sl st in last point st, ch 1, sc next 2 sts tog, sc in next 4 sts, sc next 2 sts tog, sc in last st, turn. *(7 sc made)*

Row 2: Ch 1, sc in first st, sc next 2 sts tog, sc in each of next 2 sts, sc last 2 sts tog leaving sl st unworked, turn. *(5)*

· Continued on page 116

Winter Wonder Ensemble

Continued from page 115

Row 3: Ch 1, sc first 2 sts tog, sc next 2 sts tog, sc in last st, turn. *(3)*

Row 4: Ch 1, sc 3 sts tog. **Do not turn or fasten off.**

Neck Edge

Row 1: Working across all Fill-In Triangles in sts and in ends of rows, ch 1, evenly space 70 [82, 94] sc across, turn.

Row 2: Ch 1, skip first st, sc in next st, (sc next 2 sts tog) across. Fasten off. *(35) [41, 47]*

HOOD

Row 1: With ch 40 [60, 60], repeat row 1 of Skirt. *(39 sc made) [59 sc made, 59 sc made]*

Rows 2–9 [2–11, 2–13]: Repeat rows 2–5 of Skirt consecutively, ending with row 5 [3, 5]. At end of last row, **do not fasten off.**

Top Fill-In Triangles

Work First Fill-In Triangle.

Work Second Fill-In Triangle, repeating across to last point.

Work Last Fill-In Triangle.

Top Edge

Row 1: Working across all Fill-In Triangles in sts and in ends of rows, ch 1, evenly space 22 [34, 34] sc across. Fasten off.

Fold Top Edge in half, matching sts; sew edges together forming top seam of Hood.

Bottom Fill-In Triangles

Working in remaining lps on opposite side of starting ch on row 1 of Hood, work Second Fill-In Triangle, repeating across to end. **Do not fasten off.**

Bottom Edge

Row 1: Working across all Fill-In Triangles in sts and in ends of rows, join with sc in first sl st of last row on first Fill-In Triangle, evenly space 24 [36, 36] more sc across, turn. *(25 sc made) [37 sc made, 37 sc made]*

Row 2: Ch 4, skip next st, dc in next st, (ch 1, skip next st, dc in next st) across. Fasten off.

Easing Skirt to fit, sew Neck Edge of Skirt to Bottom Edge of Hood.

VERTICAL RUFFLE

Row 1: With right side of work facing you, hold yarn on wrong side of Skirt; working vertically across in decreases and in sps between sts on dc rows, starting at bottom edge of row 1 on Skirt, join with sl st in first skipped ch below first dec; working loosely enough to keep piece flat, sl st in each row across to last row on Fill-In Triangle at top of Skirt. Fasten off. *(58 sl sts made) [62 sl sts made, 66 sl sts made]*

Row 2: Working in **back lps** *(see Stitch Guide)* of sl sts on row 1, join with sc in first st, skip next st, (5 dc in next st, sc in next st) across, turn; continuing in **front lps** of sl sts on row 1, sc in next st, skip next st, (5 dc in next st, sc in next st) across. Fasten off.

Repeat Vertical Ruffle across each decrease section of Skirt.

Starting at Top Edge and working across to Bottom Edge, repeat Vertical Ruffle across each point section on Hood.

FRONT TRIM

Row 1: With right side of work facing you, join with sc in end of row 1 on Skirt, evenly space 178 [192, 206] more sc across Skirt and Hood to opposite end of row 1, turn. *(179 sc made) [193 sc made, 207 sc made]*

Row 2: Ch 1, sc in each of first 2 [3, 2] sts, (skip next st, 5 sc in next st, skip next st, sc in next st) across to last 1 [2, 1] st, sc in last 1 [2, 1] st. Fasten off.

FINISHING

Working behind Vertical Ruffles, weave ⅜" ribbon through each beading row on Skirt and Hood leaving ½" ends. Turn ends under and tack in place.

For each **Bow,** cut 6" piece from ¼" ribbon and tie in a 1½" bow. Working in desired staggered pattern, sew Bows across each point section on Skirt.

Weave ⅞" ribbon through last row on Bottom Edge of Hood, leaving long ends for tying in bow.

Dress & Booties

Sizes: Infant's 0–3 mos. fits 16" chest and 2¼"-long Sole. Infant's 3–6 mos. fits 18" chest and 2½"-long Sole. Infant's 6–9 mos. fits 20" chest and 2¾"-long Sole.

Materials:
- ❑ White baby yarn:
    - 14 oz. for 0–3 mos.
    - 16 oz. for 3–6 mos.
    - 18 oz. for 6–9 mos.
- ❑ White satin ribbon:
    - 24 yds. of ⅜"-wide
    - 10 yds. of ¼"-wide
- ❑ 3 white ½" buttons
- ❑ White sewing thread
- ❑ Tapestry and sewing needles
- ❑ E and F hooks or hook needed to obtain gauge

Gauge: F hook, 9 sts = 2"; (3 sc, 1 dc) row pattern =1".

Basic Stitches: Ch, sl st, sc, hdc, dc, tr.

Notes: Instructions are for Infant's 0–3 mos. Changes for 3–6 mos. and 6–9 mos. are in [ ].
Use F hook unless otherwise stated.

DRESS
Skirt
Row 1: With ch 180 [200, 220], work row 1 of Cape Skirt on page 115. *(179 sc made)* [*199 sc made, 219 sc made*]

Rows 2–47 [2–51, 2–55]: Work rows 2–5 of Cape Skirt consecutively, ending with row 3. **Do not fasten off.**

First, Second & Last Fill-In Triangles
Work First Cape Fill-In Triangle on page 115.
Work Second Cape Fill-In Triangle and repeat 6 [7, 8] more times.
Work Last Cape Fill-In Triangle.

Top Edge
Row 1: Working across all Triangles in sts and in ends of rows, ch 1, evenly space 106 [118, 130] sc across, turn.

Row 2: Ch 1, sc in each of first 3 sts, (sc next st, sc next 2 sts tog) across to last 4 sts, sc in last 4 sts, turn. **Do not fasten off.** *(73) [81, 89]*

Bodice
Row 1: Ch 1, sc in each st across, turn.

Row 2: For **Ribbon Casing,** ch 4, tr in each st across, turn.

Row 3: For **Left Back,** ch 1, sc in first 16 [17, 18] sts leaving remaining sts unworked, turn. *Front of row 3 is right side of work.*

Rows 4–20: Ch 1, sc in each st across, turn. At end of last row, fasten off.

Row 3: For **Front,** skip next 4 [6, 8] unworked sts on row 2; join with sc in next st, sc in next 32 [34, 36] sts leaving remaining sts unworked, turn. *(33) [35, 37]*

Rows 4–13: Ch 1, sc in each st across, turn.

Row 14: For **First Shoulder,** ch 1, sc in first 10 [11, 12] sts leaving remaining sts unworked, turn.

Row 15: Ch 1, skip first st, sc in each st across, turn. *(9) [10, 11]*

Row 16: Ch 1, sc in each st across to last 2 sts, sc last 2 sts tog, turn. *(8) [9, 10]*

Rows 17–20: Ch 1, sc in each st across, turn. At end of last row, fasten off. **Do not turn.**

Row 14: For **Neck Edge,** skip next 13 unworked sts on row 13 of Front; for **Second Shoulder,** join with sc in next st, sc in each st across, turn. *(10) [11, 12]*

Row 15: Ch 1, sc in each st across to last 2 sts, sc last 2 sts tog, turn. *(9) [10, 11]*

Row 16: Ch 1, skip first st, sc in each st across, turn. *(8) [9, 10]*

Rows 17–20: Ch 1, sc in each st across, turn. At end of last row, fasten off.

Row 3: For **Right Back,** skip next 4 [6, 8] unworked

sts on row 2; join with sc in next st, sc in each st across, turn. *(16) [17, 18]*

Rows 4–20: Ch 1, sc in each st across, turn. At end of last row, fasten off.
For Shoulder seams, matching sts on last rows, sew Front Shoulders to each Back.

Neck Band
Row 1: With E hook, join with sc in first st at left back corner of neckline, evenly space 44 more sc around neckline to last st at right back corner, turn. *(45 sc made)*

Row 2: Ch 3, dc in each st across, turn.

Row 3: Ch 1, sc in each st across, turn.

Row 4: Ch 1, sc in first st, (skip next st, 5 dc in next st, skip next st, sc in next st) across, **do not turn or fasten off.**

Button Placket
Row 1: Working in ends of rows on Left Back edge, ch 1, sc in each sc row, 3 sc in tr row and 2 sc in dc row across to row 1 on Bodice, turn. *(27 sc made)*

Row 2: Ch 1, sc in each st across. Fasten off.

Buttonhole Placket
Row 1: Working in ends of rows on Right Back edge, with E hook, join with sl st in first st of row 4 on Neck Band and repeat row 1 of Button Placket.

Row 2: Ch 1, sc in each of first 2 sts, *ch 1, skip next st *(buttonhole made),* sc in next 10 sts; repeat from *, ch 1, skip next st, sc in each of last 2 sts. Fasten off.
Lapping Buttonhole Placket over Button Placket, match and sew ends of rows on Skirt together.
Sew buttons to Button Placket to match buttonholes.

Sleeve (make 2)
Row 1: Ch 40, sc in second ch from hook, sc next 2 chs tog, sc in next 6 chs, 3 sc in next ch, sc in next 8 chs, **dec** *(see Special Stitch for Cape on page 115),* sc in next 8 chs, 3 sc in next ch, sc in next 6 chs, sc next 2 chs tog, sc in last ch, turn. *(39 sc made)*

Rows 2–3: Ch 1, sc first 2 sts tog, sc in next 7 sts, 3 sc in next st, sc in next 8 sts, dec, sc in next 8 sts, 3 sc in next st, sc in next 7 sts, sc last 2 sts tog, turn.

Row 4: Ch 4, skip next st, dc in next st, (ch 1, skip next st, dc in next st) 3 times, dc in next point st, dc in next st, (ch 1, skip next st, dc in next st) 4 times, skip next st, dc in next st, (ch 1, skip next st, dc in next st) 4 times, dc in next point st, dc in next st, (ch 1, skip next st, dc in next st) 4 times, turn. *(38 sts and ch sps)*

Row 5: Working in sts and in ch sps, ch 1, sc first st and next ch sp tog, sc in next 7 sts and ch sps, 3 sc in next st, sc in next 8 sts and ch sps, sc next 2 sts tog, sc in next 8 sts and ch sps, 3 sc in next st, sc in next 7 sts and ch sps, sc next 2 chs of ch-4 tog, turn. *(39 sc)*

• • • • • • • • • • • • • • • • • • Continued on page 118

Winter Wonder Ensemble

Continued from page 117

Rows 6–22 [6–25, 6–29]: Or to desired length; repeat rows 2–5 consecutively, ending with row 2 [5, 5]. Fasten off.

For Underarm seam, sew ends of rows together.

Top Fill-In Triangles

Working in last row of Sleeve, work Cape Second Fill-In Triangle in each space between points. At end of last row, **do not fasten off.**

For **Top Edge,** working in ends of rows and in sts of Fill-In Triangles, ch 1, evenly space 24 sc around, join with sl st in first sc. Fasten off.

Bottom Fill-In Triangles

Working in remaining lps on opposite side of starting ch on Sleeve, work Cape Second Fill-In Triangle in each space between points. At end of last row, **do not fasten off.**

Wristband

Rnd 1: Working around edge in ends of rows and in sts of Bottom Fill-In Triangles, with E hook, ch 1, evenly space 24 sc around, join with sl st in first sc, **turn.**

Rnd 2: Ch 3, dc in each st around, join with sl st in top of ch-3, **turn.**

Rnds 3–4: Ch 3, **dc front post (dc fp—see Stitch Guide)** around next st, **dc back post (dc bp—see Stitch Guide)** around next st, dc fp around next st, (dc bp around next st, dc fp around next st) around, join, **turn.** At end of last rnd, fasten off.

Easing Top Edge to fit, sew Sleeves in armholes on Bodice.

Vertical Ruffles

Work Cape Vertical Ruffle across each decrease section and across center back seam of Skirt on Dress.

Bodice Vertical Ruffles

Row 1: For **First Ruffle,** holding yarn behind work, join with sl st in center st on row 3 of Bodice Front, sl st in next 9 rows. Fasten off.

Row 2: Repeat row 2 of Cape Vertical Ruffle on page 116.

For **Second Ruffle,** skip four sts to the left of First Ruffle and repeat First Ruffle.

For **Third Ruffle,** skip four sts to the right of First Ruffle and repeat First Ruffle.

Dress Finishing

Weave ⅜" ribbon through sts of row 2 on Bodice leaving ½" ends. Fold ends to wrong side and tack in place. Repeat in each beading row on Skirt and Sleeves.

Weave ¼" ribbon through row 2 of Neck Band. Secure ends same as on Skirt.

Make and attach ribbon Bows same as for Cape.

BOOTIE (make 2)

Vamp

Row 1: Ch 7, sc in second ch from hook, sc in each ch across, turn. *(6 sc made)*

Row 2: Ch 1, 2 sc in first st, sc in next 4 sts, 2 sc in last st, turn. *(8)*

Rows 3–6 [3–7, 3–8]: Ch 1, sc in each st across, turn. At end of last row, fasten off.

Sole

Rows 1–2: Repeat rows 1–2 of Vamp.

Rows 3–12 [3–13, 3–14]: Ch 1, sc in each st across, turn. At end of last row, fasten off.

Sides

Rnd 1: Working around outer edge of Sole, join with sc in fourth st on last row, sc in each st and in end of each row around, join with sl st in first sc, **turn.** *(38 sc made)* [40 sc made, 42 sc made]

Rnds 2–3: Ch 1, sc in each st around, join, **turn.**

Rnd 4: To join Sides and Vamp, ch 1, sc in first 10 sts, sc next st and first st on last row of Vamp tog, sc in next 6 sts on Vamp; skipping next 16 [18, 20] sts on Sides, sc last st on Vamp and next st on Sides tog, sc in last 10 sts on Sides, join, **turn.** *(28)*

Rnd 5: Ch 3, dc in each st around, join with sl st in top of ch-3. Fasten off.

Sew sts and ends of rows on Vamp to Skipped sts on rnd 4.

Top

Rows 1–7: Work rows 1–7 of Dress Sleeve on page 117. At end of last row, fasten off.

Top Fill-In Triangles

Working in remaining lps on opposite side of starting ch on Top, work Cape Skirt Second Fill-In Triangle *(see page 115)* in spaces between points. At end of last row, **do not fasten off.**

For **Bottom Edge,** working across edge of Fill-In Triangles, ch 1, sc in each st and in end of each row across. Fasten off.

Finishing

Sew ends of rows on Top together. Easing Bottom Edge to fit, sew Top and Sides together.

Weave ⅜" ribbon through beading row and secure ends same as for Cape Skirt.

Make two ribbon Bows same as for Cape. Sew Bows to ⅜" ribbon at point on each side of Top.

Cut 20" piece from ¼" ribbon. Beginning and ending at center front, weave through sts of rnd 5 on Sides. Tie ends in bow. ✪

CHAPTER 6

Shower Stoppers

Pat A Cake

Pat a cake, pat a cake, baker's man,
Bake me a cake as fast as you can.
Roll it and pat it, and mark it with a B,
And put it in the oven for baby and me.

A variation of this ever-popular hand clapping game was widely known as early as 1698.

Baby Bow Trims

Designed by Barbara Anderson

Finished Size: Baby is 3½" tall.

Materials For Both:
- ❑ Baby yarn:
  - 2 oz. lt. peach
  - Small amount each of white, lt. blue and lt. pink
- ❑ Black and pink embroidery floss
- ❑ 4 black 6mm beads
- ❑ 4 small gold safety pins
- ❑ 1 blue and 1 pink 4½" gift bow
- ❑ Powdered blush
- ❑ Polyester fiberfill
- ❑ Tapestry and embroidery needles
- ❑ D hook or hook needed to obtain gauge

Gauge: 5 sc = 1; 6 sc rows = 1".

Basic Stitches: Ch, sl st, sc, hdc.

Note: Work in continuous rnds; do not join or turn unless otherwise stated. Mark first st of each rnd.

BABY (make 2)
Head
Rnd 1: With lt. peach, ch 2, 5 sc in second ch from hook. *(5 sc made)*

Rnd 2: 2 sc in first st, sc in each of next 3 sts, 2 sc in last st. *(7)*

Rnd 3: Sc in each of first 2 sts; for **Top**, 2 sc in each of next 3 sts; sc in each of last 2 sts. *(10)*

Rnd 4: Sc in each of first 2 sts, 2 sc in each of next 6 sts, sc in each of last 2 sts. *(16)*

Rnd 5: Sc in each of first 2 sts, 2 sc in each of next 12 sts, sc in each of last 2 sts. *(28)*

Rnd 6: Sc in each of first 3 sts; for **Cheek**, 2 sc in each of next 4 sts; sc in next 14 sts; for **Cheek**, 2 sc in each of next 4 sts; sc in each of last 3 sts. *(36)*

Rnd 7: Sc in each st around.

Rnd 8: Sc in each of first 3 sts, (sc next 2 sts tog) 4 times, sc in next 14 sts, (sc next 2 sts tog) 4 times, sc in each of last 3 sts. *(28)*

Rnds 9–14: Sc in each st around.

Rnd 15: (Sc next 2 sts tog) 2 times, (sc in next st, sc next 2 sts tog) around. *(18)*

Rnd 16: Sc in each st around. Stuff.

Rnd 17: (Sc next 2 sts tog) around. *(9)*

Rnd 18: Sc in each st around, join with sl st in first sc. Fasten off. Sew opening closed.

Facial Features
With two strands lt. peach held together, using satin stitch *(see Stitch Guide),* working from side to side, embroider ¼" nose over rnd 1 of Head according to photo.

With three strands pink floss, using outline stitch *(see Stitch Guide),* embroider mouth between rnds 4 and 5.

With black floss, sew beads 1" apart above Cheeks between rnds 4 and 5 for eyes.

For **Sculpting**, thread tapestry needle with lt. peach yarn. Leaving 6" end, insert needle under one bead, push needle through Head and out under second bead, make a small stitch and push needle back through Head and out under first bead. Pull thread until beads are ¾" apart. Tie ends of thread to secure and hide ends inside Head.

Apply powdered blush to each Cheek *(see photo)*.

Body

Rnd 1: With lt. peach, ch 10, sl st in first ch to form ring, ch 1, sc in each ch around. *(10 sc made)*

Rnd 2: Sc in each st around.

Rnd 3: Sc in each of first 3 sts; for **Tummy,** 2 sc in each of next 4 sts; sc in leach of last 3 sts. *(14)*

Rnd 4: (2 sc in next st, sc in next st) around. *(21)*

Rnds 5–8: Sc in each st around.

Rnd 9: (Sc next 2 sts tog, sc in next st) around. *(14)*

Rnd 10: Sc in each st around.

Rnd 11: (Sc next 2 sts tog) around. *(7)*

Rnd 12: (Sc next 2 sts tog) 3 times, sc in last st, join with sl st in first sc. Fasten off. Sew opening closed. Stuff.

With Tummy in front, sew bottom of rnds 8–13 on Head to rnd 1 on Body.

Arm (make 2)

Rnd 1: With lt. peach, ch 7, sl st in first ch to form ring, ch 1, sc in each ch around. *(7 sc made)*

Rnds 2–4: Sc in each st around.

Rnd 5: For **Hand,** sc in first st, (2 sc in next st, sc in next st) around. *(10)*

Rnds 6–7: Sc in each st around.

Rnd 8: (Sc next 2 sts tog) around, join with sl st in first sc. Fasten off. Sew opening closed. Stuff.

Sew rnd 1 of Arms over rnds 2–4 on each side of Body.

Foot & Leg (make 2)

Rnd 1: With lt. peach, ch 4, 2 sc in second ch from hook, sc in next ch, 3 hdc in last ch; working in remaining lps on opposite side of starting ch, 2 hdc in next ch, sc in next ch, 2 sc in last ch. *(11 sts made)*

Rnd 2: Sc in each st around.

Rnd 3: Sc in first 4 sts, (sc next 2 sts tog) 2 times, sc in each of last 3 sts. *(9)*

Rnd 4: Sc in first 4 sts, sc next 2 sts tog, sc in each of last 3 sts. *(8)*

Rnd 5: Sc in each st around.

Rnd 6: Sc in each of first 2 sts, 2 sc in each of next 4 sts, sc in each of last 2 sts. *(12)*

Rnds 7–8: Sc in each st around.

Rnd 9: (Sc next 2 sts tog) around, join with sl st in first sc. Fasten off. Stuff. Sew opening closed.

With Foot pointing up *(see photo)*, sew rnds 8–9 of Legs over rnds 8–11 on each side of Body.

DIAPER (make 2)

Row 1: With white, ch 5, sc in second ch from hook, sc in each ch across, turn. *(4 sc made)*

Rows 2–3: Ch 1, sc in each st across, turn.

Rows 4–11: Ch 1, 2 sc in first st, sc in each st across to last st, 2 sc in last st, turn. At end of last row, fasten off. *(20)*

With row 1 in front, place Diaper on one Baby, lap each end of row 11 over each end of row 1 and tack in place. Fasten safety pins over tacked ends of Diaper. Repeat on other Baby.

NECK TIE (make 1 lt. pink, 1 lt. blue)

Ch 55. Fasten off. Tie in bow around Baby's neck.

GIRL'S HEAD BOW

With lt. pink, ch 24. Fasten off. Tie in bow and tack to top of Girl Baby's Head. ✪

Baby's Bunting & Bonnet

Bunting Designed by Ruth Holloway
Bonnet Designed by Deborah Levy-Hamburg

Finished Size: Fits up to 12 mos.

Materials:
- ❑ 12 oz. pink baby yarn
- ❑ Ribbon:
    - 3 yds. pink ¼-wide
    - 1 yd. pink ⅜"-wide
- ❑ 2" piece cardboard
- ❑ Tapestry needle
- ❑ G and I hooks or hooks needed to obtain gauges

Gauges: G hook, 2 shells and 2 dc = 2"; 5 pattern rows = 2". **I hook,** 2 shells and 2 dc = 2½"; 4 pattern rows = 2".

Basic Stitches: Ch, sl st, sc, dc.

Special Stitch: For **shell,** 5 dc in specified ch or st.

BUNTING
Center
Row 1: With I hook, ch 140, dc in fourth ch from hook, (skip next 2 chs, **shell**—*see Special Stitch*—in next ch, skip next 2 chs, dc in each of next 2 chs) across to last 3 chs, skip next 2 chs, 3 dc in last ch, turn. *(19 shells, 43 dc made)*

Rows 2–52: Ch 3, dc in next st, skip next st, shell in sp between next 2 sts, skip next 2 sts on next shell, dc in each of next 2 sts, skip next st) across to last 2 sts, 3 dc in sp between last 2 sts, turn. At end of last row, **do not turn or fasten off.**

Border
Rnd 1: Working in ends of rows and in sts around outer edge of Center, with I hook, ch 1, *3 sc in next row *(corner made),* evenly space 55 sc across edge to last row, 3 sc in last row *(corner made)**; working in remaining lps on opposite side of starting ch, evenly space 83 sc across edge; repeat between first *, evenly space 83 sc across last row, join with sl st in first sc. *(288 sc made)*

NOTE: Work remaining rows of Border in **back lps** *(see Stitch Guide).*

Rnds 2–8: Ch 1, sc in each st around with 3 sc in center st of each corner, join. At end of last rnd *(344).*

Rnd 9: Sl st in each st across to center st of next corner, (sl st, ch 3, 4 dc) in center st of corner, skip next st, shell in next st, *[skip next 2 sts, dc in each of next 2 sts, skip next 2 sts, (shell in next st, skip next 2 sts, dc in each of next 2 sts, skip next 2 sts) across to next 3 corner sts], shell in next st, skip next st, shell in next st; repeat from * 2 more times; repeat between [ ], join. Fasten off.

Cut 2¼ yds. from ¼" ribbon. Fold Bunting piece in half, matching sts and shells; starting at one corner, lace ribbon through sts along both edges across to middle of Bunting edge *(see photo).* Tie ends of ribbon in bow. Trim ends to desired length.

Working on bottom edge, weave ⅜" ribbon through sts along edge; pull tight to gather edge. Tie ends of ribbon in bow. Trim ends to desired length.

BONNET
Row 1: With G hook, ch 73, shell in third ch from hook, (skip next 2 chs, dc in each of next 2 chs, skip next 2 chs, shell in next ch) across, turn. *(11 shells, 29 dc made) Beginning ch-2 is not counted or used as a st.*

Row 2: Ch 2, skip first st, dc in each of next 2 sts, (skip next 2 sts, shell in sp between next 2 sts, skip next st on next shell, dc in each of next 2 sts) across leaving last 2 sts unworked, turn.

Row 3: Ch 2, shell in sp between first 2 sts, (skip next st on next shell, dc in each of next 2 sts, skip next 2 sts, shell in sp between next 2 sts) across turn.

Rows 4–15: Repeat rows 2 and 3 alternately.

Row 16: Ch 5, skip first 2 sts, dc in next st, ch 1, skip next st, dc in next st, ch 1, dc in sp between next 2 sts, *ch 1, dc in next st on next shell, (ch 1, skip next st, dc in next st) 2 times, ch 1, dc in sp between next 2 sts; repeat from * across to last shell, dc in next st on last shell, ch 1, skip next st, dc in next st leaving last 2 sts unworked, turn. *(41 ch sps)*

Row 17: Ch 2, shell in first ch sp, (skip next ch sp, 2 dc in next ch sp, skip next ch sp, shell in next ch sp) across, sl st in same ch sp as last shell. Fasten off.

Fold row 1 in half, matching shells; sew edges together forming center back seam.

Weave remaining ribbon through sts on row 16, leaving ends long for tying.

POM-POM
Wrap yarn around cardboard about 50 times. Slide loops off cardboard and tie a separate strand of yarn around center of all loops. Cut ends of loops. Trim to shape.

Sew Pom-pom to end of center back seam at top of Bonnet. ✪

Bubble Bath Bear Bag

Designed by Michele Wilcox

Finished Size: 10½" × 11¼" without Handles.

Materials:
- ❏ Worsted yarn:
    - 8 oz. blue
    - 1 oz. each of off-white, lt. brown, tan and white
    - Small amount each of yellow, lt. beige, lt. pink, dk. pink, black and orange
- ❏ Polyester fiberfill
- ❏ Items for optional Lining:
    - ⅓ yd. lightweight vinyl or fabric
    - 2 standard-size sheets plastic canvas
    - Sewing needle and thread to match fabric
- ❏ Tapestry needle
- ❏ F hook or hook needed to obtain gauge

Gauge: 9 sc = 2"; 9 sc rows = 2".

Basic Stitches: Ch, sl st, sc, dc.

BACK
Row 1: With blue, ch 46, sc in second ch from hook, sc in each ch across, turn. *(45 sc made)*
Rows 2–49: Ch 1, sc in each st across, turn.
Rnd 50: Working around outer edge, ch 1, sc in each st and in end of each row around with 3 sc in each corner, join with sl st in first sc. Fasten off.

LINING (optional)
From vinyl or fabric, using crochet piece as pattern, cut two pieces ½" larger around all edges. Allowing ½" for seams, sew pieces right sides together around side and bottom edges. Fold top edge down ½" and press.

For reinforced Lining, cut two pieces from plastic canvas slightly smaller than outer edge of crochet piece. Sew side and bottom edges together with blue yarn. This Lining can be used alone or with fabric Lining.

FRONT
Row 1: With tan, ch 46, sc in second ch from hook, sc in each ch across, turn. *(45 sc made)*
Rows 2–16: Ch 1, sc in each st across, turn. At end of last row, fasten off.

Row 17: Join blue with sc in first st, sc in each st across, turn.
NOTE: *When changing colors (see Stitch Guide), drop first color to wrong side of work, pick up when needed. Fasten off each color when no longer needed.*
Row 18: Ch 1, sc in each of first 3 sts changing to lt. pink in last st made, sc in next st changing to blue, (sc in each of next 3 sts changing to lt. pink in last st made, sc in next st changing to blue) 10 times, sc in last st, turn.
Row 19: Ch 1, sc in each st across, turn.
Rows 20–49: Repeat rows 18 and 19 alternately.
Rnd 50: Working in rnds, changing colors to match colors on outer edge of piece, ch 1, sc in each st and in end of each row around with 3 sc in each corner, join with sl st in first sc. Fasten off.
Rnd 51: Working in **front lps** *(see Stitch Guide)*, join lt. pink with sc in any st, ch 3, skip next st, (sc in next st, ch 3, skip next st) around, join with sl st in first sc. Fasten off.

HANDLE (make 2)
Row 1: With blue, ch 6, sc in second ch from hook, sc in each ch across, turn. *(5 sc made)*
Rows 2–48: Ch 1, sc in each st across, turn.
Rnd 49: Working around outer edge, ch 1, sc in each st and in end of each row around with 3 sc in each corner, join with sl st in first sc. Fasten off.

APPLIQUÉS
Bear's Body & Head
Row 1: With lt. brown, ch 10, sc in second ch from hook, sc in each ch across, turn. *(9 sc made)*
Rows 2–3: Ch 1, sc in each st across, turn.
Row 4: Ch 1, sc first 2 sts tog, sc in each st across to last 2 sts, sc last 2 sts tog, turn. *(7)*
Row 5: Ch 1, sc in each st across, turn.
Rows 6–7: Repeat row 4. At end of last row *(3)*.
Rows 8–10: Ch 1, 2 sc in first st, sc in each st across to last st, 2 sc in last st, turn. At end of last row *(9)*.
Rows 11–13: Ch 1, sc in each st across, turn.
Rows 14–15: Repeat row 4. At end of last row, **do not turn**.

• • • • • • • • • • • • • • • • Continued on page 126

Bubble Bath Bear Bag

Continued from page 124

Rnd 16: Working around outer edge, ch 1, sc in end of each row and in each st around with 3 sc in each bottom corner, join with sl st in first sc. Fasten off.

Bear's Ear (make 2)
Row 1: With lt. brown, ch 2, 6 sc in second ch from hook, turn. *(6 sc made)*
Row 2: Ch 1, 2 sc in each st across. Fasten off.

Bear's Arm
Row 1: With lt. brown, ch 4, sc in second ch from hook, sc in each ch across, turn. *(3 sc made)*
Rows 2–12: Ch 1, sc in each st across, turn.
Row 13: Ch 1, sc 3 sts tog. Fasten off.

Bear's Muzzle
Rnd 1: With lt. beige, ch 2, 6 sc in second ch from hook, **do not join rnd.** *(6 sc made)*
Rnd 2: (Sc in next st, 2 sc in next st) around, join with sl st in first sc. Fasten off.
Sew to Bear's Head over rnds 9–12 *(see photo).*
With black, using satin stitch *(see Stitch Guide),* embroider eyes on row 12 of Head ¾" apart and embroider nose over top half of rnd 1 on Muzzle.
With black, using straight stitch, embroider mouth over bottom half of rnds 1 and 2 as shown in photo.

Brush
With dk. pink, ch 12, sc in second ch from hook, sc in each of next 2 chs, sl st in next 4 chs, dc in each of next 3 chs, sc in last ch. Fasten off.

Duck
Row 1: With yellow, ch 6, sc in second ch from hook, sc in each ch across, turn. *(5 sc made)*
Row 2: Ch 1, 2 sc in first st, sc in each st across to last st, 2 sc in last st, turn. *(7)*
Row 3: Ch 1, sc in each st across, turn.
Row 4: Ch 1, sc first 2 sts tog, sc in next st leaving last 4 sts unworked, turn. *(2)*
Row 5: Ch 1, 2 sc in each st across, turn. *(4)*
Row 6: Ch 1, sc 4 sts tog. Fasten off.
With black, using French knot *(see Stitch Guide),* embroider eye on row 5.

Tub
Row 1: With off-white, ch 20, sc in second ch from hook, sc in each ch across, turn. *(19 sc made)*
Row 2: Ch 1, 2 sc in first st, sc in each st across to last st, 2 sc in last st, turn. *(21)*
Row 3: Ch 1, sc in each st across, turn.
Rows 4–7: Repeat rows 2 and 3 alternately. At end of last row *(25).*

Rows 8–12: Ch 1, sc in each st across, turn.
Row 13: Ch 1, 2 sc in first st, (sc in next st, 2 sc in next st) across, **do not turn.** *(38)*
Rnd 14: Working around outer edge, ch 1 sc in end of each row and in each st around, join with sl st in first sc. Fasten off.

Tub Leg (make 2)
Rnd 1: With off-white, ch 2, 6 sc in second ch from hook, **do not join rnds.** *(6 sc made)*
Rnds 2–3: Sc in each st around.
Rnd 4: (Sc in next st, 2 sc in next st) around. *(9)*
Rnds 5–6: Sc in each st around. At end of last rnd, fasten off. Sew opening closed.

Bubbles
For **Large Bubbles,** with white, (ch 4, 5 dc in fourth ch from hook, drop lp from hook, insert hook in top of ch-4, pull dropped lp through) 39 times. Fasten off.
For **Small Bubbles,** with white, (ch 3, 3 dc in third ch from hook, drop lp from hook, insert hook in top of ch-3, pull dropped lp through) 10 times. Fasten off.

Appliqué Assembly
Fold center of last 4 rows down forming rim of Tub as shown in photo; tack edge in place to side of Tub.
Sew side and bottom edges of Tub over rows 11–26 on Front.
Insert rows 1 and 2 of Bear's Body inside one end of Tub. Stuffing Head lightly, sew Body & Head in place.
Sew remaining Appliqué pieces on Front as shown in photo.
With orange, using lazy-daisy stitch *(see Stitch Guide),* embroider beak on Duck as shown in photo.
With black, using straight stitch, embroider bristles on Brush.

FINISHING
Hold Front and Back wrong sides together, matching sts and rows; working in **back lps** *(see illustration),* sew side and bottom edges together.

Insert desired Linings into finished Bag, sew top edge to inside of Bag.
Sew each end of one Handle to top edge of Front 2" apart. Repeat on Back. ✪

Bathtime Buddy

Designed by Ann Parnell

Finished Size: 5" wide and 11" long.

Materials:
- ❏ 4-ply cotton worsted yarn:
  - 2½ oz. green
  - 1 oz. orange
- ❏ Buttons:
  - 2 white ¾" flat
  - 2 black ⅝" flat
- ❏ Black sewing thread
- ❏ Tapestry and sewing needles
- ❏ G hook or hook needed to obtain gauge

Gauge: 4 sc = 1"; 9 sc rows = 2".

Basic Stitches: Ch, sl st, sc.

TOP
Row 1: With green, ch 23, sc in second ch from hook, sc in each ch across, turn. *(22 sc made)*
Rows 2–5: Ch 1, skip first st, sc in each st across, turn. At end of last row *(18)*.
Rows 6–37: Ch 1, sc in each st across, turn.
Rows 38–39: Ch 1, skip first st, sc in each st across, turn. *(17, 16)*
Rows 40–41: Ch 1, sc in each st across, turn.
Rows 42–43: Ch 1, skip first st, sc in each st across, turn. *(15, 14)*
Rows 44–45: Ch 1, sc in each st across, turn.
Rows 46–49: Ch 1, skip first st, sc in each st across, turn. At end of last row *(10)*.
Row 50: Ch 1, skip first st, sc in next st, (skip next st, sc in next st) across. Fasten off.

BOTTOM
Rows 1–33: Repeat rows 1–33 of Top.
Row 34: Ch 1, skip first st, sl st in next st, ch 1, sc in next 15 sts leaving last st unworked, turn. *(15 sc)*
Rows 35–41: Ch 1, skip first st, sc in each st across, turn. At end of last row *(8)*.
Row 42: Ch 1, skip first st, sc in next st, (skip next st, sc in next st) across. Fasten off.

MOUTH
Row 1: With orange, ch 5, 2 sc in second ch from hook, 2 sc in each ch across, turn. *(8 sc made)*
Rows 2–9: Ch 1, sc in each st across to last st, 2 sc in last st, turn. At end of last row *(16)*.
Row 10: Ch 1, sc in each st across, turn.
Row 11: Working this row in **back lps** *(see Stitch Guide)*, for **Fold,** ch 1, sc in each st across, turn.
Rows 12–19: Ch 1, sc in each st across, turn.
Rows 20–28: Repeat rows 42-50 of Top.

FINISHING
For **Eyes,** place each black button over each white button, matching holes. With black sewing thread, sew Eyes centered over rows 34–37 of Top about 1" apart.

Sew ends of rows 1–33 on Top and Bottom together.

Match row 1 of Mouth to row 42 of Bottom, match row 28 of Mouth to row 50 of Top and match fold to end of side seams; easing to fit, sew edges of Mouth to Bottom and Top.

For **Hanger,** with orange, ch 10. Leaving an 8" end for sewing, fasten off.

Fold Hanger in half and sew ends to rnd 1 on inside at one seam. ✪

Sweet Tees Trimmings

Designed by Rosemarie Walter

Girl's Tee Trim

Finished Size: Fits small infant shirt.

Materials:
- ❏ 150 yds. white size 10 crochet cotton thread
- ❏ 1 small pink infant T-shirt
- ❏ 4 small pink ribbon roses
- ❏ 2¼ yds. of pink ¼" picot ribbon
- ❏ White sewing thread
- ❏ Sewing needle
- ❏ No. 9 steel hook or hook needed to obtain gauge

Gauge: 3 dtr groups = 1"; dtr is ⅝" tall.

Basic Stitches: Ch, sl st, sc, dc, dtr *(see Stitch Guide).*

BOTTOM RUFFLE
Rnd 1: Inserting hook through fabric as you work, join with sc at center back of bottom edge on shirt; spacing sts ¼" apart, ch 3, (sc, ch 3) 65 times around edge, join with sl st in first sc. *(66 ch sps made)*

Rnd 2: (Sl st, ch 5, 2 dtr) in first ch sp, 3 dtr in each ch sp around, join with sl st in top of ch-5.

Rnd 3: For **Beading,** (sl st, ch 1, sc) in next st, ch 4, sc in next sp between dtr groups, ch 4, (sc in center st of next dtr group, ch 4, sc in next sp between dtr groups, ch 4) around, join with sl st in first sc.

Rnd 4: (Sl st, ch 1, 3 sc) in first ch sp, ch 1, (3 sc in next ch sp, ch 1) around, join. Fasten off.

SLEEVE RUFFLES
Rnd 1: Working around edge of shirt sleeve, join with sc at underarm seam; spacing sts ¼" apart, ch 3, (sc, ch 3) 26 times around edge, join with sl st in first sc. *(27 ch sps made)*

Rnds 2–4: Repeat rnds 2–4 of Bottom Ruffle. Repeat on other shirt sleeve.

FRONT RUFFLE
Row 1: For **Center Casing,** ch 6, dc in sixth ch from hook, turn. *(5 chs count as first dc and ch sp—2 dc made.)*

Rows 2–27: Ch 4 *(counts as first dc and ch sp),* skip next ch, dc in next ch, turn. At end of last row, **do not turn.** *(2 dc, 1 ch sp)*

Rnd 28: Working in ends of rows along side of Center Casing, (ch 5, 2 dtr) in next row, 3 dtr in each row across to row 1, (2 dtr, ch 5, sl st) in end of row 1, ch 2; working along opposite side of Center Casing, (sl st, ch 5, 2 dtr) in end of row 1, 3 dtr in each row across to last row, (2 dtr, ch 5, sl st) in end of last row, ch 2, join with sl st in last dc of last row.

Rnd 29: Sl st in each ch of first ch-5, *ch 4, (sc in next sp between dtr groups, ch 4, sc in center st of next dtr group, ch 4) 25 times, sc in next sp between dtr groups, ch 4, sl st in each ch of next ch-5, ch 2, sl st in next ch-2 sp*, ch 2, sl st in each ch of next ch-5; repeat between first *, ch 2, join with sl st in first sl st.

Rnd 30: Covering sl sts, ch 1, 5 sc in first ch-5 sp of rnd 28, 5 sc in first ch-4 sp of last rnd, *(ch 1, 3 sc) in each ch-4 sp across to next ch-5 sp of rnd 28, 5 sc in next ch-5 sp, ch 1, sc in each of next 2 ch-2 sps, ch 1*, 5 sc in next ch-5 sp of rnd 28; repeat between first *, join with sl st in first sc. Fasten off.

FINISHING
Cut piece from ribbon 1" longer than Center Casing. Weave ribbon through Center Casing, going over three rows and under one. Fold ends to wrong side of Casing and tack in place.

Cut two pieces from ribbon to fit Beading on each Sleeve. Weave through ch sps on Beading rnds. Overlap ends and tack together on wrong side of Sleeves.

Cut one piece from ribbon to fit Beading on Bottom Ruffle and weave same as on Sleeves.

Sew ribbon roses evenly spaced across Center Casing. Sew Front Ruffle to center front of T-shirt *(see photo).*

Girl's Panties Trim

Finished Size: 7½" across.

- ❏ Size 10 crochet cotton thread:
  - 40 yds. white
  - 30 yds. pink
- ❏ 1 pair of small pink infant panties
- ❏ 2 small pink ribbon roses

Continued on page 130

Sweet Tees Trimmings

Continued from page 129

❑ 23" of pink ¼" picot ribbon
❑ White sewing thread
❑ Sewing needle
❑ No. 9 steel hook or hook needed to obtain gauge

Gauge: 3 dtr groups = 1"; dtr is ⅝" tall.

Basic Stitches: Ch, sl st, sc, dc, dtr *(see Stitch Guide).*

CENTER CASING
Row 1: With pink, ch 6, dc in sixth ch from hook, turn. *(5 chs count as first dc and ch sp—2 dc made.)*
Rows 2–26: Ch 4 *(counts as first dc and ch sp),* skip next ch, dc in next ch, turn. At end of last row, **do not turn.** *(2 dc, 1 ch sp)*

TOP EDGING
Row 1: Working in ends of rows along side of Center Casing, (ch 4, sc in next row) across to row 1, ch 4, (sc, ch 4, sc) in end of row 1, turn.
Row 2: (Ch 1, 3 sc) in each ch sp across. Fasten off.

BOTTOM RUFFLE
Row 1: Working in ends of rows on opposite side of Center Casing, join white with sl st in end of row 1, (ch 5, 2 dtr) in same row, 3 dtr in each row across, turn.
Row 2: For **Beading,** ch 4, sc in center st of next dtr group, (ch 4, sc in next sp between dtr groups, ch 4, sc in center st of next dtr group) across, ch 4, sc in last st of last dtr group, turn.
Row 3: (Sl st, ch 1, 3 sc) in first ch sp, (ch 1, 3 sc) in each ch sp across. Fasten off.

FINISHING
Cut piece from ribbon 1" longer than Center Casing. Weave ribbon through Center Casing, going over two rows and under one. Fold ends to wrong side of Casing and tack in place.
Weave remaining ribbon through ch sps on Beading row, fold ends to wrong side and tack in place.
Sew ribbon roses to each end of Center Casing. Sew Center Casing across back of panties just above leg openings *(see photo).*

Girl's Sock Trim

Materials:
❑ 75 yds. white size 10 crochet cotton thread
❑ 1 pair pink infant socks
❑ 2 small pink ribbon roses
❑ 24" of pink ¼" picot ribbon
❑ White sewing thread

❑ Sewing needle
❑ No. 9 steel hook or hook needed to obtain gauge

Gauge: 3 dtr groups = 1"; dtr is ⅝" tall.

Basic Stitches: Ch, sl st, sc, dc, dtr *(see Stitch Guide).*

RUFFLE
Rnd 1: Fold top of sock down to form cuff. Inserting hook through fabric as you work, join with sc at center back of edge on sock; spacing sts ¼" apart, ch 3, (sc, ch 3) 19 times around edge, join with sl st in first sc. *(20 ch sps made)*
Rnds 2–4: Work rnds 2–4 of Bottom Ruffle for Girl's Tee Trim.
Repeat on other sock.

FINISHING
Cut ribbon in half. Weave each piece through Beading on each Ruffle. Overlap ends and tack together on wrong side.
Sew ribbon roses to each outer side of each cuff *(see photo).*

Boy's Tee Trim
Finished Size: Fits small infant shirt.

❑ Size 10 crochet cotton thread:
    40 yds. white
    25 yds. med. blue
    20 yds. dk. blue
❑ 1 small white infant T-shirt
❑ 5 dk. blue ⅜" flat buttons
❑ White and dk. blue sewing thread
❑ Sewing needle
❑ No. 7 steel hook or hook needed to obtain gauge

Gauge: 7 dc = 1"; 4 dc rows = 1".

Basic Stitches: Ch, sl st, sc, dc.

BUTTON PLACKET
Row 1: With white, ch 6, dc in fourth ch from hook, dc in each ch across, turn. *(4 dc made)*
Rows 2–29: Ch 3, dc in each st across, turn. At end of last row, **do not turn.**
Row 30: Working in ends of rows, ch 3, dc in next row, 2 dc in each row across to row 1, dc in end of row 1, ch 3; working in remaining lps on opposite side of starting ch, sl st in each ch across, ch 3; working in ends of rows, dc in end of row 1, 2 dc in each row across, turn.
Row 31: Working in **front lps** *(see Stitch Guide),* ch 3, dc in next 56 sts, ch 3, sl st in next dc, sl st in

each of next 3 chs, sl st in next 4 sl sts, sl st in each of next 3 chs, ch 3, dc in each st across, turn.

Row 32: Working in **back lps**, ch 3, dc in next 56 sts, ch 3, sl st in next dc, sl st in next 10 sl sts across bottom edge, ch 3, dc in each st across. Fasten off.

Side Edgings

Working from top to bottom in remaining lps of row 30, join med. blue with sc in first st, (ch 1, sc) in each st across to sl sts at bottom edge. Fasten off.

Repeat on row 31 and in **back lps** on row 32 of same side *(see photo)*.

Working from bottom to top in remaining lps of row 30, join med. blue with sc in st just past sl sts at bottom edge, (ch 1, sc) in each st across to top. Fasten off.

Repeat on row 31 and in **back lps** on row 32 of same side.

BOW TIE

Row 1: With dk. blue, ch 12, sc in second ch from hook, sc in each ch across, turn. *(11 sc made)*

Rows 2–29: Ch 1, sc in each st across, turn.

Rnd 30: Ch 1, sc in first 10 sts, 3 sc in last st *(corner made)*, sc in end of next 28 rows; working in remaining lps on opposite side of starting ch, 3 sc in first ch, sc in each ch across to last ch, 3 sc in last ch, sc in end of next 10 rows; fold piece in half lengthwise, matching ends of rows; working through both thicknesses, sc in next 7 rows; working in unfinished edge only, sc in next 10 rows, 2 sc in same st as first sc, join with sl st in first sc. Fasten off.

FINISHING

Sew buttons evenly spaced across center of Button Placket. Sew Placket across center front of T-shirt *(see photo)*.

Sew Bow Tie over top edge of Button Placket.

Boy's Pants Trim

Finished Size: Each Pocket Flap is 2½" across.

❏ Size 10 crochet cotton thread:
 29 yds. white
 10 yds. med. blue
 10 yds. dk. blue
❏ 1 pair of small blue infant panties
❏ 2 dk. blue ⅜" flat buttons
❏ White and dk. blue sewing thread
❏ Sewing needle
❏ No. 7 steel hook or hook needed to obtain gauge

Gauge: 7 dc = 1"; 4 dc rows = 1".

Basic Stitches: Ch, sl st, sc, dc.

POCKET FLAP *(make 2)*

Row 1: With white, ch 16, dc in fourth ch from hook, dc in each ch across, turn. *(14 dc made)*

Rows 2–4: (Ch 3, dc) in first st, dc in each st across to last st, 2 dc in last st, turn. *(16, 18, 20)*

Row 5: Ch 1, sc in each st across. Fasten off. **Do not turn.**

Row 6: Working in ends of rows and in sts on outer edge, join dk. blue with sc in end of row 5, sc in same row, 2 sc in next 4 rows; working in remaining lps on opposite side of starting ch, sc in each ch across, 2 sc in each row across. Fasten off.

Row 6: Working in **back lps** *(see Stitch Guide)*, join white with sc in first st of last row, sc in each st across. Fasten off.

Row 7: Working in **both lps,** join med. blue with sc in first st of last row, sc in each st across. Fasten off.

Sew Pocket Flaps evenly spaced apart on center back of panties *(see photo)*.

Sew buttons to center of Pocket Flaps.

Boy's Sock Trim

Materials:
❏ Size 10 crochet cotton thread:
 20 yds. white
 20 yds. med. blue
 20 yds. dk. blue
❏ 1 pair of small white infant socks
❏ No. 7 steel hook or hook needed to obtain gauge

Gauge: 7 dc = 1"; 4 dc rows = 1".

Basic Stitches: Ch, sl st, sc, dc.

EDGING

Rnd 1: Fold top of sock down to form cuff. Inserting hook through fabric as you work, join dk. blue with sc at center back of edge on sock; spacing sts ⅛" apart, work 39 sc around edge, join with sl st in first sc. Fasten off. *(40 sc made)*

Rnd 2: Working in **back lps** *(see Stitch Guide),* join white with sl st in any st, ch 3, dc in each st around, join with sl st in top of ch-3. Fasten off.

Rnd 3: Working in **both lps,** join med. blue with sc in first st, ch 1, (sc, ch 1) in each st around, join. Fasten off.

Repeat on other sock. ✪

Nannie's Paddle

Designed by Diane Simpson

Finished Size: 14½" long including Ruffle.

Materials:
- ❑ Sport yarn:
  - 3½ oz. yellow
  - 2 oz. each of white and peach
  - Small amount green
- ❑ Polyester fiberfill
- ❑ Wooden paint stir stick
- ❑ Sharp knife
- ❑ Tapestry needle
- ❑ G crochet hook
- ❑ H afghan hook or hook needed to obtain gauge

Gauge: H afghan hook, 7 afghan sts = 2"; 5 afghan st rows = 2".

Basic Stitches: Ch, sl st, sc, dc.

Special Stitches:
Afghan stitch rows are worked in two stages as follows:

For **row 1 of afghan stitch,** ch length needed, insert hook in second ch from hook, yo, pull through ch, (insert hook in next ch, yo, pull through ch) across leaving all lps on hook; to **work lps off hook,** yo, pull through first lp on hook, (yo, pull through 2 lps on hook—*see illustration 1*) across leaving last lp on hook (*this lp is first st of next row*).

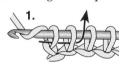

For **row 2 of afghan stitch,** skip first vertical bar, (insert hook under next vertical bar, yo, pull through bar—*see illustration 2*) across to last bar, insert hook under last bar and lp directly behind it (*see illustration 3*), yo, pull through bar and lp; work lps off hook.

Repeat row 2 until piece is desired size.

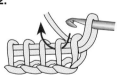 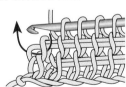

For afghan stitch **increase (inc),** insert hook under next horizontal bar, yo, pull lp through. Always skip first vertical bar when working inc at beginning of row.

For afghan stitch **decrease (dec),** insert hook under each of next 2 vertical bars, yo, pull lp through both bars.

For **reverse sc,** working from left to right, insert hook in next st (*see illustration 1*), yo, pull through, yo and pull through both loops on hook (*see illustration 2*).

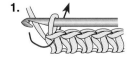 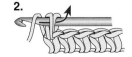

HEART SIDE (make 2)
Row 1: With H afghan hook and yellow, ch 3, work afghan stitch (*see Special Stitches*). (*3 sts made*)

Row 2: Skip first vertical bar, **inc** (*see Special Stitches*), work next lp on hook, inc, work last last lp on hook; work lps off hook. (*5*)

Row 3: (Inc, work next lp on hook) across; work lps off hook. (*9*)

Rows 4–5: Inc, work lps on across to last st, inc, work last lp on hook; work lps off hook. (*11, 13*)

Row 6: (Inc, work next lp on hook) 2 times, work lps on hook across to last 2 sts, (inc, work next lp on hook) 2 times; work lps off hook. (*17*)

Rows 7–14: Repeat rows 4–6 consecutively, ending with row 5 and 37 sts.

Rows 15–17: Work afghan stitch.

Row 18: Dec (*see Special Stitches*), work lps on hook across to last 3 sts, dec, work last lp on hook; work lps off hook. (*35*)

Rows 19–20: Work afghan stitch.

Row 21: For **First Side,** dec, work next 12 lps on hook, dec leaving last 18 lps unworked; work lps off hook. (*15*)

Row 22: Work afghan stitch.

Rows 23–24: (Insert hook under next 3 vertical bars, yo, pull all 3 bars), work lps on hook across to last 4 sts; repeat between ( ), work last lp on hook; work lps off hook. (*11, 7*)

Row 25: Sl st in each st across. Fasten off.

Row 21: For **Second Side,** skip next st on row 20, join with sl st in next st, dec, work lps on hook across to last 3 sts, dec, work last lp on hook; work lps off hook. (*15*)

Rows 22–25: Repeat rows 22–25 of First Side.

Rnd 26: Working in ends of rows and in sts around outer edge, with G hook and yellow, join with sc in end of row 1, 2 sc in next row, (sc in next row, 2 sc in next row) 11 times, 2 sc in first st on row 25, sc in next 5 sts, 2 sc in next st; repeat between ( ) 2 times, sc in skipped st at center of row 20; repeat between ( ) 2 times, 2 sc in next st on row 25, sc in next 5 sts, 2 sc in next st, (2 sc in next row, sc in next row) 12 times; working in remaining lps of starting ch, sc in each of next 3 chs, join with sl st in first sc. Fasten off.

FRONT DECORATION
With green, using straight stitch and French knot (*see Stitch Guide*), embroider lettering on one Heart Side according to graph on page 134.

With peach and green, using lazy-daisy stitch, embroider petals and leaves according to graph.

With white, using French knot, embroider center of each flower according to graph.

EDGING
Hold Heart Sides wrong sides together with Front facing you; working through both thicknesses, with G hook and yellow, join with st in fourth st from center on left-hand side, sc in each st

• • • • • • • • • • • • • • • • Continued on page 134

Nannie's Paddle

Continued from page 133

around to fourth st from center on right-hand side, stuffing as you work; working on Front edge only, sc in next 6 sts, turn; working on back edge only, sc in next 6 sts. Leaving an 8" end, fasten off.

With sharp knife, cut notches on each side of paint stick 4" from handle end. Insert stick inside Heart through opening at top of Heart up to notches. Weave 8" end through 6 sts on back, wrap end around stick and pull to tighten opening around stick. Secure end.

YARN:
- ⬚ = GREEN
- ⬚ = PEACH

FRENCH KNOTS:
- ◯ = GREEN
- ● = WHITE

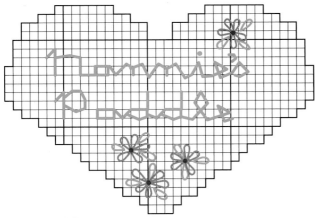

RUFFLES

Rnd 1: With Front facing you, join yellow with sc in first st of 6 sc worked on Front at top opening, sc in next 5 sts, sc in each st around, join with sc in first sc. Fasten off.

Rnd 2: Working in **front lps** *(see Stitch Guide),* join peach with sl st in any st, ch 3, 4 dc in same st, 5 dc in each st around, join with sl st in top of ch-3. Fasten off.

Rnd 3: Working in **back lps** of rnd 1, join white with sl st in any st, ch 3, 2 dc in same st, 3 dc in each st around, join.

Rnds 4–5: Ch 3, dc in each st around, join. At end of last rnd, fasten off.

Rnd 6: Join green with sc in any st; working from left to right, **reverse sc** *(see Special Stitches)* in each st around, join with sl st in first sc. Fasten off.

HANGER

With G hook and yellow, ch 35. Fasten off.

With sharp knife, cut hole in wooden stick ½" from end.

Insert one end of ch-35 in hole. Tie ends of ch in small bow. ✪

 **Shower Stoppers**

Bootie & Basket Party Favors

Designed by Leslie Jacoby

Finished Sizes: Bootie is 2" tall. Basket is 2¾" long.

Materials For One Each:
- ❑ 150 yds. size 10 crochet cotton thread
- ❑ 1 yd. of matching ⅛" ribbon
- ❑ 3 small silk flowers
- ❑ Fabric Stiffener
- ❑ Plastic Wrap
- ❑ No. 9 steel hook or hook needed to obtain gauge

Gauge: 9 dc = 1"; 6 dc rows = 1¼".

Basic Stitches: Ch, sl st, hdc, dc.

BOOTIE

Rnd 1: Ch 15, 4 dc in fourth ch from hook dc in next 10 chs, 8 dc in last ch; working in remaining lps on opposite side of starting ch, dc in next 10 chs, 3 dc in last ch, join with sl st in top of ch-3. *(36 dc made)*

Rnd 2: Ch 3, 2 dc in next st, 3 dc in next st, (2 dc in next st, dc in next 12 sts, 2 dc in next st), 3 dc in each of next 3 sts; repeat between ( ), 3 dc in next st, 2 dc in last st, join. *(52)*

Rnd 3: (Ch 3, dc) in first st, 2 dc in each of next 3 sts, dc in next 18 sts, 2 dc in each of next 8 sts, dc in next 18 sts, 2 dc in each of last 4 sts, join. *(68)*

Rnd 4: Working this rnd in **back lps** *(see Stitch Guide),* for **Sides,** (ch 3, dc, ch 1, 2 dc) in first st, skip next 3 sts; *for **shell,** (2 dc, ch 1, 2 dc) in next st *(shell made),* skip next 3 sts; repeat from * around, join. *(17 shells)*

Rnds 5–7: Sl st in next st, (sl st, ch 3, dc, ch 1, dc) in next ch sp, shell in ch sp of each shell around, join.

Rnd 8: Sl st in next st and in next ch sp, ch 3, (sl st in ch sp of next shell, ch 3) around, join with sl st in second sl st. Fasten off. *(17 ch sps)*

Row 9: For **Instep,** skip first 6 ch sps, join with sl st in next sl st, (ch 3, dc in next sl st) 4 times, ch 3, sl st in next sl st, sl st in each of next 3 chs, sl st in next sl st, turn.

Row 10: (Ch 3, skip next ch sp, dc in next dc) 4 times, ch 3, sl st in next sl st on rnd 8, sl st in each of next 3 chs, sl st in next sl st, turn.

Row 11: (Ch 3, skip next ch sp, dc in next dc) 4 times, ch 3, sl st in next sl st on rnd 8, **do not turn.**

Rnd 12: Ch 4, dc in second ch of next ch-3, ch 1, (dc in next sl st, ch 1, dc in second ch of next ch-3, ch 1) 7 times, (dc in second ch of next ch-3, ch 1, dc in next dc, ch 1) 4 times, skip last ch-3, join with sl st in third ch of first ch-3. *(24 dc)*

Rnd 13: Ch 3, (dc, ch 1, 2 dc) in first st, skip next st, (shell in next st, skip next st) around, join. *(12 shells)*

Rnds 14–15: Sl st in next st, (sl st, ch 3, dc, ch 1, 2 dc) in next ch sp, shell in ch sp of each shell around, join. At end of last rnd, fasten off.

BASKET

Rnd 1: Ch 15, 4 dc in fourth ch from hook dc in next 10 chs, 8 dc in last ch; working in remaining lps on opposite side of starting ch, dc in next 10 chs, 3 dc in last ch, join with sl st in top of ch-3. *(36 dc made)*

Rnd 2: (Ch 3, dc) in first st, 2 dc in each of next 4 sts, dc in next 10 sts, 2 dc in next 8 sts, dc in next 10 sts, 2 dc in each of last 3 sts, join. *(52)*

Rnd 3: Ch 3, (2 dc in next st, dc in next st) 4 times, dc in next 14 sts, (2 dc in next st, dc in next st) 6 times, dc in next 14 sts, 2 dc in next st, dc in next st, 2 dc in last st, join. *(64)*

Rnd 4: Working this rnd in **back lps,** ch 3, dc in each st around, join.

Rnd 5: Ch 3, dc in each st around, join.

Rnd 6: Ch 4, skip next st, (dc in next st, ch 1, skip next st) around, join with sl st in third ch of ch-4.

Rnd 7: Ch 3, dc in each st and in each ch around, join.

Rnd 8: Ch 3, dc in each st around, join.

Rnd 9: (Ch 3, dc, ch 1, 2 dc) in first st, skip next 3 sts, (shell in next st, skip next 3 sts) around, join. Fasten off.

Handle

Working inside Basket, join with sl st in dc on rnd 8 at center of one side, ch 25, sl st in dc on opposite side of rnd 8, turn; working over ch-25 *(see illustration),* work 50 hdc, sl st in joining sl st. Fasten off.

FINISHING

Apply fabric stiffener to Basket and Bootie according to manufacturer's directions.

Stuff Basket and Bootie with plastic wrap and shape. Let dry completely. Remove plastic wrap.

Cut 12" piece from ribbon. Beginning and ending at center front, weave through sts on rnd 12 of Bootie. Tie ends in bow.

Cut 12" piece from ribbon. Weave ribbon through sts of rnd 6 on Basket. Secure ends on inside.

Cut three 4" pieces from ribbon. Tie each flower to Handle with each piece of ribbon. ✪

Pretty Powder Puff

Designed by Janet Wright

Finished Size: 8½" tall including puff.

Materials:
- Worsted yarn:
    - 1½ oz. off-white
    - ¼ oz. each of lavender and lt. green
- 2"-diameter circle of quilt batting
- 8 oz. plastic seasoning container with removable shaker disk
- Baby powder
- Craft glue
- G hook or size needed to obtain gauge

Gauge: 4 hdc = 1"; 5 hdc rows = 2".

Basic Stitches: Ch, sl st, sc, hdc, dc, tr.

COVER
Rnd 1: With off-white, ch 4, sl st in first ch to form ring, ch 3, 11 dc in ring, join with sl st in top of ch-3. *(12 dc made)*

Rnd 2: Ch 4, (dc, ch 1) in each st around, join with sl st in third ch of ch-4. *(12 dc, 12 chs)*

Rnd 3: Working in **back lps** *(see Stitch Guide)*, ch 2, hdc in each st and in each ch around, join with sl st in top of ch-2. *(24 hdc)*

Rnd 4: Ch 2, hdc in each st around, join.

Rnd 5: Ch 3, dc in next 4 sts, 2 dc in next st, (dc in next 5 sts, 2 dc in next st) 3 times, join. *(28)*

Rnd 6: Ch 2, hdc in next 4 sts, hdc next 2 sts tog, (hdc in next 5 sts, hdc next 2 sts tog) 3 times, join with sl st in top of ch-2. *(24)*

Rnds 7–14: Ch 2, hdc in each st around, join.

Rnd 15: Ch 3, dc in next 4 sts, 2 dc in next st, (dc in next 5 sts, 2 dc in next st) 3 times, join. *(28)*

Rnd 16: Working in **back lps**, ch 2, (dc next 2 sts tog) 3 times, dc in next st, skip ch-2, join with sl st in first dc. Fasten off.

Top Trim
Rnd 1: With rnd 1 facing you, working in remaining **front lps** of rnd 2, join lt. green with sl st in any st, (ch 2, dc, tr, dc, hdc) in same st, skip next st, *(hdc, dc, tr, dc, hdc) in next st, skip next st; repeat from * around, join with sl st in top of ch-2. Fasten off.

Rnd 2: Working in front of sts on rnd 1, in remaining skipped **front lps** of rnd 2, join lavender with sc in any st, (hdc, dc, hdc, sc) in same st, (sc, hdc, dc, hdc, sc) in each skipped st around, join with sl st in first sc. Fasten off.

PUFF
For each **fringe,** cut three 4" strands off-white. Fold all strands held together in half, insert hook around post of st *(see illustration)*, pull fold through, pull ends through fold. Tighten. Fringe around each st on rnds 1 and 2 of Cover. Brush strands of yarn to fluff. Trim ends evenly.

FINISHING
Being careful not to glue holes closed, glue batting circle over shaker disk. Fill container with baby powder. Replace shaker disk.

For **Tie,** with lavender, ch 75. Fasten off.

Place container inside Cover.

Wrap Tie around Cover below rnd 1 of Trim, tie ends in bow. ✪

CHAPTER 7

First Fashions

Lavender Blue

Lavender's blue, dilly, dilly, lavender's green,
When I am king, dilly dilly, you shall be queen.

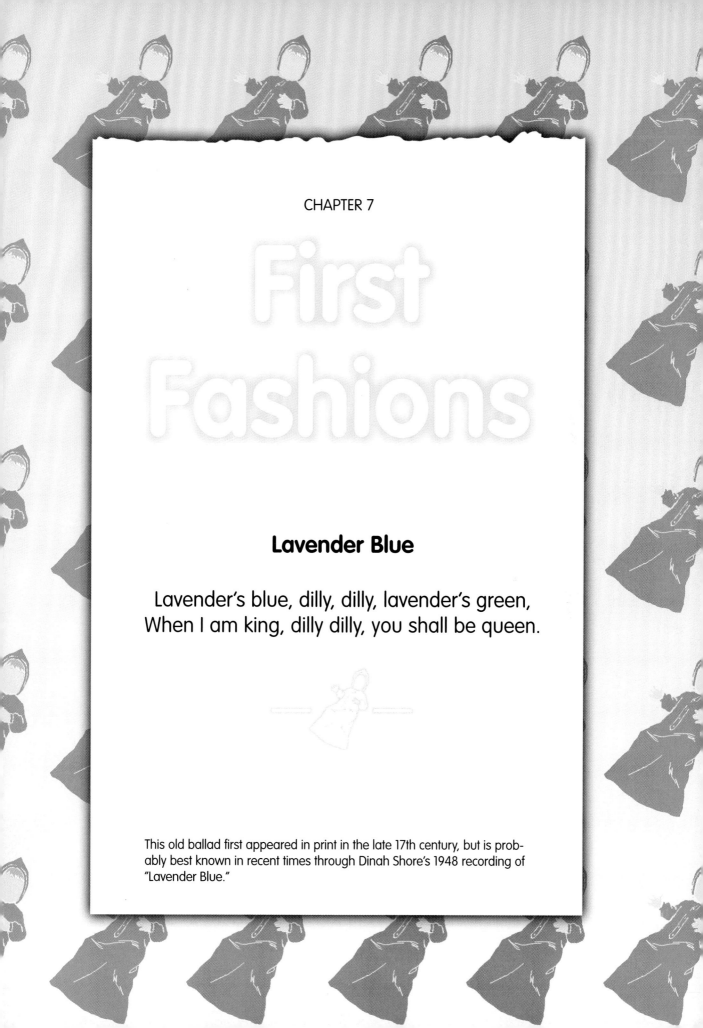

This old ballad first appeared in print in the late 17th century, but is probably best known in recent times through Dinah Shore's 1948 recording of "Lavender Blue."

Sailor Suit Designed by Michele Lupo
Sailor Dress Designed by Beth Ahlberg

Sailor Suit

Sizes: Infant's 3–6 mos., 6–9 mos. and 9–12 mos.

Materials:
- ❑ Sport yarn:
    - 5 oz. blue
    - 2 oz. white
    - Small amount red
- ❑ 3 small red star appliqués
- ❑ 2 pieces thread elastic to fit waist plus 1"
- ❑ Tapestry needle
- ❑ I hook or hook needed to obtain gauge

Gauge: 7 sc = 2"; 4 sc rows = 1".

Basic Stitches: Ch, sl st, sc, dc.

Note: Instructions are for Infant's 3–6 mos. Changes for 6–9 mos. and 9–12 mos. are in [ ].

TOP

Row 1: With blue, ch 34, [36, 38], sc in second ch from hook, sc in each ch across, turn. *(33 sc made) [35 sc made, 37 sc made]*

Rows 2–28 [2–27, 2–26]: Ch 1, sc in each st across, turn. At end of last row, fasten off.

Row 29 [28, 27]: With blue, ch 8, sc in each st across last row, ch 9, turn. *(33 sc, 17 chs) [35 sc, 17 chs, 37 sc, 17 chs]*

Row 30 [29, 28]: Sc in second ch from hook, sc in each ch and in each st across, turn. *(49) [51, 53]*

Rows 31–44 [30–44, 29–44]: Ch 1, sc in each st across, turn.

Row 45: Ch 1, sc in first 17 sts, ch 15 [17, 19], skip next 15 [17, 19] sts, sc in last 17 sts, turn. *(34)*

Row 46: Ch 1, sc in each st and in each ch across, turn. *(49) [51, 53]*

Rows 47–60 [47–61, 47–62]: Ch 1, sc in each st across, turn. At end of last row, fasten off.

Row 61 [62, 63]: Skip first 8 sts, join blue with sc in next st, sc in next 32 [34, 36] sts leaving last 8 sts unworked, turn. *(33) [35, 37]*

Rows 62–89 [63–89, 64–89]: Ch 1, sc in each st across, turn. At end of last row, fasten off.

Sew sleeve and side seams. Working in ends of rows, join blue with sc in row at bottom of sleeve,
sc in each row around, join with sl st in first st. Fasten off. Repeat on other sleeve.

COLLAR

Row 1: Starting at back, with white, ch 24 [26, 28], sc in second ch from hook, sc in each ch across, turn. *(23 sc made) [25 sc made, 27 sc made]*

Rows 2–11 [2–13, 2–15]: Ch 1, sc in each st across, turn.

Row 12 [14, 16]: For **Right Front, do not ch 1,** sc in first 4 sts leaving last 19 [21, 23] sts unworked, turn. *(4)*

Row 13 [15, 17]: Ch 1, 2 sc in first st, sc in each of next 2 sts leaving last st unworked, turn. *(4)*

Row 14 [16, 18]: Do not ch 1, skip first st, sc in each of next 2 sts, 2 sc in last st, turn. *(4)*

Rows 15–22 [17–26, 19–30]: Repeat rows 13 and 14 [15 and 16, 17 and 18] alternately. At end of last row, **do not turn.** Fasten off.

Row 12 [14, 16]: For **Left Front,** skip next 15 [17, 19] sts on row 11 [13, 15], join white with sc in next st, sc in each st across, turn. *(4)*

Rows 13–22 [15–26, 17–30]: Repeat rows 14 and 13 [16 and 15, 18 and 17] alternately.

Rnd 23 [27, 31]: For **Edging,** working in sts and in ends of rows, sc around entire Collar with sc 2 sts tog at each inside corner and 3 sc in each outside corner, join with sl st in first sc. Fasten off.

Row 24 [28, 32]: Working in rows, for **Trim,** join red with sc in first st on left front point, sc in each st across outside edge to last st on right front point with 3 sc in center st of each back corner. Leaving inside sts of row 33 [27, 31] unworked, fasten off.

Row 25 [29, 33]: Working in **back lps** *(see Stitch Guide),* join white with sc in first st of row 24 [28, 32], sc in each st across with 3 sc in center st of each back corner. Fasten off.

Skip 1 [3, 5] chs on row 45 of top; matching sts on inside neck edge of Collar back and next 13 [15, 17] chs on row 45 of Top, sew Collar to Top. Sew front points of Collar tog, sew points to Top. Sew one star inside each corner on back of Collar.

TIE

Row 1: With red, ch 36, sc in second ch from hook, sc in each ch across to last ch, 2 sc in last ch, turn. *(36 sc made)*

Continued on page 140

Play "Maties" Sailor Ensembles

Continued from page 139

Row 2: Ch 1, 2 sc in first st, sc in each st across to last 2 sts, sc last 2 sts tog, turn.

Row 3: Do not ch 1, skip first st, sc in next st, sc in each st across to last st, 2 sc in last st. Fasten off.

Tie knot in center of Tie. Sew knot over points of Collar, sew ends of Tie to Top.

PANTS
Back
Row 1: With blue, ch 34, [36, 38], sc in second ch from hook, sc in each ch across, turn. *(33 sc made) [35 sc made, 37 sc made]*

Rows 2–29 [2–31, 2–33]: Ch 1, sc in each st across, turn. At end of last row, fasten off.

Front
Rows 1–25 [1–27, 1–29]: Repeat rows 1–25 [1–27, 1–29] of Back.

Rows 26–28 [28–30, 30–32]: Sl st in first 4 sts, sc in each st across leaving last 4 sts unworked, turn. At end of last row *(9) [11, 13]*.

Rows 29–32 [31–34, 33–36]: Ch 1, sc in each st across, turn. At end of last row, fasten off.

Matching ends of rows 1–15 on Back to rows 1–15 on Front and easing rows 16–29 [16–31, 16–33] on Back to rows 16–25 [16–27, 16–29] on Front, sew side seams.

For **Crotch**, sew last row on Front to middle 9 [11, 13] sts of last row on Back.

Leg Edging
Rnd 1: Working in sts and in ends of rows around leg opening, join blue with sc in any st, sc in each st around, join with sl st in first sc.

Rnd 2: Ch 1, sc in each st around, join. Fasten off. Repeat on other leg opening.

Waist
With tapestry needle, thread one piece elastic through back of sts on row 1. Tie ends tog. Repeat with other strand through back of sts on row 2.

Stripe (make 2)
Row 1: With white, ch 22 [24, 26], sc in second ch from hook, sc in each ch across, **do not turn.** Fasten off. *(21 sc made) [23 sc made, 25 sc made]*

Row 2: Join red with sc in first st, sc in each st across, **do not turn.** Fasten off.

Row 3: Working in **back lps,** join white with sc in first st, sc in each st across. Fasten off.

Sew one Stripe over each side seam.

HAT
NOTE: *Do not join rnds unless otherwise stated. Mark first st of each rnd.*

Rnd 1: With white, ch 2, 8 sc in second ch from hook. *(8 sc made)*

Rnd 2: 2 sc in each st around. *(16)*

Rnd 3: (2 sc in next st, sc in next st) around. *(24)*

Rnd 4: Sc in each st around.

Rnd 5: (Sc in each of next 2 sts, 2 sc in next st) around. *(32)*

Rnd 6: Sc in each st around.

Rnd 7: Sc in next st, (2 sc in next st, sc in each of next 3 sts) 7 times, 2 sc in next st, sc in each of next 2 sts. *(40)*

Rnd 8: (Sc in next 4 sts, 2 sc in next st) around. *(48)*

Rnd 9: Sc in each of next 2 sts, (2 sc in next st, sc in next 5 sts) 7 times, 2 sc in next st, sc in each of next 3 sts. *(56).*

Rnd [10, 10]: For **sizes 6–9 mos. and 9–12 mos.** only, (sc in next 13 sts, 2 sc in next st) around. *(60)*

Rnd [11]: For **size 9–12 mos.** only, sc in next 7 sts, 2 sc in next st, (sc in next 14 sts, 2 sc in next st) 3 times, sc in next 7 sts. *(64)*

Rnds 10–19 [11–20, 12–21]: For **all sizes,** sc in each st around. At end of last rnd, join with sl st in first sc, **turn.** *(56) [60, 64]*

Rnd 20 [21, 22]: For **Brim,** working in **back lps,** ch 1, sc in each st around.

Rnd 21 [22, 23]: (Sc in each of next 3 sts, 2 sc in next st) around. *(70) [75, 80]*

Rnd 22 [23, 24]: Sc in each st around.

Rnd 23 [24, 25]: (Sc in next 13 [14, 15] sts, 2 sc in next st) around. *(75) [80, 85]*

Rnds 24–26 [25–27, 26–28]: Sc in each st around.

Rnd 27 [28, 29]: Working in **back lps,** sl st in each st around, join with sl st in first sl st. Fasten off.

Sew star on front of brim. ✪

Sailor Dress

Sizes: Infant's 3–6 mos, 6–9 mos. and 9–12 mos.

Materials:
- ❑ Sport yarn:
  - 5½ oz. blue
  - 3 oz. white
- ❑ 2 yds. of ⅝" ribbon
- ❑ ¼" elastic to fit waist plus 1"
- ❑ 4 small star appliqués
- ❑ Tapestry needle
- ❑ Hook size needed to obtain gauge:
  - E hook for 3–6 mos.
  - F hook for 6–9 mos.
  - G hook for 9–12 mos.

Gauges: E hook, 5 dc = 1"; 5 dc rows = 2". **F hook,** 9 dc = 2"; 5 dc rows = 2". **G hook,** 4 dc = 1"; 2 dc rows = 1".

Basic Stitches: Ch, sl st, sc, hdc, dc.

Note: Instructions are for Infant's 3–6 mos. Changes for 6–9 mos. and 9–12 mos. are in [ ].

DRESS
Bodice Front
Row 1: With blue, ch 56, dc in fourth ch from hook, dc in each ch across, turn. *(54 dc made)*

Rows 2–4: Ch 3, dc in each st across to last 2 sts, dc last 2 sts tog, turn. *(53, 52, 51)*

Row 5: Ch 3, dc in each st across, turn.

Rows 6–13: Repeat rows 3–5 consecutively, ending with row 4 and 45 sts.

Row 14: For **Armhole Shaping,** sl st in each of first 2 sts, (sl st, ch 1, sc) in next st, hdc in next st, dc in next 37 sts, hdc in next st, sc in next st leaving last 2 sts unworked, turn. *(41 sts)*

Row 15: Sl st in each of first 3 sts, ch 2, dc in next 35 sts, hdc in next st leaving last 2 sts unworked, turn. *(37)*

Row 16: Sl st in each of first 2 sts, ch 3, dc in next 34 sts leaving last st unworked, turn. *(35)*

Rows 17–20: Ch 3, dc in each st across, turn.

Row 21: For **Right Shoulder,** ch 3, dc in next 11 sts leaving last 23 sts unworked, turn. *(12)*

Row 22: Ch 3, dc next 2 sts tog, dc in each st across, turn. *(11)*

Row 23: Ch 3, dc in each st across to last 2 sts, dc last 2 sts tog, turn. *(10)*

Row 24: Ch 3, dc in each st across, turn.

Row 25: Sl st in each of first 3 sts, sc in next 4 sts, dc in each of last 3 sts. Fasten off.

Row 21: For **Left Shoulder,** skip next 11 sts on row 20, join with sl st in next st, ch 3, dc in each st across, turn. *(12)*

Rows 22–23: Repeat rows 23 and 22 of Right Shoulder. *(11, 10)*

Row 24: Ch 3, dc in each st across, turn.

Row 25: Ch 3, dc in each of next 2 sts, sc in next 4 sts, sl st in next st leaving last 2 sts unworked. Fasten off.

Bodice Back
Rows 1–20: Repeat rows 1–20 of Bodice Front.

Row 21: Ch 3, dc in each st across, turn.

Row 22: For **Left Shoulder,** ch 3, dc in next 10 sts leaving remaining 24 sts unworked, turn. *(11)*

Row 23: Ch 3, dc next 2 sts tog, dc in each st across, turn. *(10)*

Rows 24–25: Repeat rows 24–25 of Bodice Front Left Shoulder.

Row 22: For **Right Shoulder,** skip next 13 st son row 21, join with sl st in next st, ch 3, dc in each st across, turn. *(11)*

Rows 23–25: Repeat rows 23–25 of bodice Front Right Shoulder.

Matching sts and ends of rows, sew shoulder and side seams.

Sleeve (make 2)
NOTE: *Do not join rnds unless otherwise stated. Mark first st of each rnd.*

Rnd 1: With blue, ch 48, sl st in first ch to form ring, ch 1, sc in first ch, sc in each of next 3 chs, hdc in next 4 chs, dc in next 32 chs, hdc in next 4 chs, sc in last 4 chs. *(48 sts made)*

Rnd 2: Sc in first 4 sts, hdc in next 4 sts, (dc in next st, 2 dc in next st) 16 times, hdc in next 4 sts, sc in last 4 sts. *(64)*

Rnd 3: Sc in first 4 sts, hdc in next 4 sts, dc in next 48 sts, hdc in next 4 sts, sc in last 4 sts.

Rnd 4: Sc in first 4 sts, hdc in next 4 sts, (dc in next st, dc next 2 sts tog) 16 times, hdc in next 4 sts, sc in last 4 sts, join with sl st in first sc. *(48)*

Rnd 5: (Ch 3, dc) in first st, dc in next 7 sts, dc next 2 sts tog, (dc in each of next 2 sts, dc next 2 sts tog) 8 times, dc in last 6 sts, join with sl st in top of ch-3. *(40)*

Rnd 6: Ch 3, dc in next st, dc next 2 sts tog, (dc in each of next 2 sts, dc next 2 sts tog) around, join. *(30)*

Rnd 7: Ch 3, dc in each st around, join. Fasten off.

Rnd 8: Join white with sc in first st, sc in each st around.

Rnds 9–11: Sc in each st around. At end of last rnd, join with sl st in first sc. Fasten off.

Sew Sleeves in armholes.

Skirt
Rnd 1: Working in opposite side of starting ch on Dress Front and Back, join white with sl st at center back, ch 3, dc in each ch around, join with sl st in top of ch-3. *(108 dc made)*

Rnd 2: Ch 3, dc in next 4 sts, 2 dc in next st, (dc in next 5 sts, 2 dc in next st) around, join. *(126)*

Rnd 3: Ch 3, dc in each of next 2 sts, 2 dc in next st, (dc in next 6 sts, 2 dc in next st) 17 times, dc in each of last 3 sts, join. *(144)*

Rnd 4: Ch 3, dc in next 4 sts, 2 dc in next st, (dc in next 7 sts, 2 dc in next st) 17 times, dc in each of last 2 sts, join. *(162)*

Rnd 5: Ch 3, dc in each st around, join.

Rnd 6: Ch 3, dc in next 7 sts, 2 dc in next st, (dc in next 8 sts, 2 dc in next st) around. *(180)*

Rnds 7–10: Ch 3, dc in each st around, join. At end of last rnd, fasten off.

Collar Left Front
Row 1: With white, ch 22, dc in fourth ch from hook, dc in each ch across, turn. *(20 dc made)*

Row 2: (Ch 3, dc) in first st, dc in each st across to last 2 sts, dc last 2 sts tog, turn.

Row 3: Ch 3, dc next 2 sts tog, dc in each st across to last st, 2 dc in last st, turn.

Rows 4–8: Repeat rows 2 and 3 alternately. At end of last row, fasten off.

Continued on page 144

Ribbons & Ruffles

Designed by Beth Ahlberg

Size: Infant's 6–9 mos.

Materials:
- ❑ Baby yarn:
  - 3 oz. white
  - 2 oz. pink
- ❑ 26" of ¼"-wide elastic
- ❑ ¾ yd. each of pink, lavender, yellow and aqua ¼" ribbon
- ❑ Sewing needle and thread
- ❑ G hook or hook needed to obtain gauge

Gauge: 6 dc = 1"; 3 dc rows = 1".

Basic Stitches: Ch, sl st, sc, hdc, dc.

DRESS
Front
Row 1: With white, ch 57, dc in third ch from hook, dc in each ch across, turn. *(56 dc made)*

Rows 2–3: Ch 3, dc in each st across, dc last 2 sts tog, turn. *(55, 54)*

Row 4: Ch 4, skip next st, dc in next st, (ch 1, skip next st, dc in next st) across to last 2 sts, dc last 2 sts tog, turn.

Rows 5–6: Ch 3, dc in each st across to last 2 sts, dc last 2 sts tog, turn. *(53)*

Row 7: Ch 4, skip next st, dc in next st, (ch 1, skip next st, dc in next st) across, turn.

Rows 8–13: Repeat rows 5–7 consecutively. *(52, 51)*

Row 14: Ch 1, sc in next st, hdc in next st, ch 1, dc in each ch and in each st across to last 3 sts, ch 1, hdc in next st, sc in next st, sl st in last st, turn.

Row 15: Sl st in next sc and hdc, ch 3, dc in each st across to last 3 sts leaving last 3 sts unworked, turn.

Rows 16–18: Ch 2, dc in each st across to last 2 sts, dc last 2 sts tog, turn.

Row 19: For **First Shoulder,** ch 3, dc in next 11 sts leaving remaining sts unworked, turn.

Row 20: Ch 2, dc in next 9 sts, dc last 2 sts tog, turn.

Rows 21–24: Ch 3, dc in each st across, turn. At end of last row, leaving 12" end for sewing, fasten off.

Row 19: For **Second Shoulder,** join white with sc in 12th st from end on row 19, ch 1, dc in next 11 sts, turn.

Row 20: Ch 2, dc in next 9 sts, dc last 2 sts tog, turn.

Rows 21–24: Ch 3, dc in each st across, turn. At end of last row, leaving 12" end for sewing, fasten off.

Back
Row 1: With white, ch 57, dc in third ch from hook, dc in each ch across, turn. *(56 dc made)*

Rows 2–4: Ch 3, dc in each st across to last 2 sts, dc last 2 sts tog, turn. *(55, 54, 53)*

Row 5: Ch 2, dc in each st across, turn.

Rows 6–13: Repeat rows 5 and 2 alternately.

Row 14: Ch 1, sc in next st, hdc in next st, dc in each st across to last 3 sts, hdc in next st, sc in next st, sl st in last st, turn.

Rows 15–24: Repeat rows 15–24 of Front.

Sew Front to Back at sides and shoulders.

Skirt
Rnd 1: Working on opposite side of starting ch on Dress Front and Back, join pink with sl st in first st, ch 2, dc in each st and in each seam around, join with sl st in top of ch-2. *(112 dc made)*

Rnd 2: Ch 3, dc in next 4 sts, 2 dc in next st, (dc in next 5 sts, 2 dc in next st) around, join with sl st in top of ch-3.

Rnd 3: Ch 3, dc in next 5 sts, 2 dc in next st, (dc in next 6 sts, 2 dc in next st) around, join.

Rnd 4: Ch 3, dc in next 6 sts, 2 dc in next st, (dc in next 7 sts, 2 dc in next st) around, join.

Rnd 5: Ch 3, dc in each st around, join.

Rnd 6: Ch 3, dc in next 7 sts, 2 dc in next st, (dc in next 8 sts, 2 dc in next st) around, join.

Rnd 7: Ch 3, dc in each st around, join.

Rnd 8: Ch 3, dc in next 7 sts, dc next 2 sts tog, (dc in next 8 sts, dc next 2 sts tog) around, join.

Rnd 9: Ch 3, dc in next 6 sts, dc next 2 sts tog, (dc in next 7 sts, dc next 2 sts tog) around, join.

Rnd 10: Ch 3, dc in each st around, join. Fasten off.

Sleeve (make 2)
Rnd 1: With pink, ch 50, sl st in first ch to form ring, sc in first 5 chs, hdc in next 5 chs, dc in next 30 chs, hdc in next 5 chs, sc in last 5 chs, **do not join.** *(50 sts made)*

Rnd 2: Sc in next 5 sts, hdc in next 5 sts, (dc in next st, 2 dc in next st) 15 times, hdc in next 5 sts, sc in last 5 sts, **do not join.**

Rnd 3: Sc in next 5 sts, hdc in next 5 sts, dc in next 45 sts, hdc in next 5 sts, sc in next 5 sts, **do not join.**

Rnd 4: Sc in next 5 sts, hdc in next 5 sts, (dc in next st, dc next 2 sts tog) 15 times, hdc in next 5 sts, sc in last 5 sts, join with sl st in first sc.

Rnd 5: Ch 2, dc in next 6 sts, dc next 2 sts tog, (dc in each of next 2 sts, dc next 2 sts tog) 8 times, dc in next 9 sts, join with sl st in top of ch-2.

Rnd 6: Ch 2, dc in next st, dc next 2 sts tog, (dc in each of next 2 sts, dc next 2 sts tog) around, join.

Rnd 7: Ch 2, dc in each st around, join.

Continued on page 144

Ribbons & Ruffles

Continued from page 142

Rnd 8: Sew ends of 5" piece of elastic together; working over elastic *(see Stitch Guide)*, sc in each st around, join.

Rnd 9: Ch 3, 2 dc in each st around, join. Fasten off. With right sides tog, sew Sleeves to Dress.

Edging

Rnd 1: Join pink with sc in center Back, sc in each st with 2 sc in side of dc at shoulders around, join with sl st in first sc.

Rnd 2: Ch 1, sc in each of first 3 sts, sc next 2 sts tog, (sc in each of next 3 sts, sc next 2 sts tog) around, join. Fasten off.

Cut a 4" piece from each ribbon and tie in a 1" bow. Weave ribbons through rows 5, 8, 11 and 14 on Front of Dress *(see photo)*. Tack each ribbon in place at side seams. Tack 1" bows to matching color ribbon in a diagonal direction across Front.

RUFFLED PANTIES

Front

Row 1: With white, ch 52, dc in third ch from hook, dc in each ch across, turn. *(50 dc made)*

Rows 2–8: Ch 3, dc in each st across, turn.

Rows 9–13: Ch 3, dc next 2 sts tog, dc in each st across to last 2 sts, dc last 2 sts tog, turn.

Row 14: Sl st in first 4 sts, ch 3, dc in each st across leaving last 4 sts unworked, turn.

Rows 15–18: Ch 2 *(not counted as st)*, dc next 2 sts tog, dc in each st across to last 3 sts, dc next 2 sts tog leaving last st unworked, turn.

Row 19: Ch 3, dc in each st across. Leaving 12" end for sewing, fasten off.

Back

Row 1: With white, ch 56, dc in third ch from hook, dc in each ch across, turn. *(54 dc made)*

Rows 2–6: Ch 3, dc in each st across, turn.

Row 7: Working in **back lps** *(see Stitch Guide)*, ch 3, dc in each st across, turn.

Row 8: Ch 3, dc in each st across, turn.

Row 9: Working in **back lps**, ch 3, dc in each st across, turn.

Row 10: Working in **back lps**, ch 3, dc next 2 sts tog, dc in each st across to last 2 sts, dc last 2 sts tog, turn.

Rows 11–13: Repeat rows 7 and 10 alternately, ending with row 7.

Row 14: Sl st in first 5 sts, ch 3, dc in each st across to last 4 sts leaving last 4 sts unworked, turn.

Rows 15–20: Ch 2 *(not counted as st)*, dc next 2 sts tog, dc in each st across to last 3 sts, dc next 2 sts tog leaving last st unworked, turn. At end of last row, fasten off.

Back Ruffles

Row 1: Working in **front lps**, join white with sl st in first st on row 6 of Back, ch 3, 2 dc in first st, 3 dc in each st across, sl st in last st. Fasten off.

Row 2: Join pink with sc in first st, sc in each st across. Fasten off.

Repeat on rows 8, 10 and 12.

With right sides facing, sew Front and Back together at sides and crotch.

Sew 14" piece of elastic into a circle with ¼" seam.

Hold elastic circle over top edge of Front and Back; working over elastic and into remaining lps on opposite side of starting ch on Front and Back *(see illustration)*, join white with sc in any ch, 2 sc in same ch, 3 sc in each ch around, join. Fasten off.

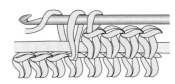

Leg Ruffles

Join white with sl st in end of any row around one leg opening, (ch 3, dc) in same row, 2 dc in end of each row around, join with sl st in top of ch-3. Fasten off.

Repeat on other leg opening. ✪

Play "Maties" Sailor Ensembles

Continued from page 141

Collar Right Front

Row 1: With white, ch 22, dc in fourth ch from hook, dc in each ch across, turn. *(20 dc made)*

Rows 2–8: Repeat rows 3 and 2 of Collar Left Front alternately. At end of last row, fasten off.

Row 9: Working across row 8 of Right and Left Front pieces, join with sl st in last st on row 8 on Left Front, ch 3, dc in each st across to first st, dc next st of Left Front and last st of row 8 on Right Front

tog, dc in each st across, turn. *(39)*

Row 10: For **Right Shoulder Shaping**, ch 3, dc in next 13 sts leaving last 25 sts unworked, turn. *(14)*

Row 11: Ch 2, dc in each st across, turn. *(13 dc)*

Row 12: Ch 3, dc in next 10 sts, dc next 2 sts tog leaving ch-2 unworked. *(12)*

Row 13: Ch 2, dc in each st across, turn. *(11 dc)*

Row 14: Ch 3, dc in each st across leaving ch-2 unworked. Fasten off.

Row 10: For **Left Shoulder Shaping,** skip next 11 sts on row 9, join with sl st in next st, ch 3, dc in each st across, turn. *(14)*

Row 11: Ch 3, dc in each st across to last 2 sts, dc last 2 sts tog, turn. *(13)*

Row 12: Ch 2, dc in each st across, turn. *(12 dc)*

Row 13: Ch 3, dc in next 9 sts, dc next 2 sts tog leaving ch-3 unworked, turn. *(11)*

Row 14: Ch 3, dc in each st across. Fasten off.

Collar Back

Row 1: With white, ch 50, dc in fourth ch from hook, dc in each ch across, turn. *(48 dc made)*

Rows 2–10: Ch 3, dc next 2 sts tog, dc in each st across, turn. At end of last row *(39)*.

Rows 11–12: Ch 3, dc in each st across, turn.

Row 13: For **Right Shoulder Shaping,** ch 3, dc in next 12 sts leaving last 26 sts unworked, turn. *(13)*

Row 14: Ch 3, dc in each st across to last 2 sts, dc last 2 sts tog, turn. *(12)*

Row 15: Ch 2, dc in each st across, turn. *(11 dc)*

Row 16: Ch 3, dc in each st across. Fasten off.

Row 13: For **Left Shoulder Shaping,** skip next 13 sts on row 12, join with sl st in next st, ch 3, dc in each st across, turn. *(13)*

Row 14: Ch 3, dc in each st across to last 2 sts, dc last 2 sts tog, turn. *(12)*

Row 15: Ch 2, dc in each st across, turn. *(11 dc)*

Row 16: Ch 3, dc in each st across leaving ch-2 unworked. Fasten off.

Matching sts, sew row 16 of Back to row 14 of Front on each shoulder. Place Collar over Dress with right sides of both pieces facing you.

Matching shoulder seams, working through both thicknesses, join white with sc in shoulder seam; spacing sts evenly, sc in each st and 2 sc in end of each row around neck opening, join with sl st in first sc. Fasten off.

Finishing

Working around outside edge of Collar, join white with sl st at center front; spacing sts evenly, sc in each st and 2 sc in end of each row around with 3 sc in each corner, join with sl st in first sc. Fasten off.

Cut 45" of ribbon. Place middle of ribbon at center front over starting ch of Dress, sew in place across starting ch, tie in bow at center back. Sew one star at each outer corner of Collar. Cut 16" of ribbon, tie in bow, sew to center front of Collar on row 9.

PANTIES
Front

Row 1: With white, ch 51, dc in fourth ch from hook, dc in each ch across, turn. *(49 dc made)*

Rows 2–8: Ch 3, dc in each st across, turn.

Rows 9–13: Ch 3, dc next 2 sts tog, dc in each st across to last 2 sts, dc last 2 sts tog, turn. At end of last row *(39)*.

Row 14: Sl st in first 5 sts, ch 3, dc in each st across to last 4 sts leaving last 4 sts unworked, turn. *(31)*

Rows 15–19: Ch 3, (dc next 2 sts tog) 2 times, dc in each st across to last 4 sts, (dc next 2 sts tog) 2 times, turn. At end of last row *(11)*.

Rows 20–21: Ch 3, dc in each st across, turn. At end of last row, fasten off.

Back

Row 1: With blue, ch 57, dc in fourth ch from hook, dc in each ch across, turn. *(55 dc made)*

Rows 2–5: Ch 3, dc in each st across, turn.

Row 6: Working in **back lps** *(see Stitch Guide),* ch 3, dc in each st across, turn.

Row 7: Ch 3, dc in each st across, turn.

Row 8: Working in **back lps,** ch 3, dc in each st across, turn.

Row 9: Ch 3, dc next 2 sts tog, dc in each st across to last 2 sts, dc last 2 sts tog, turn. *(53)*

Rows 10–22: Ch 3, (dc next 2 sts tog) 2 times, dc in each st across to last 4 sts, (dc next 2 sts tog) 2 times, turn. At end of last row, fasten off *(11)*.

Ruffle

Row 1: Working in **front lps** of row 6 on Back, join blue with sl st in first st, ch 3, 2 dc in same st, 3 dc in each st across to last st, (2 dc, ch 3, sl st) in last st. Fasten off.

Row 2: Join white with sc in first st, sc in each st across. Fasten off.

Repeat Ruffle on rows 8, 10 and 12 of Back.

Matching ends of rows and sts, sew side and crotch seams.

Finishing

For **waistband,** overlap ends of elastic 1", sew tog. Working over elastic *(see Stitch Guide)* and on opposite side of starting ch, join blue with sc at center back, sc in each ch around top of Panties, join with sl st in first sc. Fasten off.

For **leg,** join blue with sc at crotch seam; spacing sts evenly, sc around leg, join with sl st in first sc. Fasten off. Repeat on other leg. ✪

Sizes: Infant's 3–6 mos., 6–9 mos. and 9–12 mos.

Materials:
- ❑ 16 oz. baby yarn
- ❑ 22" zipper
- ❑ 2½ yds. of ¼" ribbon
- ❑ Sewing and tapestry needles
- ❑ Hook or size needed to obtain gauge:
    - D hook for 3–6 mos.
    - E hook for 6–9 mos.
    - F hook for 9–12 mos.

Gauges: D hook, 11 sts = 2"; 3 patterns rows = 1"; Granny Square = 1⅞" square. **E hook,** 5 sts = 1"; 5½ pattern rows = 2"; Granny Square = 2" square. **F hook,** 9 sts = 2"; 5 pattern rows = 2"; Granny Square = 2⅛" square.

Basic Stitches: Ch, sl st, sc, dc.

GRANNY SQUARE *(make 10)*
Rnd 1: Ch 4, 2 dc in fourth ch from hook, ch 2, (3 dc, ch 2) 3 times in same ch, join with sl st in top of ch-3. *(12 dc made)*

Rnd 2: Ch 4, *(3 dc, ch 2, 3 dc) in next ch-2 sp, ch 1; repeat from * around to last ch sp, (3 dc, ch 2, 2 dc) in last ch sp, join with sl st in third ch of ch-4. *(24)*

Rnd 3: Ch 1, sc in each ch-1 and in each st around with 3 sc in each ch-2 sp, join with sl st in first sc. Fasten off. *(40 sc)*

YOKE

Hold two Squares right sides tog, matching sts; working through both thicknesses, join with sl st in corner, sl st in each st across. Fasten off.

BACK

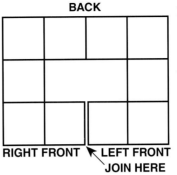

RIGHT FRONT ◄ LEFT FRONT
JOIN HERE

Repeat with remaining Squares according to diagram.

BODY

Row 1: With wrong side of yoke facing you, join with sl st in center sc on corner at lower edge of right front, ch 3; for **dc loop st (dlp**—*see illustration),* **yo, insert hook in next st, yo, pull through st (3 lps on hook); wrap yarn one time around finger, insert hook from right to left through second lp on finger, pull second lp only through 2 lps on hook, yo, pull through remaining 2 lps on hook, drop lp from finger;** evenly space 19 dlp across to next center corner st, (3 dlp in next st, evenly space 31 dlp across to next corner st, 3 dlp in next st), evenly space 42 dlp across to next corner st; repeat between ( ), evenly space 20 dlp across to next center corner st on lower corner of left front, dc in corner st, turn. *(158 sts)*

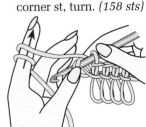

Row 2: Ch 3; for **front dlp (fr dlp), work same as dlp, pulling lp to front while you remove finger;** fr dlp in each st across to last st with 3 fr dlp in each center corner st, dc in last st, turn. *(166)*

Row 3: Ch 3, dlp in each st across to last st with 3 dlp in each center corner st, dc in last st, turn. *(174)*

⬩⬩⬩ Continued on page 150

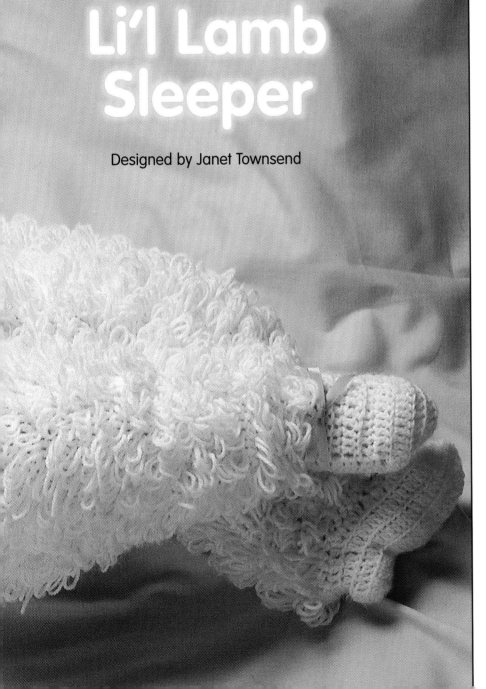

Li'l Lamb Sleeper

Designed by Janet Townsend

Sugar & Spice

Designed by Dawn Shaw

Sizes: Infant's 3–6 mos. and 6–9 mos.

Materials:
❑ Sport yarn:
     6 oz. main color (MC)
     2 oz. contrasting color (CC)
❑ Three ½" and three ¾" buttons
❑ Tapestry needle
❑ Hook or size hook needed to obtain gauge:
     D hook for 3–6 mos.
     E hook for 6–9 mos.

Gauges: **D hook,** 11 hdc = 2"; 4 hdc rows = 1". **E hook,** 5 hdc = 1"; 7 hdc rows = 2".

Basic Stitches: Ch, sl st, sc, hdc, dc.

BODICE
NOTE: CC trim rows are worked after Bodice is complete.
Row 1: Starting at waist, with MC, ch 107, hdc in third ch from hook, hdc in each ch across, turn. *(106 hdc made)*

Rows 2–8: Ch 2, hdc in each st across, turn.

Row 9: For **Left Back,** ch 2, hdc in next 21 sts, hdc next 2 sts tog leaving last 82 sts unworked, turn. *(23)*

Rows 10–21: Ch 2, hdc in each st across, turn.

Row 22: For **Shoulder Shaping,** ch 2, hdc in next 13 sts leaving last 9 sts unworked. Fasten off. *(14)*

Row 9: For **Front,** skip next 5 sts on row 8, join MC with sl st in next st, ch 2, hdc next 2 sts tog, hdc in next 43 sts, hdc next 2 sts tog leaving next 29 sts unworked, turn. *(46)*

Rows 10–13: Ch 2, hdc in each st across, turn.

Row 14: For **Right Front Shoulder,** ch 2, hdc in next 16 sts leaving next 29 sts unworked, turn. *(17)*

Row 15: Ch 2, hdc next 2 sts tog, hdc in each st across, turn.

Row 16: Ch 2, hdc in each st across to last 2 sts, hdc last 2 sts tog, turn. *(15)*

Row 17: Ch 2, hdc next 2 sts tog, hdc in each st across, turn. *(14)*

Rows 18–22: Ch 2, hdc in each st across, turn. At end of last row, fasten off.

Row 14: For **Left Front Shoulder,** skip next 12 sts on row 13, join MC with sl st in next st, ch 2, hdc in each st across, turn. *(17)*

Rows 15–17: Repeat rows 16 and 15 of Right Front Shoulder alternately.

Rows 18–22: Repeat rows 18–22 of Right Front Shoulder.

Row 9: For **Right Back,** skip next 5 sts on row 8, join MC with sl st in next st, ch 2, hdc next 2 sts tog, hdc in each st across, turn. *(23)*

Rows 10–21: Ch 2, hdc in each st across, turn.

Row 22: For **Shoulder Shaping,** sl st in first 10 sts, ch 2, hdc in each st across. Fasten off. *(14)*

For **CC trim,** with right side facing you, working across top of sts on odd-numbered rows up through row 11, hold CC underneath work and starting at right side of each section, *insert hook in next sp, yo, pull lp through st and lp on hook; repeat from * across. Fasten off. Sew shoulder seams tog.

SLEEVE (make 2)
Row 1: With CC, ch 13, hdc in third ch from hook, 2 hdc in next ch, hdc in next 7 chs, 2 hdc in each of last 2 chs, turn. *(15 hdc made)*

Rows 2–7: (Ch 2, hdc) in first st, hdc in each st across to last st, 2 hdc in last st, turn. At end of last row, fasten off. *(27)*

Row 8: With CC, ch 5, 2 hdc in last st on row 7, hdc in each st across to last st, 2 hdc in last st, turn. *(29)*

Row 9: Ch 6, hdc in third ch from hook, hdc in each of next 3 chs, hdc in next 29 sts, hdc in last 5 chs, turn. *(39)*

Rows 10–12: Ch 2, hdc in each st across, turn. At end of row 12, fasten off.

Row 13: Join MC with sc in first st, sc in each st across, turn.

Row 14: (Ch 3, skip next st, sl st in next st) across. Fasten off. *(19 ch sps)*

Matching ends of rows, sew ends of rows 9–14 tog. Easing sts on row 1 across shoulder, sew Sleeve in armhole.

COLLAR (make 2)
Row 1: With CC, ch 42, sc in second ch from hook, sc in next ch, hdc in each of next 3 chs, dc in next 31 chs, hdc in each of next 3 chs, sc in each of last 2 chs, turn. *(41 sts made)*

Row 2: Ch 1, sc in each of first 2 sts, hdc in each of next 3 sts, dc in next 31 sts, hdc in each of next 3 sts, sc in each of last 2 sts, turn.

Row 3: Sl st in each of first 2 sts, sc in each of next 3 sts, hdc in next 5 sts, dc in next 21 sts, hdc in next 5 sts, sc in each of next 3 sts, sl st in each of last 2 sts. Fasten off.

Row 4: Join MC with sc in end of row 1, sc in end of next row, skip next row, 2 sc in next st, sc in next 39 sts, 2 sc in next st, skip next row, sc in end of rows 2 and 1, turn. *(47)*

Continued on page 150

Sugar & Spice

Continued from page 149

Row 5: (Ch 3, skip next st, sl st in next st) across. Fasten off. *(23 ch sps)*

With right side of first Collar up, match end st on one end of row 5 to center of unworked sts on row 13 of Front and end st on opposite end of row 5 to last st on row 21 of Back; repeat on other side with second Collar. Working through both thicknesses and easing to fit, join CC with sl st in first st, sl st in each st across neck opening. Fasten off.

BUTTONHOLE PLACKET

Row 1: Join MC with sc in end of row 1 on left side of back, (2 sc in end of next row, sc in end of next row) across, turn. *(31 sc made)*

Row 2: Ch 1, sc in each of first 2 sts, (ch 3, skip next 3 sts, sc in next 9 sts) 2 times, ch 3, skip next 3 sts, sc in each of last 2 sts, turn. *(3 buttonholes)*

Row 3: Ch 1, sc in each st and in each ch across. Fasten off. *(31)*

Sew ¾" buttons on corresponding rows of Right Back to match buttonholes.

SKIRT

Row 1: Working on opposite side of starting ch of Bodice, join MC with sc in first ch; for **shell, 3 dc in next ch;** (sc in next ch, shell in next ch) 51 times, sc next 2 sts tog, turn. *(52 shells made)*

Rows 2–5: Ch 3, 2 dc in next st, (sc in center st of next shell, shell in next sc) 51 times, sc in center st of next shell, 2 dc in last st, turn.

Rnds 6–24: Working in rnds, ch 3, 2 dc in next st, (sc in center st of next shell, shell in next sc) 51 times, sc in center st of next shell, join with sl st in top of ch-3, **turn.** At end of last rnd, fasten off. *(52 shells)*

Rnd 25: Join CC with sl st in first st, ch 2, hdc in each st around, join with sl st in top of ch-2, **turn.** *(208 hdc)*

Rnd 26: (Ch 3, skip next st, sl st in next st) around, join with sl st in same st as ch-3. Fasten off. *(77 ch sps)*

POCKET

Row 1: With CC, ch 10, hdc in third ch from hook, hdc in each ch across, turn. *(9 hdc made)*

Rows 2–3: (Ch 2, hdc) in first st, hdc in each st across to last st, 2 hdc in last st, turn. *(11, 13)*

Rows 4–5: Ch 1, sc in each st across, turn.

Rnd 6: Working around outside edge, ch 1, 2 sc in first st, sc in next 11 sts, 2 sc in next st, sc in end of next 2 rows, 2 sc in end of next row, sc in end of next row, 2 sc in end of next row; working on opposite side of starting ch, 2 sc in first ch, sc in next 7 chs, 2 sc in next ch, (2 sc in end of next row, sc in end of next row) 2 times, sc in end of next row, join with sl st in first sc, **turn.**

Row 7: (Ch 3, skip next st, sl st in next st) 13 times leaving remaining sts unworked. Fasten off. *(13 ch sps)*

For **MC trim,** working across rows 3–5, work same as CC trim on Bodice. Sew pocket on left front Bodice over rnds 3–8. Sew ½" buttons evenly spaced down front of Bodice. ✪

Li'l Lamb Sleeper

Continued from page 147

Rows 4–5: Repeat rows 2–3. *(182, 190)*

Row 6: Ch 3, fr dlp in next 25 sts; for **armhole,** skip next 43 sts; fr dlp in next 52 sts; for **armhole,** skip next 43 sts; fr dlp in next 24 sts, dc in last st, turn. *(104)*

Row 7: Ch 3, dlp in each st across to last st, dc in last st, turn.

Row 8: Ch 3, fr dlp in each st across to last st, dc in last st, turn.

Rows 9–14: Repeat rows 7 and 8 alternately.

Row 15: Ch 3, dlp in next 6 sts, 2 dlp in next st, (dlp in next 9 sts, 2 dlp in next st) 9 times, dlp in next 5 sts, dc in st st, turn. *(114)*

Rows 16–22: Repeat rows 8 and 7 alternately, ending with row 8.

Row 23: Ch 3, dlp in next 6 sts, 2 dlp in next st, (dlp in next 10 sts, 2 dlp in next st) 9 times, dlp in next 6 sts, dc in last st, turn. *(124)*

Rows 24–31: Repeat rows 8 and 7 alternately.

Row 32: Ch 3, fr dlp in next 6 sts, 2 fr dlp in next st, (fr dlp in next 11 sts, 2 fr dlp in next st) 9 times, fr dlp in next 7 sts, dc in last st, turn. *(134)*

Rows 33–36: Repeat rows 7 and 8 alternately.

Rnd 37: For **right leg,** working in rnds, ch 3, dlp in next 66 sts, skip next 67 sts, join with sl st in top of ch-3. *(67)*

Rnd 38: Ch 3, skip next st, dlp in each st around, join. *(66)*

Rnd 39: Ch 3, skip next st, dlp in each st around to last st, skip last st, join. *(64)*

Rnds 40–55: Repeat rnds 38 and 39 alternately. At end of last rnd *(40)*.

Rnds 56–59: Repeat rnd 39. At end of last rnd, fasten off. *(32)*.

Row 60: For **foot,** working in rows, join with sl st in fifth st of rnd 59, ch 3, dc in next 9 sts leaving last 18 sts unworked, turn. *(10)*

Rows 61–64: Working in **back lps** (see Stitch Guide), ch 3, dc in each st across, turn. At end of last row, **do not turn.**

Rnd 65: For **sole,** working around outer edge of foot and bottom of leg in ends of rows and in sts, ch 3, dc in first row, 2 dc in each of next 4 rows, dc in next 22 unworked sts on rnd 59, 2 dc in each of next 4 rows, dc in last row, 3 dc in next st, dc in **front lp** of next 8 sts, 2 dc in same st as ch-3, join with sl st in top of ch-3, **turn.** (54)

Rnds 66–67: Working in **back lps,** ch 3, dc in each st around, join. At end of last rnd, **turn.**

Rnd 68: Working in **front lps,** ch 3, *dc in next 14 sts, (dc next 2 sts tog) 6 times; repeat from *, dc in last st, join. Fasten off.

With right sides tog, fold sole between third and fourth decrease sts on each end; working through both thicknesses, matching sts, sl st opening closed.

Row 37: For **left leg,** join with sl st in first skipped st on rows 36, ch 3, dlp in each st across, turn. **Do not join.** (67)

Row 38: Ch 3, skip first st, fr dlp in each st across, turn. (66)

Row 39: Ch 3, skip next st, dlp in each st across leaving last st unworked, turn. (64)

Rows 40–55: Repeat rows 38 and 39 alternately. At end of last row (40).

Row 56: Ch 3, skip next st, fr dlp in each st across leaving last st unworked, turn. (38)

Rows 57–59: Repeat rows 39 and 56 alternately, ending with row 39 and 32 sts. At end of last row, **do not turn.** Fasten off.

Row 60: For **foot,** join with sl st in 19th st of row 59, ch 3, dc in next 9 sts leaving last 4 sts unworked, turn. (10)

Rows 61–64: Repeat rows 61–64 of right leg.

Rnd 65: For **sole,** working around outer edge of foot in ends of rows and in sts, ch 3, dc in first row, 2 dc in each of next 4 rows, dc in next 4 unworked sts on row 59, dc in first 18 sts of row 59, 2 dc in each of next 4 rows, dc in next row, 3 dc in next st, dc in **front lp** of next 8 sts, 2 dc in same st as first ch-3, join with sl st in top of ch-3, **turn.** (54)

Rnds 66–68: Repeat rnds 66–68 of right leg.

Turn right side out.

SLEEVE

Rnd 1: Working around armhole, with wrong side facing you, join with sl st in first skipped st on row 6, ch 3, dlp in each skipped st around, dlp in side of st on row 6, dlp between sts on row 5, dlp in side of other st on row 6, join with sl st in top of ch-3. (46 sts made)

Rnds 2–16: Ch 3, dlp in each st around, join.

*NOTE: To **dlp next 2 sts tog,** yo, insert hook in next st, yo, pull through st, yo, pull through 2 lps on hook, yo, insert hook in next st, yo, pull through st (4 lps on hook), wrap yarn one time around finger, insert hook from right to left through second lp on*

finger, pull second lp only through 2 lps on hook, yo, pull through all 3 lps on hook, drop lp from finger.

Rnd 17: Ch 3, dlp in next st, (dlp next 2 sts tog, dlp in each of next 2 sts) around, join. (35)

Rnd 18: Ch 3, (dlp next 2 sts tog, dlp in each of next 2 sts) across to last 2 sts, dlp last 2 sts tog, join. (26)

Rnd 19: Ch 1, sc in each st around, join. Fasten off.

Turn right side out.

Repeat on other armhole.

HOOD

Row 1: With wrong side facing you, join with sl st in third st from right-hand corner of neck opening, ch 3, evenly space 64 dlp across neck opening to 4 sts from left-hand corner of neck edge, dc in next st leaving last 3 sts unworked, turn. (66 sts)

Row 2: Ch 3, fr dlp in next 4 sts, (2 fr dlp in next st, fr dlp in next 10 sts) 5 times, 2 fr dlp in next st, fr dlp in next 4 sts, dc in last sts, turn. (72)

Row 3: Ch 3, dlp in each st across to last st, dc in last st, turn.

Row 4: Ch 3, fr dlp in each st across to last st, dc in last st, turn.

Rows 5–16: Repeat rows 3 and 4 alternately. At end of last row, fold row 16 right sides tog, matching sts; sl st across. Fasten off.

FINISHING

For zipper, measure 22" down front from neck; matching ends of rows, sew remaining rows of left leg together. Sew first and last sts of rnd 37 on right leg together.

Border

Rnd 1: With right side facing you, join with sc in top of seam on left leg, 2 sc in end of each row across to Yoke, sc in each st on Yoke, 3 sc in corner sp, sc in each of next 2 sts, sc next st and end of next row tog, 2 sc in end of each row around Hood to last row, sc end of last row and next st on Yoke tog, sc in each of next 2 sts, 3 sc in corner sp, sc in each st across Yoke, 2 sc in end of each row down front, join with sl st in first sc.

Rnd 2: Ch 1, sc next 2 sts tog, sc in each st across to center corner st, 3 sc in next st, skip next 3 sts, (dc in next st, ch 1, skip next st) 31 times, skip next 3 sts, 3 sc in corner, sc in each st across to last 2 sts, sc last 2 sts tog, join.

Rnd 3: Ch 1, sc next 2 sts tog, sc in each st around to last 2 sts, sc last 2 sts tog, join. Fasten off.

Fold top ends of zipper under. Pin zipper in place under Border on front, sew in place. Cut 36" ribbon, weave through rnd 2 of Hood Border. Cut two 9" pieces ribbon. Tie in bow, sew to top of each foot. Cut two 18" pieces ribbon, weave one through last rnd on each Sleeve, tie in bow. ✿

Rodeo Rider

Designed by Michele Lupo

Sizes: Infant's 6 mos., 9 mos. and 12 mos.

Materials:
- ❑ Sport yarn:
  - 5 oz. dark
  - 3 oz. light
  - 2 oz. off-white
  - Small amount red
- ❑ 3 strands thread elastic to fit waist
- ❑ 3 brown and 1 red ⅜" buttons
- ❑ Tapestry needle
- ❑ G hook or hook needed to obtain gauge

Gauges: 9 sc = 2"; 11 sc rows = 2".

Basic Stitches: Ch, sl st, sc.

Note: Instructions are for 6 mos. Changes for 9 mos. and 12 mos. are in [ ].

BIB

Front (make 2)
Row 1: With dark, ch 15 [16, 17], 2 sc in second ch from hook, sc in each ch across, turn. *(15 sc made) [16 sc made, 17 sc made]*

Row 2: Ch 1, sc in each st across to last st, 2 sc in last st, turn. *(16) [17, 18]*

Row 3: Ch 1, 2 sc in first st, sc in each st across, turn. *(17) [18, 10]*

Rows 4–6: Repeat rows 2 and 3 alternately, ending with 20 [21, 22] sts in last row.

Rows 7–28 [7–30, 7–32]: Ch 1, sc in each st across, turn.

Row 29 [31, 33]: For **armhole shaping,** ch 1, sc in each st across to last 2 sts leaving last 2 sts unworked, turn. *(18) [19, 20]*

Row 30 [32, 34]: Ch 1, sc first 2 sts tog, sc in each st across, turn. *(17) [18, 19]*

Row 31 [33, 35]: Ch 1, sc in each st across to last 2 sts, sc last 2 sts tog, turn. *(16) [17, 18]*

Rows 32–34 [34–45, 36–47]: Ch 1, sc in each st across, turn.

Row 44 [46, 48]: For **neck shaping,** ch 1, sc in each st across to last 4 sts leaving last 4 sts unworked, turn. *(12) [13, 14]*

Rows 45–47 [47–49, 49–51]: Repeat rows 30 and 31 alternately, ending with 9 [10, 11] sts in last row.

Row 48 [50, 52]: Ch 1, sc in each st across, turn.

Row 49 [51, 53]: Ch 1, sc in first 4 [5, 6] sts, sl st in next st leaving last 4 sts unworked, turn.

Row 50 [52, 54]: Sl st in each of first 3 sts, sc in each st across. Fasten off.

Center Front
Row 1: With off-white, ch 15, sl st in second ch from hook, sl st in next ch, ch 1, sc in same ch, sc in each ch across leaving last ch unworked, turn. *(12 sc made)*

Rows 2–5: Ch 1, sc first 2 sts tog, sc in each st across to last 2 sts, sc last 2 sts tog, turn. At end of last row *(4).*

Rows 6–43 [6–45, 6–47]: Ch 1, sc in each st across, turn. At end of last row, fasten off.

Matching ends of rows 1–43 [1–45, 1–47] on each piece, sew Center Front to two Front pieces.

Back
Row 1: With dark, ch 45 [47, 49], sc in second ch from hook, sc in each ch across, turn. *(44 sc made) [46 sc made, 48 sc made]*

Rows 2–28 [2–30, 2–32]: Ch 1, sc in each st across, turn.

Row 29 [31, 33]: For **armhole shaping,** sl st in each of first 2 sts, (sl st, ch 1, sc) in next st, sc in each st across leaving last 2 sts unworked, turn. *(40) [42, 44]*

Row 30 [32, 34]: Ch 1, sc first 2 sts tog, sc in each st across to last 2 sts, sc last 2 sts tog, turn. *(38) [40, 42]*

Rows 31–49 [33–51, 35–53]: Ch 1, sc in each st across, turn.

Row 50 [52, 54]: Sl st in first 4 [5, 6] sts, sc in next st, sc in each st across to last 5 [6, 7] sts, sl st in next st. Fasten off.

Matching sts, sew last 9 [10, 11] sts on right back to right front shoulder.

Buttonhole Flap
Row 1: With right side facing you, join dark with sc in first st on left front shoulder, sc in each st across, turn. *(9 sc made) [10 sc made, 11 sc made]*

Row 2: Ch 1, sc in first st; for **buttonholes,** ch 2, skip next st, (sc in each of next 2 sts, ch 2, skip next st) 2 times, sc in each st across. Fasten off. Overlapping ends of rows at shoulder, sew ends of rows 2 and 2 of buttonhole flap and ends of last 2 rows on back left shoulder tog at armhole edge.

Sleeve (make 2)
Row 1: With off-white, ch 31 [36, 41], sc in second ch from hook, sc in each ch across, turn. *(30 sc made) [35 sc made, 40 sc made]*

Rows 2–6 [2–8, 2–10]: Ch 1, sc in each st across, turn.

Continued on page 159

Peach & Pineapple Dress Set

Designed by Mary Layfield

Sizes: Infant's 6–12 mos. Finished measurement: 19½" chest.

Materials:
- ❑ Baby or fingering yarn:
  - 10 oz. peach
  - ½ oz. white
- ❑ Ribbon:
  - 2 yds. of ¼" white
  - 10" of ⅛" lt. blue
- ❑ 12 blue 18mm ribbon roses or rosebuds
- ❑ 4 snaps
- ❑ Four tiny peach buttons
- ❑ 6" square of iron-on flexible vinyl
- ❑ Peach sewing thread
- ❑ Sewing and embroidery needles
- ❑ D hook or hook need to obtain gauge

Gauge: 7 sts or chs = 1"; 5 diagonal st rows and 4 sc rows = 2".

Basic Stitches: Ch, sl st, sc, dc, tr.

Special Stitches:
For **diagonal st (d-st),** skip next 2 sts, tr in next st; working behind tr, dc in 2 skipped sts.
For **reverse diagonal st (reverse d-st),** skip next st, dc in each of next 2 sts; working behind last 2 dc, tr in skipped st.
For **beginning shell (beg shell),** sl st across to first ch sp, (sl st, ch 3, dc, ch 2, 2 dc) in ch sp.
For **shell,** (2 dc, ch 2, 2 dc) in ch sp of next shell.

DRESS
Bodice Front
Row 1: With peach, ch 66, sc in second ch from hook, sc in each ch across, turn. *(65 sc made)*
Row 2: Ch 3 *(counts as dc),* (**d-st**—*see Special Stitches,* dc in next st) across, turn. *(65 sts—each d-st is counted as 3 dc).* **Front** *of row 2 is right side of work.*
Row 3: Ch 1, sc in each st across, turn.
Rows 4–5: Repeat rows 2–3.
Row 6: For **Armhole,** sl st in first 5 sts, ch 3, (d-st, dc in next st) across to last 4 sts leaving last 4 sts unworked for **Armhole,** turn. *(57 sts)*
Row 7: Ch 1, sc in each st across, turn.
Rows 8–9: Repeat rows 2–3.
Row 10: Sl st in first 3 sts, ch 3, dc in next 2 sts, (d-st in next st) across to last 4 sts, dc in next 2 sts leaving last 2 sts, turn. *(53)*
Rows 11–12: Repeat rows 3 and 2.
Row 13: Ch 1, skip first st, sc in each st across to last 2 sts, sc last 2 sts tog, turn. *(51)*
Row 14: Sl st in first 2 sts, ch 3, (d-st, dc in next st) across leaving last st unworked, turn. *(49)*
Rows 15–19: Repeat rows 3 and 2 alternately, ending with row 3.
Row 20: For **first shoulder,** ch 1, sc in first 22 sts leaving remaining sts unworked, turn. *(22)*
Row 21: Ch 1, sc in each st across, turn.
Row 22: Ch 3, (d-st, dc in next st) 4 times, sc in next st leaving last 4 sts unworked, turn. *(18)*
Row 23: Sl st in next st, ch 3, dc in each of next 3 sts, sc in each st across, turn. *(17)*
Row 24: Ch 3, (d-st, dc in next st) 2 times, (skip next 2 sts, dtr in next st, tr in each of 2 skipped sts, tr in next st) 2 times, turn.
Row 25: Ch 3, dc in each of next 3 sts, sc in each st across. Fasten off.
Row 20: For **Second Shoulder,** with front of row 19 facing you, join with sl st in opposite end of row 19, repeat row 20 of First Shoulder.
Rows 21–25: Repeat rows 21–25 of First Shoulder. working **reverse d-sts** *(see Special Stitches)* instead of d-sts.

First Bodice Back
Row 1: With peach, ch 37, sc in second ch from hook, sc in each ch across, turn. *(36 sc made)*
Row 2: Ch 3, d-st, (dc in next st, d-st) across, turn. *(36 sts) Front of row 2 is right side of work.*
Row 3: Ch 1, sc in each st across, turn.
Rows 4–5: Repeat rows 2–3.
Row 6: Ch 3, d-st, (dc in next st, d-st) across leaving last 4 sts unworked for **Armhole,** turn. *(32)*
Row 7: Ch 1, sc in each st across, turn.
Rows 8–9: Repeat rows 2–3.
Row 10: Ch 3, d-st, (dc in next st, d-st) across to last 4 sts, dc in next 2 sts leaving last 2 sts, turn. *(30)*
Row 11: Ch 1, sc in each st across, turn.
Row 12: Ch 3, d-st, (dc in next st, d-st) across leaving last st unworked, turn. *(29)*
Row 13: Ch 1, sc in each st across, turn.
Row 14: Ch 2 *(not worked into or counted as st),* (d-st, dc in next st) across, turn. *(28)*
Rows 15–20: Repeat rows 3 and 2 alternately.

• • • • • • • • • • • • • • • • • • • Continued on page 156

Peach & Pineapple Dress Set

Continued from page 155

Row 21: Ch 1, sc in each st across, turn. Fasten off.
Row 22: For **Shoulder,** skip first 11 sts, join peach with sl st in next st, ch 3, (d-st, dc in next st) across, turn. *(17)*
Row 23: Ch 1, sc in each st across, turn.
Row 24: Ch 3, dc in each st across, turn.
Rows 25–26: Ch 1, sc in each st across, turn. At end of last row, fasten off.

Second Bodice Back
Rows 1–5: Repeat rows 1–5 of First Bodice Back.
Row 6: For **Armhole,** sl st in first 5 sts, ch 3, d-st, (dc in next st, d-st) across, turn. *(32)*
Row 7: Ch 1, sc in each st across, turn.
Rows 8–9: Repeat rows 2–3 of First Bodice Back.
Row 10: Sl st in each of first 3 sts, ch 3, (d-st, dc in next st) across with dc in last st, turn. *(30)*
Row 11: Ch 1, sc in each st across, turn.
Row 12: Ch 3, d-st, (dc in next st, d-st) across to last 2 sts, dc in next st leaving last st unworked, turn. *(29)*
Row 13: Ch 1, sc in each st across, turn.
Row 14: Sl st in each of first 2 sts, ch 3, d-st, (dc in next st, d-st) across, turn. *(28)*
Rows 15–21: Repeat rows 3 and 2 of First Bodice Back alternately, ending with row 3.
Row 22: For **Shoulder,** ch 3, (d-st, dc in next st) 4 times leaving remaining sts unworked, turn. *(17)*
Rows 23–26: Repeat rows 23–26 of First Bodice Back.
Sew one Back to each side of Front across ends of rows 1–5.
For shoulder seams on each side, sew last rows on Backs and Fronts together.

Skirt
Row 1: Working on opposite side of starting ch on Backs and Front, with wrong side of work facing you, join peach with sc in first ch at center back; skipping 2 chs at one seam and one ch at other seam, sc in each ch across, turn. *(134 sc made)*
Row 2: (Ch 3, dc) in first st, ch 2, 2 dc in next st, (skip next st, 2 dc in next st, ch 2, 2 dc in next st) across, turn. *(45 ch-2 sps)*
Row 3: Beg shell *(see Special Stitches),* (ch 2, **shell**— *see Special Stitches*—in next ch sp) across, turn. *(45 shells, 44 ch sps)*
Row 4: Beg shell, (ch 2, sc in next ch sp, ch 2, shell) across, turn. *(45 shells, 88 ch sps)*
Row 5: Beg shell, (ch 3, sc in next ch sp, ch 2, sc in next ch sp, ch 3, shell) across, turn. *(45 shells, 132 ch sps)*
Row 6: Beg shell, (ch 3, skip next 3 ch sps, shell) across, turn. *(45 shells, 44 ch sps)*
Row 7: Beg shell, (ch 3, sc in next ch sp, ch 3, shell) across, turn. *(45 shells, 88 ch sps)*
Row 8: Repeat row 5.

Row 9: Beg shell, (ch 4, skip next 3 ch sps, shell) across, turn. *(45 shells, 44 ch sps)*
Row 10: Beg shell, (ch 3, sc in next ch sp, ch 3, shell) across, turn. *(45 shells, 88 ch sps)*
Row 11: Beg shell, (ch 4, sc in next ch sp, ch 2, sc in next ch sp, ch 4, shell) across, turn. *(45 shells, 132 ch sps)*
Rnd 12: Beg shell, (ch 4, skip next 3 ch sps, shell) across, ch 2, join with dc in top of ch-3, **do not turn.** *(Ch-2 and dc count as joining ch sp—45 shells, 45 ch sps.)*
Rnd 13: Ch 1, sc in joining ch sp, ch 3, (3 dc, ch 2, 3 dc) in next shell, *ch 3, sc in next ch sp, ch 3, (3 dc, ch 2, 3 dc) in next shell; repeat from * around, ending with ch 3, join with sl st in first sc. *(135 ch sps)*
Rnd 14: Sl st in next ch, ch 1, sc in next ch, ch 4, (3 dc, ch 2, 3 dc) in next ch sp, *ch 4, sc in next ch sp, ch 2, sc in next ch sp, ch 4, (3 dc, ch 2, 3 dc) in next ch sp; repeat from * around, ending with ch 4, sc in next ch sp, ch 2, join. *(180 ch sps)*
Rnd 15: Sl st across to next dc, ch 3, dc in each of next 2 dc, 6 dc in next ch sp, dc in each of next 3 dc, ch 3, skip next 3 ch sps, (dc in each of next 3 dc, 6 dc in next ch sp, dc in each of next 3 dc, ch 3, skip next 3 ch sps) around, join with sl st in top of ch-3. *(12 dc and 1 ch sp in each repeat)*
Rnd 16: Ch 3, dc in each of next 2 dc, ch 3, dc in next dc, (ch 1, dc in next dc) 5 times, ch 3, dc in each of next 3 dc, skip next ch sp, *dc in each of next 3 dc, ch 3, dc in next dc, (ch 1, dc in next dc) 5 times, ch 3, dc in each of next 3 dc, skip next ch sp; repeat from * around, join. *(12 dc, 7 ch sps in each repeat)*
Rnd 17: Sl st across to next ch sp, (sl st, ch 3, 2 dc) in ch sp, (ch 5, sc in next ch sp) 5 times, ch 5, 3 dc in next ch sp, *3 dc in next ch sp, (ch 5, sc in next ch sp) 5 times, ch 5, 3 dc in next ch sp; repeat from * around, join. *(6 ch sps in each repeat)*
Rnd 18: Sl st across to next ch sp, (sl st, ch 3, 2 dc) in ch sp, (ch 5, sc in next ch sp) 4 times, ch 5, 3 dc in next ch sp, *3 dc in next ch sp, (ch 5, sc in next ch sp) 4 times, ch 5, 3 dc in next ch sp; repeat from * around, join. *(5 ch sps in each repeat)*
Rnd 19: Sl st across to next ch sp, (sl st, ch 3, 2 dc) in ch sp, (ch 5, sc in next ch sp) 3 times, ch 5, 3 dc in next ch sp, ch 3, *3 dc in next ch sp, (ch 5, sc in next ch sp) 3 times, ch 5, 3 dc in next ch sp, ch 3; repeat from * around, join.
Rnd 20: Sl st across to next ch sp, (sl st, ch 3, 2 dc) in ch sp, (ch 5, sc in next ch sp) 2 times, ch 5, 3 dc in next ch sp, ch 3, dc in next ch sp, ch 3, *3 dc in next ch sp, (ch 5, sc in next ch sp) 2 times, ch 5, 3 dc in next ch sp, ch 3, dc in next ch sp, ch 3; repeat from * around, join.
Rnd 21: Sl st across to next ch sp, (sl st, ch 3, 2 dc) in ch sp, ch 5, sc in next ch sp, (ch 5, sc in next ch sp) 2 times, *3 dc in next ch sp, ch 5, sc in next ch sp,

ch 5, 3 dc in next ch sp, ch 3, (dc in next ch sp, ch 3) 2 times; repeat from * around, join.

Rnd 22: Sl st across to next ch sp, (sl st, ch 3, 2 dc) in ch sp, ch 3, 3 dc in next ch sp, ch 5, (dc in next ch sp, ch 5) 3 times, *3 dc in next ch sp, ch 3, 3 dc in next ch sp, ch 5, (dc in next ch sp, ch 5) 3 times; repeat from * around, join.

Rnd 23: Sl st across to next ch sp, (sl st, ch 3, 2 dc) in ch sp, ch 6, sl st in fourth ch from hook, ch 2, (3 dc in next ch sp, ch 6, sl st in fourth ch from hook, ch 2) around, join. Fasten off.

Sleeve (make 2)

Row 1: With peach, ch 58, sc in second ch from hook, sc in each ch across, turn. *(57 sc made)*

Row 2: Ch 4 *(counts as dc and ch-1)*, skip next st, dc in next st, (ch 1, skip next st, dc in next st) across, turn. *(29 dc, 28 ch sps)*

Row 3: Ch 1, sc in each st across, turn. *(57 sc)*

Row 4: Ch 3, dc in next st, (ch 2, skip next st, dc in next st) 3 times, (ch 2, dc in next st) across to last 7 sts, (ch 2, skip next st, dc in next st) 3 times, dc in last st, turn. *(51 dc)*

NOTE: Skip each ch sp unless otherwise stated.

Row 5: Ch 3, dc in next st, (ch 2, dc in next st) across to last st, dc in last st, turn.

Row 6: For **Cap of Sleeve**, sl st in first 3 sts and 1 ch, ch 5 *(sl sts are not worked into or counted as sts)*, dc in next st, (ch 2, dc in next st) across leaving last 2 sts unworked, turn. *(47 dc)*

Row 7: Sl st in first 2 sts and 1 ch, ch 5, dc in next st, (ch 2, dc in next st) across leaving last st unworked, turn. *(45)*

Rows 8–21: Sl st in first 2 sts and 1 ch, ch 5, dc in next st, (ch 2, dc in next st) across leaving last 2 sts unworked, turn. At end of last row, fasten off. *(3 dc)*

Sew ends of rows 1–5 together at underarm.

Row 22: To gather Cap of Sleeve, join peach with sc in end of row 7, 2 sc in each ch sp across Cap of Sleeve to other end of row 7. Fasten off.

Matching underarm seam to top of side seam on Bodice, easing cap of sleeve to fit, sew Sleeve in Armhole.

For **Sleeve Trim**, working around one Sleeve in opposite side of starting ch on row 1, join peach with sc at seam, ch 4, (sc in next ch, ch 4) around, join with sl st in first sc. Fasten off. Repeat on other Sleeve.

Neck Trim

Row 1: Working in sts and in ends of rows around neck edge, join peach with sc at center back neck edge; placing one sc in each st and in end of each sc row with 2 sc in end of each dc row and 3 sc in end of each tr row, sc across neck edge to center back on other side.

Row 2: Ch 1, sc in first st, (ch 4, sc in next st) across. Fasten off.

Row 3: Join white with sc in first ch sp, (ch 4, sc in next ch sp) across. Fasten off.

Dress Finishing

Sew one ribbon rose to center of row 18 on Bodice Front.

Lapping left Back over right Back, sew four snaps evenly spaced on center back edges between Bodice Backs, sew one button over each snap on outside of left Back.

Cut two 18" pieces of white ribbon, weave one piece through row 2 on each Sleeve, tie ends in bow at center of Sleeve.

PINAFORE
Overskirt

Row 1: With white, ch 117, sc in second ch from hook, sc in each ch across, **do not turn.** Fasten off. *(116 sc made)*

Row 2: Join peach with sc in first st, sc in each st across, turn.

Row 3: (Ch 3, dc) in first st, ch 2, 2 dc in next st, (skip next st, 2 dc in next st, ch 2, 2 dc in next st) across, turn. *(39 ch sps)*

Rows 4–12: Repeat rows 3–11 of Dress Skirt on page 156.

Rows 13–15: Repeat rows 9–11 of Dress Skirt. At end of last row, fasten off. *(45 shells)*

Row 16: Working on opposite side of starting ch on row 1, join peach with sc in first ch, sc in each ch across. Fasten off.

Front Bib

Row 1: Join peach with sl st in 42nd st on row 16 of Overskirt, ch 3, dc in next st, (d-st, dc in next st) 8 times, dc in next st leaving last 40 sts unworked, turn. *(35 sts made)*

Row 2: Ch 1, sc in each st across, turn.

Row 3: Ch 3, dc in each st across, turn.

Rows 4–10: Repeat rows 2 and 3 alternately.

Row 11: Ch 3, dc in next st, (d-st, dc in next st) 8 times, dc in next st, turn.

Row 12: Ch 1, sc in each st across, turn. Fasten off.

Row 13: Join white with sc in first st, sc in each st across, turn. Fasten off.

Row 14: Join peach with sc in first st, sc in each st across, turn.

Row 15: Working over row 14 into sts of row 13, ch 1, sc in each st across, turn.

Row 16: Working in row 15, ch 1, sc in first st, (ch 3, sc in next st) across. Fasten off.

Strap (make 2)

Row 1: With white, ch 78, sc in second ch from hook, sc in each ch across, turn. Fasten off. *(77 sc made)* *Front of row 1 is right side of work.*

Row 2: Join peach with sc in first st, sc in each st across, turn.

Row 3: For **ruffle**, ch 1, sc in first 7 sts, ch 2, (dc, ch 2, 2 dc) in next st, *skip next st, (2 dc, ch 2, 2 dc) in next st; repeat from * 30 more times leaving last 7 sts unworked, turn. *(32 ch sps)*

Continued on page 158

Peach & Pineapple Dress Set

Continued from page 157

Row 4: Beg shell, (ch 2, shell in next ch sp) across, turn. *(32 shells, 31 ch sps)*

Row 5: Beg shell, (ch 2, sc in next ch sp, ch 2, shell) across, turn. *(32 shells, 63 ch sps)*

Row 6: Beg shell, (ch 3, skip next 2 ch sps, shell) across, turn. *(32 shells, 31 ch sps)*

Row 7: Sl st across to next ch sp, (sl st, ch 3, 2 dc) in next ch sp, *ch 4, (sc, ch 4, sc) in next ch sp, 3 dc in next ch sp; repeat from * across. Fasten off.

Row 8: With wrong side of row 1 facing you, working on opposite side of starting ch, join peach with sc in first ch, sc in each ch across, turn. *(77 sc)*

Row 9: Ch 3, (d-st, dc in next st) across, turn.

Row 10: Ch 1, sc in each st across, turn. Fasten off.

Row 11: Join white with sc in first st, sc in each st across, turn. Fasten off.

Row 12: Join peach with sc in first st, sc in each st across. Fasten off.

Pinafore Finishing

On each end of each Strap, sew ends of rows 4–7 to wrong side of seven stitches at end of row 2.

On each side of Pinafore Bib, with right sides of all pieces facing you, sew one end of one Strap over 2 stitches at ends of rows 1–15 on Bib; sew ends of rows on Strap under edge of waistband on Overskirt.

Cut two pieces of blue ribbon each 2½" long, sew one ribbon rose ¼" from each end of each piece.

Tack the four roses to center front of Pinafore Bib forming an "X" with the ribbons.

Tack two ribbon roses to waistband at ends of Straps.

Place Pinafore on Dress and baste tog around waist. Tack Straps in place over shoulders, sew ends of Straps under waistband at center of each Back Bodice.

Sew Pinafore and Dress tog around waist; sew back opening on Overskirt and Skirt tog. Remove basting.

BIB

Row 1: With peach, ch 18, sc in second ch from hook, sc in each ch across, turn. *(17 sc made)*

Rows 2–12: Ch 1, 2 sc in first st, sc in each st across to last st, 2 sc in last st, turn. At end of last row *(39)*.

Row 13: Ch 1, sc in each st across, turn.

Row 14: Ch 1, 2 sc in first st, sc in each st across to last st, 2 sc in last st, turn. *(41)*

Rows 15–28: Ch 1, sc in each st across, turn.

Row 29: For **first strap**, ch 1, sc in first 16 sts leaving remaining sts unworked, turn. *(16)*

Row 30: Ch 1, sc in each st across, turn.

Row 31: Ch 1, skip first st, sc in each st across, turn. *(15)*

Rows 32–41: Repeat rows 30 and 31 alternately. At end of last row *(10)*.

Rows 42–46: Ch 1, sc in each st across, turn.

Row 47: Ch 1, sc in each st across to last st, 2 sc in last st, turn. *(11)*

Row 48: Ch 1, 2 sc in first st, sc in each st across leaving last st unworked, turn.

Row 49: Ch 1, sc in each st across to last st, 2 sc in last st, turn. *(12)*

Row 50: Ch 1, sc in each st across, turn.

Row 51: Ch 1, sc in each st across to last st, 2 sc in last st, turn. *(13)*

Row 52: Ch 1, sc in each st across leaving last st unworked, turn. *(12)*

Rows 53–55: Repeat rows 51, 52 and 51. *(13, 12, 13)*

Row 56: Ch 3, sc in second ch from hook, sc in next ch, sc in each st across leaving last st unworked, turn. *(14)*

Row 57: Ch 1, sc in each st across, turn.

Rows 58–61: Repeat rows 56 and 57 alternately. *(15, 16)*

Rows 62–63: Ch 1, sc in each st across leaving last st unworked, turn. At end of last row, fasten off. *(15, 14)*

Row 29: For **second strap,** with right side of row 28 facing you, join with sc in first st at opposite end of row 28, sc in next 15 sts leaving remaining sts unworked, turn. *(16)*

Rows 30–63: Repeat rows 30–63 of first strap. At end of last row, **do not fasten off.** Remove loop from hook.

For **lining,** using rows 1–46 as pattern, cut a piece of flexible vinyl ½" smaller than Bib on all edges and lay aside.

Border

Rnd 1: Return loop to hook, ch 1; working around outer edge, sc in each st and in end of each row around entire Bib, join with sl st in first sc.

Rnd 2: Ch 1, sc in first st, ch 4, (sc, ch 4) in each st around, join with sl st in first sc. Fasten off.

Row 3: Join white with sc in first ch sp, ch 4, sc in same ch sp, ch 4, (sc, ch 4, sc, ch 4) in each ch sp around, join. Fasten off.

Trim

Row 1: Ch 5, sl st in first ch to form ring, (ch 3, 2 dc, ch 2, 3 dc) in ring, turn. *(6 dc, 1 ch sp made)*

Row 2: Ch 3, dc in each of next 2 sts, ch 1, 6 dc in next ch sp, ch 1, dc in each of last 3 sts, turn. *(12 dc, 2 ch sps)*

Row 3: Ch 3, dc in each of next 2 sts, ch 1, dc in next dc, (ch 1, dc in next dc) 5 times, ch 1, dc in each of last 3 sts, turn. *(12 dc, 7 ch sps)*

Rows 4–8: Sl st across to first ch sp, (sl st, ch 3, 2 dc) in ch sp, (ch 5, sc in next ch sp) across to last ch sp, ch 5, 3 dc in last ch sp, turn. At end of last row *(2 ch sps)*.

Row 9: Sl st across to first ch sp, (ch 3, 2 dc) in ch sp, ch 5, 3 dc in last ch sp, turn. *(1 ch sp)*

Row 10: Sl st across to ch sp, (ch 3, 2 dc) in ch sp, **turn,** sl st in top of ch-3. Fasten off.

Bib Finishing

1: Fuse flexible vinyl lining centered on back of Bib according to manufacturer's instructions.

2: Cut two pieces of blue ribbon each 2½" long, sew ribbon rose ¼" from each end of each piece.

3: Hold one piece of ribbon with roses behind Trim, push one rose to front of Trim through ch sp at one end of row 6, push other rose through center of row 8, tack both roses in place; repeat with other piece of ribbon with roses on other end of row 6.

4: Tack one ribbon rose to center of row 1 on Trim.

5: Matching row 1 on Trim to center of row 26 on Bib, tack Trim to Bib being careful not to puncture vinyl backing.

6: Cut a 10" piece of white ribbon and tie into a 1½"-wide bow, tack to center of row 28 on Bib.

7: Cut two 10" pieces of white ribbon. With each piece, fold one end under ½" and tack together ¼" from fold, tack to end of one Strap. ✪

Rodeo Rider

Continued from page 152

Row 7 [9, 11]: Sl st in each of first 2 sts, (sl st, ch 1, sc) in next st, sc in each st across leaving last 2 sts unworked, turn. *(26) [31, 36]*

Rows 8–15 [10–17, 12–19]: Ch 1, sc first 2 sts tog, sc in each st across to last 2 sts, sc last 2 sts tog, turn. At end of last row, fasten off. *(10) [15, 20]*

Easing to fit, sew Sleeves in armholes, sew Sleeve and side seams.

Neck Band

Row 1: With right side facing you, working in ends of rows and sts, join red with sc in end of last row on left Front, 19 sc evenly spaced across to rows on next shoulder; for **tie loop,** ch 1, skip next row, sc in each row and st across shoulder and back leaving last 9 [10, 11] sts on left shoulder unworked, turn.

Row 2: Ch 1, sc in each st and in each ch across, turn.

Rows 3–4: Ch 1, sc in each st across, turn. At end of last row, for **buttonhole,** ch 3, join with sl st in end of first row. Fasten off.

Tie

With red, ch 50, sc in second ch from hook, sc in each ch across to end ch, (sc, ch 3, sc) in end ch; working on opposite side of ch, sc in each ch across with (sc, ch 3) in same ch as first sc, join with sl st in first sc. Fasten off. Slip Tie through ch-1 sp on row 1 of Neck Band, tie in knot at center. Tack ends to front.

Trim

With right side facing you and dark, hold yarn at back of work; insert hook between sts of first row on left shoulder at Neck Band, yo, pull through to front, *insert hook between next 2 sts, yo, pull through to front and through lp on hook; repeat from * around outer edge of front and back sections to opposite shoulder. Fasten off.

Repeat Trim around each armhole, join with sl st in first sl st. Fasten off.

Sew brown buttons across back left shoulder to correspond with buttonholes. Sew red button to end of Neck Band.

PANTS

Front

Row 1: With light, ch 47 [49, 51], sc in second ch from hook, sc in each ch across, turn. *(46 sc made) [48 sc made, 50 sc made]*

Rows 2–35 [2–37, 2–39]: Ch 1, sc in each st across, turn.

Row 36 [38, 40]: For **first leg,** ch 1, sc in first 23 [24, 25] sts leaving last 23 [24, 25] sts unworked, turn. *(23) [24, 25]*

Rows 37–71 [39–75, 41–79]: Or to desired length; ch 1, sc in each st across, turn. At end of last row, fasten off.

Row 36 [38, 40]: For **second leg,** join light with sc in first unworked st, sc in each st across, turn. *(23) [24, 25]*

Rows 37–71 [39–75, 41–79]: Or to desired length; ch 1, sc in each st across, turn. At end of last row, fasten off.

Back

With dark, work same as Pants Front.

Trim

Row 1: Place Front and Back tog; matching ends of rows and working through both thicknesses, join light with sc in end of last row on outside edge of leg, sc in each row up leg, turn. *(71 sc made) [75 sc made, 79 sc made]*

Row 2: Ch 1, sc in each st across, turn.

Row 3: Ch 1, sc in each of first 3 sts, *(ch 1, dc) in each of next 2 sts, ch 1, sc in each of next 2 sts; repeat from * across. Fasten off.

Repeat on other leg.

Matching ends of rows, sew inseams tog.

With tapestry needle, weave elastic thread through each st on row 1 of Front and Back, tie ends tog. Repeat in rows 2 and 3. ✪

Stitch Guide

Crochet Stitches

Chain—ch: Yo, pull through lp on hook.

Slip stitch—sl st: Insert hook in st, yo, pull through both lps on hook.

Single crochet—sc: Insert hook in st, yo, pull through st, yo, pull through both lps on hook.

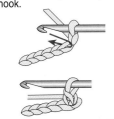

Front loop—front lp: Back loop—back lp:

FRONT LOOP   BACK LOOP

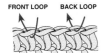

Half double crochet—hdc: Yo, insert hook in st, yo, pull through st, yo, pull through all 3 lps on hook.

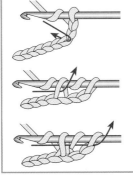

Double crochet—dc: Yo, insert hook in st, yo, pull through st, (yo, pull through 2 lps) 2 times.

Change colors: Drop first color; with 2nd color, pull through last 2 lps of st.

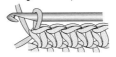

Treble crochet—tr: Yo 2 times, insert hook in st, yo, pull through st, (yo, pull through 2 lps) 3 times.

Double treble crochet—dtr: Yo 3 times, insert hook in st, yo, pull through st, (yo, pull through 2 lps) 4 times.

Front post stitch—fp: Back post stitch—bp: When working post st, insert hook from right to left around post of st on previous row.

Back   Front

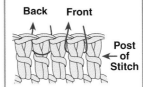

Post of Stitch

OUNCES TO GRAMS

1	=	28.4
2	=	56.7
3	=	85.0
4	=	113.4

GRAMS TO OUNCES

25	=	7/8
40	=	1²/₅
50	=	1¾
100	=	3½

HOOK AND NEEDLE SIZES

U.S.		METRIC	U.K.
	14	.60 mm.	
	12	.75 mm.	
	10	1.00 mm.	
	6	1.50 mm.	
0	5	1.75 mm.	
1	B	2.00 mm.	14
2	C	2.50 mm.	12
3	D	3.00 mm.	10
4	E	3.50 mm.	9
5	F	4.00 mm.	8
6	G	4.50 mm.	7
		4.75 mm.	
8	H	5.00 mm.	6
9	I	5.50 mm.	5
10	J	6.00 mm.	4
		6.50 mm.	3
10½	K	7.00 mm.	2
		8.00 mm.	
		9.00 mm.	
	P	10.00 mm.	
	Q	16.00 mm.	

Embroidery Stitches

Straight Stitch:

Lazy-Daisy Stitch:
1.   2.

Satin Stitch:

French Knot:

Back Stitch:

Fly Stitch:
1.   2.

Outline Stitch:

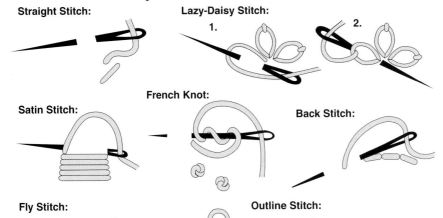

STANDARD ABBREVIATIONS

ch............................chain
dc.............double crochet
hdc ...half double crochet
lp, lps.............loop, loops
rnd, rnds...round, rounds
sc ....single crochet
sl st ....slip stitch
sp, sps.....space, spaces
st, sts ....stitch, stitches
tog.......................together
yo ....yarn over

sc next 2 sts tog....(insert hook in next st, yo, pull through st) 2 times, yo, pull through all 3 lps on hook.

hdc next 2 sts tog (yo, insert hook in next st, yo, pull through st) 2 times, yo, pull through all 5 lps on hook.

dc next 2 sts tog ....(yo, insert hook in next st, yo, pull through st, yo, pull through 2 lps on hook) 2 times, yo, pull through all 3 lps on hook.